"This is not science fiction. This is not a diatribe to frighten you. This is not an arid book of academia. This is a profound, prophetic, poetic call to arms. . . . *World War III* must not happen. Michael Tobias shows us how that is possible."

—**William Shatner**

"[A] passionate, convincing portrayal of our planet in crisis. . . . Tobias reveals points of light in the global darkness, and proposes a philosophy and ethics that could turn the tide against the approaching apocalypse."

—**Joseph Kulin, executive publisher, *Parabola* magazine**

"*World War III* may well become an animal rights classic, but even more than that, it is a stirring and comprehensive look at the global problems created by human overpopulation and overconsumption, as well as offering a desperately needed blueprint for preserving the Earth—for all its species. Please buy it, read it, and spread the word!"

—**Gretchen Wyler,
President, The Ark Trust**

"*World War III* is the most important book of the 1990s. Compassionate and brilliant, Tobias' picture is painfully, almost clinically, forthright. Whereas many other ecologists have deftly described ecological mayhem in all its particulars, no one has diagnosed the demographic trouble spots with anywhere near the contemporary range of *World War III*; nor has anyone examined the philosophical and statistical ambiguities of demography itself. *World War III* ranks with the great books of our century and should be read by every leader of every nation, religion, organization, and corporation. This thinking must be imbued in humankind."

—**Marilyn Brant Chandler, president/executive
director, Population Education Committee**

MICHAEL TOBIAS, Ph.D., is an internationally respected ecologist, author, screenwriter, director, and producer, whose more than twenty-five books and one hundred films have been read or seen in some eighty countries. In 1996 Tobias was given the "Courage of Conscience Award" by the Peace Abbey in Sherborn, Massachusetts.

WORLD WAR III

WORLD WAR III
Population
and the Biosphere
at the end
of the
Millennium

~MICHAEL TOBIAS~

CONTINUUM • NEW YORK

1998
The Continuum Publishing Company
370 Lexington Avenue
New York, NY 10017

Printed in the United States of America

Library of Congress Cataloging-in-Publication Data

Tobias, Michael.
  World War III: population and the biosphere at the end of the millennium /
by Michael Tobias. — 2nd ed. rev. and updated.
      p.   cm.
  Includes bibliographical references and index.
  ISBN 0-8264-1085-5
  1. Overpopulation. 2. Overpopulation — Enviromental aspects. 3. Population
policy. 4. Nature—Effect of human beings on. 5. Enviromental degradation—
Social aspects. I. Title.
HB871.T63   1998
363.9'1—dc21   97-47784
                                                             CIP

Photograph on page 139 by Jane Morrison; those on pages 173 and 229 by
R. Radin; and those on pages 13, 29, 47, 83, 196, and on 242 by M. Tobias.

~Contents~

〜 For Jane Gray Morrison 〜

a great artist
my soulmate, editorial conscience, and inspiration,
who labored over this book with unstinting dedication.
In eternal love, gratitude, and admiration.

~Acknowledgments~

I WANT FIRST to thank Mr. John Warren and fellow trustees of the Bixby Foundation, and Ms. Sue Stiles, for their generous support of this project. Without them, it could not have happened.

Mrs. Marilyn Brant Chandler, president and executive director of Population Education Committee, has (with the help of her many board members) worked assiduously and selflessly in assisting me, as has Mr. Robert W. Gillespie, the president of Population Communication. I owe both of them my extreme gratitude.

A special thanks goes to Nick Stonnington.

In addition, I extend my sincere appreciation to the directors and various staff of the United Nations Population Fund—in China, India, Indonesia, Kenya, and Mali—who kindly assisted me in some of my journeys.

Hundreds of scholars, family planners, and scientists gave me their time for interviews, and I can not thank all of them here. But I am particularly indebted to the following individuals:

China: Madame Peng Peiyun, Minister of the State Family Planning Commission; Huang Baoshan, director, International Relations, State Family Planning Commission; Professor Qu Geping, former head of China's Environmental Protection Agency; Mr. Shi Yuanming, State Family Planning Commission, Department of Foreign Affairs; Dr. Qian Xinzhong, former Minister of the State Family Planning Commission and Minister of Health.

Indonesia: Dr. Emil Salim, former Minister of the Environment; M. S. Zulkarnaen and the WALHI Environmental Forum; Dr. Firman Lubis and the Yayasan Kusuma Buana.

India: Ms. Maneka Gandhi, former Minister of Environment and Forests; Mrs. Usha Vohra, former secretary, Department of Family Welfare for India; Mrs. S. Bhatnagar, director, National Institute of Health and Family Welfare; Professor Ashish Bose of Nehru University; Mrs. Avabai Wadia, president, Family Planning Association of India; John J. Dumm, former director, Office of Population, Health, and Nutrition, A.I.D., New Delhi; K. Gopalakrishnan, general manager, PSI-Population Services International; Dr. V. A. Pai Panandiker, director, Centre for Policy Research, New Delhi.

Kenya: Ambassador S. B. A. Bullut, director, National Council for Population and Development, Ministry of Home Affairs; G. Z. Mzenge, executive director, Family Planning Association of Kenya; the director and staff of Chogoria Hospital; the midwives of the village of Gaatia; and Alice N. Githae.

Mali: The staff librarian of the Ministry of Environment; and John Anderson and his associates, particularly Carl-Eric Guertin of the Entraide Universitaire Mondiale du Canada (EUMC).

United States: California Department of Fish and Game, Natural Heritage Division; Joan Babbott, former executive director, Planned Parenthood of Los Angeles; Melinda Cordero, Promotoras Group; Deborah Jensen, California Policy Seminar; Jones and Stokes Associates; Dr. Maurice Van Arsdol, former chairman of the Population Education Committee, for use of the Population Research Library at the University of Southern California.

A few of the key sources included: the *World Bank Working Papers; The Kenya Wildlife Service, Policy Framework and Development Program, 1991–96; Mistaking Plantations for Indonesia's Tropical Forest: Indonesia's Pulp and Paper Industry, Communities, and Environment,* by WALHI and YLBHI; Dr. Qu Geping's book, *Environmental Management in China;* the World Resources Reports; Charlie Pye–Smith's book *In Search of Wild India;* Ramesh and Rajesh Bedi's book *Indian Wildlife;* the many writings of E. O. Wilson, particularly his book, *The Diversity of Life;* the works of Paul and Anne Ehrlich, including *The Population Explosion* and *Extinction; In Our Own Hands,* by Deborah B. Jensen, Margaret Tom, and John Harte; various UNFPA, Population Reference Bureau, and A.I.D. working papers and data sheets; and the *Los Angeles Times* newspaper.

A special, all-enduring hug goes to photographer, poet, film maker, and explorer Robert Radin for reasons only he can appreciate.

I wish to thank literary agent Julie Castiglia.

And finally, much love and profound thanks to Betty, William, Marc, Jean, and Alvaro.

~Preface~

OUR PLANET IS under seige, threatened by an ever more rapidly growing hoard of the most dangerous mammalian speicies of all time—*Homo sapiens*. Human beings have poisoned the earth, the water, and the air with a myriad of synthetic chemicals that are now present, often in highly dangerous levels, throughout the globe. Even the fragile ozone covering that, for billions of years, has protected life on earth from dangerous levels of radiation from the sun is under attack. The accumulation of the "greenhouse" gases is threatening massive global climate change. Deforestation has led to the gradual, inexorable proliferation of the world's deserts. All types of ecosystems are threatened, from coral reef and wetland, to woodland and heath and alpine meadow. Countless species of animals and plants have gone extinct—thousands more are threatened.

Many factors contribute to this ever more vicious attack on Planet Earth, among them industrialization, destructive technology, human greed, and cruelty. But without doubt the most significant factor of all, that which of itself hugely magnifies the effects of all other causes and consequences, is the explosive, terrifying growth of human populations around the world. Already there are some six billion human beings on the planet; this number is expected to double—some say triple—over the next few centuries. Already more then ninety million babies are born each year. Each one requires love and care, yet the grim reality is that thousands of them face starvation, lack of warmth and shelter, and often neglect—even abuse and death, Can we imagine a time when 180 million come into the world each year?

But even supposing such a vast hoard of humanity could be fed and clothed and housed, what would it be like? A world with twelve billion humans? What would be the effect of this staggering number of people on the natural environment—already suffering so terribly today—and on the gradually diminishing natural resources of our planet? And what of the effects of the survival needs of the growing contingent of poor, and the greed of the affluent?

This current scenario, says Michael Tobias, is tantamount to *war*. War that is being waged by humanity against the environment, by the rich against the poor—and by those of us living today against the unborn generations of the future. It is a war that is very different from the traditional wars with which we are familiar, where there are winners and losers. For in this new war all, in the long run, will be losers. It is a war during which the vast majority of life forms will lose out, helpless in the face of the destruction of the natural world. A war in which the rich diversity of life on earth will vanish. And which, in the end, will surely bring doom to the destroyers.

In this book, Michael Tobias faces up unflinchingly to all of these tough, unpleasant realities, providing ample scientific proof of the large-scale habitat destruction and loss of biodiversity that has and continues to take place. He tackles controversial issues with unfailing honesty. Readers will become angry, depressed, fatalistic. Yet, this is not a book without hope. Tobias describes for us a path that we could take—a path mapped out by a combination of scientific, logical, intuitive, and spiritual reasoning—towards a future where all is not, after all, lost.

In *World War III* Tobias raises a clarion call. A call for aid such as, in the olden days, would summon knights in shining armour to fight under the banner of their king. And now we all are summoned, each and every one of us. For we must fight together to stop this senseless assault on the natural world. We must make an effort to live in greater harmony with nature. We must do this partly because we have a responsibility to ensure that all children can enjoy what should be their birthright—a decent life with enough to eat and drink and with shelter from the elements. And because we have a responsibility to our beautiful planet, to the environment that guided our emergence as a species and, over countless thousands of years, has nurtured our gradual development and spiritual growth. And because we have a responsibility toward those who will live after us.

I hope that those reading this book will join Tobias on the path toward the more sustainable and compassionate future, trying to live again as we once did, in harmony with nature; and no longer at war.

JANE GOODALL

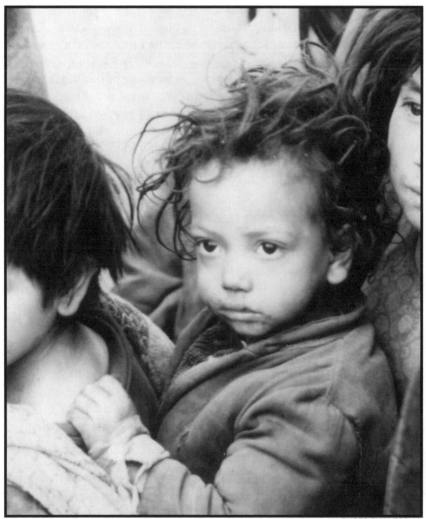

～Prologue～

F ROM THE FIRST glimpses, one is almost certain to be qualmish of demographics, or, for purposes of mental hygiene or financial gain, to try to somehow manipulate this distrust in order to shy away from the truth of overpopulation and what it means for all of us. Yet the numeric verities are not easily obscured or eluded. Leafing through countless tomes of statistics, one is impatient and skeptical. These feelings turn to real alarm as the sheer weight of numbers known vaguely to be human beings, the burden of their illimitable data, and the substantial meaning of our impact on the Earth escalate in the psyche at a speed approaching three human births every second, nearly eleven thousand per hour, or ninety-four million per year—human beings all begging for a quality of life that is increasingly impossible to satisfy. As other species quietly, rapidly, fade away, and the imbalance of human numbers continues to escalate, a hint of substantial personal peril surfaces, as if one's life were suddenly held hostage by cosmic forces totally out of our control. Yet, unlike, say, in the case of an earthquake, we alone are responsible for this situation. Only we can ameliorate, and hopefully reverse, the debacle of our unrelenting proliferation.

In the most alarming, existential sense, contact with an overpopulated human world easily dispatches reflective individuals toward unrelieved darkness, mired and subsumed in quantities, zeros, and decimal points beyond their ken. No single capability can circumvent this unimaginably teeming future. There is nothing remotely aesthetic about an infinity of humankind. Nor do such statistical aggregates make for the satisfactions of anonymity. This is the numbing day-in-day-out dilemma of family planning. Those in the social services and family health fields apply a somewhat different set of psycholinguistic rules to their practice: a nomenclature that is all but shorn, necessarily, of self-defeating nihilism. Such words and phrases as, "compassion and caring," "career challenge," "professional opportunity," or—optimistically speaking—"humanity's final chance," come immediately to mind.

The humdrum surface of family planning is imprinted with every living miracle, every child, but also totally conceals the lurking horrors of psychological and biological densification, umbrella effects of human impact. The term "family planning" and its politically correct intentions conceals something like one hundred million sex acts a day. The officialdom of family planning gives no sense of the worldly lust, the inventive positions, polyglottal gasps, redundant upward-rising ever unslaked passions, the silent enduring, and too frequent death throes which accompany the comprehensive sexual tryst, from beginning to end. Nor does the bureaucracy enshrouding population control give any clue to the crucial realm of love, family and community dynamics, religious scruples, ancient or subliminal rituals, courtship, or aggression that universally signal sexuality and its offspring.

But then comes the biological truth, beyond the mere few moments of carnal pleasure: the universal contractions, the chasm of darkness out of which the human miracle tastes the honeyed light and fresh air. In many developing countries there is no theater of technology assisting birth, but rather a single midwife, whose tools are often no more than a stone for cutting umbilical cords and cow dung for stopping bleeding. A third of all deaths among teenage women in the Third World are likely to occur during these merciless moments. Among those who survive childbirth, who are not buried and forgotten, nature honors the unwary blush of young motherhood, or conversely, in some countries, contests that innocence and reason for pride with the dismal realizations of poverty and the possibility of a child who will be scorned, oppressed, possibly even murdered if it should be a female.

By foot, or in mobile vans or boats, come the health care workers, usually too late to do more than ensure the status quo or provide nutritional advice; immunize the child; hand out rehydration supplies; or counsel on the benefits of breast-feeding, spacing, and an IUD insertion. The timing, supplies, level of counseling, and degree of contact vary, of course. One can scarcely pretend to sustain an interest in all the specifics, which range and wend, according to continent, country, region, culture, language, district, city, town, village, sub-village, family, individual, and gender.

But even the casual observer will be struck by the unthinkably acute whorl of pain directly beneath and to all sides of humanity's fertility: the collision course, long in the making, between human beings and the biosphere. I speak of nothing less than *war* in this regard. For purposes of absolute clarity I call it *World War III*. By this descriptive finality I do not mean it in the speculative sense, the war-game scenarios which have occupied the minds of countless academic and government cadres, puzzles played out in the leisure of futurism, or the sterility of think tanks. This war is already upon us and has been for some time. It is like a terminal cancer which corrodes the body from within, too often admitting no signs of itself on the surface of the person, or only at the very end. This is why the overwhelming proportion of all medical expenditures are spent during a patient's last month of life, because that is, typically, when people experience their worst agony, and rapidly succumb to the final hours of doom. Usually, nothing can save such patients. The illness has gone on too long.

All that can be done is to massively attack the mature disease with radiation; or remove a limb, an organ, large sections of tissue; or undertake a transplant. But usually science can only prepare the victims for death by dulling their senses and thus reducing pain to the extent possible.

The world is currently in the throes of a mature disease, brought on by both the best and the worst of humanity. In either case, whether best or worst, the totality of our infliction upon the Earth is akin to a war that we have waged unceasingly. It boasts of all the analogies normally associated with conventional warfare: double envelopment, vast assemblages of soldiers wreaking havoc, scorched earth strategies, aerial sorties, temporary ceasefires, paramedic corps and battlefield triage, wavering negotiations, over-crowded sanctuaries, unflinching dictators, patriotic gore, sadism, cultural madness, rapine and plunder, suicide, and near total genocide. These hostilities and absolutes are taking place at this very moment, everywhere, in every country, upon virtually every square kilometer of the planet, even where no guns are fired, no fires visible. Even where alleged wilderness remains, and the economy is booming, the atmosphere above is contaminated, or the water, or the soil; their resident wildlife and the genetic viability of their populations are increasingly cornered by advancing armies on the outer perimeters. But, unlike the previous two world wars, fought between nations, this is the final war: our species versus the entire planet. We must not imagine that there will be ticker tape parades for the victors. In 1987, when the world contained nearly seven hundred million people fewer than in 1994, the World Commission on Environment and Development described the state of "environmental decline" as a "threat second only to nuclear war." Yet, even among the most conservative of demographers our near future indicates a population of nearly eleven billion. Many others see *Homo sapiens* poised to double, possibly even triple in number, with all the attendant ecological mayhem.

The above-mentioned demographics inherent to family planning—all the obtuse quantitative calculations, census data, and fertility surveys—define a veritable war against the planet when they are coupled with realities of human impact, be they deliberate or naive. I am referring to such causes as housing starts and road-building; activities which arrogate and degrade land previously inhabited, traversed, or relied upon by far more creatures than the incoming human migrants. This sphere of conflict crescendos with the massive felling of (often old growth) forests and the horrifying operations of slaughterhouses and factory farms; the economics of poaching and complex disruptions by the tourism industry; the short-term motivations of capital goods production and commodities speculation; the intensity of agriculture that, like all forms of construction, defiles previously natural land; the putting up of fences and (leaking) pipelines which check otherwise habitual movements of animal populations; the course of vulnerable supertankers and chemical or radioactive-emitting and transporting traffic; the depletion of stratospheric ozone; the melting of glaciers; the impoverishment and desecration of nearly every organic and inorganic resource and natural sink by our extraction and consumption of energy; the countless regimes of manufacturing and waste discharge; the pathologies of defense and offense; local, tribal, ethnic, regional, and national conflicts; the feverish building of whole towns and the accretion of megacities, accompanied by a host of other energy extractions—all contributing to global warming. The death of Venice, Italy—one of the cornerstones of civilization—and the Maldivian coral reefs—the Amazon of the marine environment—are merely two icons of destruction, the tip of the iceberg, for what we're collectively doing. This approximately twelve-thousand-year-old human pattern defines the hunter, scavenger, tamperer, bulldozer, destroyer that is man and woman. They are born, suckle, dream, and want only to live. They have a soul, whatever that might mean. They avoid pain, seek out pleasure. These basic needs are biologically fixed. All animals and plants share in the gusto of life. Every population is genetically primed by these universal volitions.

And yet, for humanity, whose footprints are larger than those of the largest dinosaurs, we are plagued by our very presence in the natural world. Some are plagued more than others, of course, the "some" referring at present to probably three to four billion individuals who are poor, oppressed, in ill-health, or hungry; the "others" designating those who have thus far managed to maintain what they consider to be a dignified and pleasurable sojourn in this lifetime. Rich or poor, there is no escaping the awareness and worry of a planetary struggle, nor the appalling spasm of global extinctions that we have deliberately unleashed.

Humanity is furiously engaged in World War III at this time. Our ever-increasing numbers are bearing down on Earth's finite resilience. We are using nature as ammunition for our many struggles among ourselves (economic, political, cultural), while directly assaulting and outmaneuvering its every flank. We have defined the enemy and penetrated to her command headquarters, if you will, by razing or impaling upon a mighty guillotine all of the planet's great reservoirs of biological diversity, the rain forests, grasslands, wetlands, and coral reefs. In this offensive, humanity seems bent on taking no prisoners alive, while holding the entire world captive for another day.

This is a new kind of war, global in scope, yet remarkably concentrated wherever there is booty to be had. The booty refers to all those desirable affects, the guarantees of a way of life to which more and more people would like to become accustomed, including such things as value-added trade surpluses, secured supply lines of fossil fuels, refrigerators, skyscrapers, and intellectual property rights. For most of the world's population, however, clean water, medical supplies, electricity, and nutritious food would suffice for now. Our weapons may be as sophisticated as those used against Iraq in the Persian Gulf War, or as immemorially simple as a plough scratching a bit of hard turf in the highlands of Ethiopia. While the conflict in the Persian Gulf imposed myriad levels of stress on the environment (decimation, the better word), the Ethiopian farmer imposes an inobvious, but nonetheless war-torn burden on the land, altogether justifiable, yet tragically linked to the incremental destruction of the nonhuman world.

Not surprisingly, the fervor for this war is carried on with our most impressive instincts. What we call civilization, progress, economic prosperity, even—remarkably—human empathy, the "enemy" (our biological surroundings) more than likely views differently. Economic prosperity in China is systematically destroying Chinese environment, from snow leopards in Tibet to estuaries on the Yellow Sea. The same sorry syndrome, to varying degrees, is being perpetrated throughout every country in the world, where the differences between city and village are vanishing in the shadows of expansive and destructive development. The end-loser of all this human "progress" is nature. The runaway pressures on the biosphere of nearly six billion human bodies are converting an original, untainted world into a meaningless "resource." As we extinguish those limited resources, leveling whole ecosystems in our quest to feed, clothe, shelter, inoculate, and educate the nearly 260 thousand newborns everyday, we rely upon increasing concentrations of the machinery, monetary, or political profits of war.

The efficiency of exploitation is fundamental to human aggression, and always has been. This is a war fraught with great nerve and compulsion because our species knows that it is engulfed in conflict, has the means, possibly, to reverse the aggression, but cannot think to do so. The greed of World War III goes well beyond political ego or personal gain. It encompasses the patriotism of religious and cultural norms, lifestyles, the sense of history, which many hold sacred. That sacredness is itself steeped in battle, making it difficult today to isolate clarity, or fashion unambiguous convictions. Living with contradiction has become the hallmark of this war, whose psychological fall-out shadows everyone. And because no region, no mind, no soul is spared the ravages of this conflict, there is virtually no "clean room" left on the planet, no place where one can go to breathe unburdened. In other words, it is now next to impossible to measure in any comprehensive terms the alternatives to war, or even to take an accurate compass reading of human nature, though many well-intentioned thinkers, observers, scholars, artists, scientists, and family planners are trying to do so.

In spite of our blinders and inescapable self-interest, and the inferno all around us, we have known, at least since the time of Plato, that overpopulation is biologically and morally disastrous; that nature meets imbalance with brutality. Destabilization may have nothing to do with numbers, per se, but with excess. Morality, like the Ten Commandments, or Golden Rule (Matthew 7:12 and Luke 6:31), is a crucial human notion that has arisen, I believe, to combat excess. It is a beleaguered ideal, an even more ungainly tool. But it serves, if anything, to guide humanity toward balance in nature.

Morality disintegrates on the battlefield, which is where we are now. Yet, there are sparks of conscience, piecemeal traces of hope in every locale and country. Between countries, there are conventions, treaties, alliances, and policies that seek to stop, or slow, the war. Most importantly, there are legions of well-intended individuals, heroic, conscientious objectors. I am referring, among others, to that seemingly mundane collective of several million family planners who for much of this century have been trying urgently and humanely to curb the rate and pace of human fertility. These are people who, to varying degrees, understand the scope of this war and are determined to make a difference. One is reduced to such platitudes ("to make a difference") when confronted by such overwhelming odds. But the truth remains: it is possible to mend wounds, to change minds, to minimize suffering. Our awareness makes it our responsibility to do so. We cannot presume to make the crisis, this advanced illness, go away, or even begin to appreciate the actual danger we are in, unless we have first thoroughly diagnosed its causes and consequences. Then, like surgeons, we will have a more confident sense of where we are hemorrhaging, and whatever antidotes, policies, and resolutions we may summon will have at least some measure of credibility. Family planning has prevented the births of several hundred million humans in this century. While the projected impact of that additional contingent might be negligible, as against the nearly six billion existing people in 1998, it is, nevertheless, a nation larger than America which has not come into being. And that is ecologically (and thus morally) significant. Furthermore, it is now well understood that in simply satisfying the demand for contraceptives by those individuals presently lacking access to them (an estimated 125 million couples in the developing world), a substantial, non-Draconian hurdle will have been overcome. Free, or nearly free access to contraceptives, guided by strong political leadership, is proving to be the key to slowing down overpopulation, even more than education, which in some countries like Bangladesh and parts of Africa has proven to be of secondary importance. Nevertheless, education, consciousness raising, is key to long-term stabilization of human ethics.

Overpopulation has nothing necessarily to do with the density of people, or even the extent of their number, though the two facets seem inevitably linked to a predictable outcome. More certainly, overpopulation is a synonym for the environmental impact of our species, the result of human behavior that stems from economic goals and the ill-fitting power of individuals over nature and one another. Ecologically sound behavior, even when multiplied by large numbers of people, need not be destructive, at least in theory. Nobody knows the upper ceiling of biotic viability, or "carrying capacity," as it is called, under conditions of high human consumption. At what point does an ecosystem, and collection of ecosystems, wither and expire? The deleterious effect of radiation on a population of white pines or human blood cells is no longer a mystery. But what about the global extinction of frogs, birds, apples, and domestic animal varieties? Our relative inexperience in this is to be regarded with profound relief and adumbration. For the day we should haplessly exceed the Earth's carrying capacity will likely admit to little documentation, possibly no consciousness of any kind.

Living within the rubrics of carrying capacity requires a certain mode of agreed-to behavior, as yet to be achieved. But with ample mental and physical nurturance, cultural and economic incentives, there is reason to be optimistic. And despite an erratic record and oddly unspectacular techniques, family planning has a crucial role to play in fostering the preconditions of that sustainability.

In places like East Los Angeles, Shanghai, Bangkok, the villages of Kerala and western Java, the outbacks of Bangladesh, and the sub-Sahara, I have spent time with specialists—some trained, some less trained—who are quietly working with mothers and fathers, students and educators, village elders, community, tribal or religious leaders, local and national governments, and with numerous NGOs (nongovernmental organizations) to engender two-child families, quality health services, and appropriate ecological development. The troubled chronicle of these many diverse endeavors is often inspiring. We have no other choice but to continue working to limit human numbers as compassionately and with as much perspective as possible. We are not obligated to finish the work, simply to act as if we could. The reasons for this global exercise in sexual and egotistical restraint are obvious by now: every consumer adds kindling to a fire that is raging across the planet, destroying all that thereupon dwell.

Yet, while small families and family planning are fundamental to the planet's future (or family welfare, as some countries call it), human behavior itself is out of control, and threatens to override any and all strides in the population arena. Our consumptive frenzy is fueled by laws, taxbreaks, national economic priorities, government regulations, the very euphoria of possession, and by military paranoia. Economic growth is everywhere judged to be a good thing. And for nearly three hundred years material gain has been deemed the best form of birth control. More importantly, the accumulation of wealth has been presumed the natural evolution of humankind. Yet, those few remaining "preindustrial" communities, and the records we have of earlier ones, as well as hundreds-of-millions of existing mountain, jungle, desert, arctic, and coastal indigenous peoples, more often than not reject personal gain if at the expense of others. Human dignity, artistic enterprise, and the joys of parenthood and community need not be preconditioned by acquisitiveness and the total separation of human life from that of the surrounding environment. In America the Acoma Pueblo, an hour's drive from Albuquerque, comes immediately to my mind. Elsewhere, in India, I am drawn to the 1,495 Todas of the Nilgiri Massif in Tamil Nadu state, the last vegetarian tribe in the world—an ancient culture that reveres the Earth and refuses, and has always refused, to engage in any form of violence.

In the face of several billion have-nots plunging ever more deeply into poverty, hunger, and disease, Western politicians and cultural isolationists have stridently declared, "The American way of life is not negotiable." This credo, a defense mechanism against the incoming tide of population global pressure, has devastated women, children, and most plant and animal species, hundreds of billions of individuals, with individual souls, by a stubborn insistence that destroys, separates, and self-justifies. This destructive belief system holds that wealth is good and that the more it costs to achieve riches, the more those riches are worth. It is a disastrous, psychologically bankrupt conception of humanity and its role as a part of nature. Both developed and developing countries are allied in their war against the future, a fact often missed. A Western consumer has a far greater vested interest in the continued extraction of global resources and resulting biodiversity loss than does his counterpart in developing countries, though the Western individual is rarely, if ever in touch with the causal chain of ecological desecration of which he is a glaring part. Most, if not all, of this Western impact has no other justification than the perpetuation of consumer pleasure. Whereas for those multitudes of poor or malnourished in developing nations, consumption has an altogether different definition, namely, mere survival. Billions of people are presently stripping trees and gathering biomass for fuel, killing animals, blowing up coral reefs to more efficiently get at the fish, poaching, encroaching on national parks and sanctuaries (often their former homes from which they may have been rudely evicted), having to denude their half acre or so of farmland stranded in resource-exhausted hinterlands, or migrating jobless to the congested narrow margins of stifling urban slums.

Harrowingly, both types of consumers are killing the world, which does not provide the human heart, or policy makers, any easy choices or roadmaps. But there *are* selective choices to be made, and there is still time to make them. Perhaps not time to save 20 percent, or even eventually, half of all species on Earth, but time to save at least the other half.

I want to believe that the human population has the strength, the enthusiasm, the reasoning facility, and the conscience to alter its course. It may even be that by biological intuition, democratic impulses long-ago anticipated the ungainliness and disarray of the human presence with an eye toward correcting it. There are countless kernels of hope, but if we do not seize them, then we might well muddle onward, unable to give up the fight, addicted to ossified political boundaries out of kilter with countervailing ecological priorities, hopelessly caught up in the cry of battle, poisoned by greed and the hoarding of personal assets, undeterred by the death of nature all around us. In that case, failing to formulate a new international order of empathy, of clear-headed biological policies and imperatives, to check our numbers, and to seriously modify our laws and behavior, we will continue to fail as a species. Not contributing to the Earth, but destroying it. Not offering to the pool of life, but plundering it. Ironically, this colossal crime against the world and possibly the cosmos will be masked by ever more numbers of people, a mark of success in traditional biologic terms.

Uninhibited human fertility is surely no triumph. Depending on which projections one is inclined to believe, and in absence of any species-specific self-destruct mechanisms, *Homo sapiens* will have increased to between 10.8 and twelve billion sometime by the late twenty-first century. According to higher projections, we may attain to fifteen billion. In Africa, for example, if the number of children per couple does not come down from over six, to just over four during the next six or seven years, the difference forty years from now will amount to one billion additional people. That is some measure of the time-bomb inherent to the so-called total fertility rate (TFR), the number of live children that a woman has during her reproductive years. And if we should somehow triple our present numbers, then there will be probably nothing much to stop continued growth long into the future. The long-term biological outlook might then be best described as no bang, but a slow and agonizing whimper, with consequences better left for future environmental archaeologists to unsort.

THIS VOLUME ENDEAVORS to analyze these battlegrounds by focusing upon the major regions of the planet where particularly heavy demographic pressures are conflicting with dense plant and animal communities. I first wrote the book in 1993–94, just prior to the Cairo Population Conference. That first edition was 625 pages. In this revised edition, I have shortened the work by half, to make it more accessible, but have also had the unnerving task of updating certain data. In four years, populations in 75 percent of all countries have grown dramatically. China has even had to revise its stabilization goal by a quick one hundred million. There have been important gains. In Indonesia, for example, the contraceptive prevalence rate, or CPR, has risen over 5 percent in those four years, while per capita income has gone up approximately twenty-five dollars. As for environmental impact, key sectors have only deteriorated. The burning of Brazil's rain forest, for example, has escalated to an all-time high, despite the best-laid plans five years ago at the Rio Summit.

In this volume I first set the stage by examining the primeval backdrop and the living truth of balanced populations, most notably those in the Antarctic, as well as among certain human tribal groups of limited, but nonetheless important diagnostic value for the future. I then paint a picture of destabilizing influences and trace their history back to the origins and ephemeral nature of biological populations.

I lay greatest weight and empahsis on my analysis of China, India, Indonesia, Africa, and the United States, the five largest population hubs in the world. I view these critical ecological battlefronts through the eyes of various demographers, historians, theologians, scientists, medical specialists, family planners, politicians, and the locals themselves—farmers, cottage industry laborers, children, mothers, and teachers. The majority of the book is rooted in my contemplation of these five bioregions. Their respective dilemmas are massively suggestive of the forces and global crash occurring everywhere, but more perilous in the degree to which those pressures have already taken a toll. China, India, Indonesia, all of Africa, and the United States are together looking at a combined number of possibly as much as 60 percent of the human race, or seven billion, sometime in the middle of the coming century. At the same time, these five regions as yet harbor between them the greatest biodiversity on Earth. Destructive patterns have been set in motion. The clock is ticking. A few years are all the time left to save that precious heritage.

In China, I examine the pace of economic development and its environmental fallout. Against this context, the book recounts the political lessons from China's ambiguous history of family planning efforts and projects different possible scenarios for its future. While the nation has already made unprecedented strides toward reducing its numbers—with little encouragement from the rest of the world—the coming generations, boosted by wild spending, enormous growth, and increasing socio-economic disparities, on top of a new baby boom, offer few reassurances that the country will be able to take control of its demographic time-bomb.

Similarly, India yields a picture of intense ecological destructon. And, despite Indian family planning having been initiated in earnest nearly forty years ago, the country continues to see runaway fertility. At the same time, India's human rights violations, including an abusive regime against females, and an unmonitored, persecuted child labor class that ranks in sheer size as one of the largest nations, by itself, in the world, offer little hope of simple reconciliation or child and maternal health care antidotes.

India's several hundred million residents who are below the so-called absolute poverty line, have no choice but to strip bare the remaining forests, while the fast emerging Indian middle class is beginning to achieve a modicum of economic security—which it has been denied throughout history—but at the unfortunate price of totally undermining all remaining semi-wild habitat throughout the country.

Indonesia presents a less dire scenario, though the long-term ecological trends are terrifying. While family planning efforts have been rigorous, to date, the built-in fertility momentum, coupled with the country's unapologetic need to secure an economic future for what promises to be four hundred million Indonesians in less than thirty-five years, has targeted one of the last enormous tracts of rain forest in the world for exploitation. This blueprint for blatant development (jobs versus trees) is veiled, unfortunately, by terms that would indicate otherwise.

In Africa, I take the reader throughout Kenya, and hundreds of miles across the sub-Saharan country of Mali, as well as examining trends and data from a dozen other African nations. In Kenya, I focus upon recent demographic data, and the Agency for International Development program in the town of Chogoria, where the first substantial evidence of fertility decline emerged several years ago. In profiling the devastating decline of most ecosystems in West Africa at the hands of one species, it becomes especially clear why population remediation—with its implacable links to food insufficiency and ecological degradation—is the number one issue to contend with if Africa is ever to hope for anything like remediation.

I then proceed to question the widely shared perception that the Western, developed countries can fend for themselves, unaffected by the same forces and global links which are rapidly eroding the political and ecological stability of the rest of the world. Indeed, ecological ruination in the rapidly industrializing nations, from Mexico and Brazil to Poland and South Korea, is sounding a global wake-up call, even under those rarified conditions of zero population growth, whether in Japan, Italy, or the Netherlands. I examine the highlights of this global biodiversity crash, the logical outgrowth of continuing unmediated war. It follows from the cumulative results of runaway urbanization, energy intensity, agricultural expansion, the loss of genetic viability among countless populations, the total appropriation of forests and soil and marine vitality, and the massive tide of animal exploitation. Many have looked toward the United States for political, economic, and behavioral antidotes.

Millions of immigrants still dream of the good life in America. But, in the United States, with a focus on Los Angeles, I profile the true meaning of human impact, dispelling any illusions that a mere 260 million plus Americans are somehow magically immune to the biological dynamics of population growth, or have any compelling or obvious answers for the rest of the world.

In chapter 7, "Demographic Madness," I consider the demographic future, according to current best-guess projections by the World Bank, the United Nations, and other organizations. Much is made of the so-called "stabilization" phase in the middle of the next century, whence "classic demographic transition" should effectively bring to halt our species' continued numeric growth. This assumption is based only sporadically on readable precedent. It has taken place in some forty-five countries, most of them very small countries, with the notable exceptions of Italy, Spain, Germany, and Japan. But many competent demographers have dismissed demographic transition as less and less reliable, or even relevant. Much of demography is mere guesswork, the lodging of logical hope based upon imputed behavioral characteristics of humankind that may, or may not, hold true. In fact, as I shall reveal, future projections harbor enormous discrepancy and ambiguity. It has proven impossible to statistically account for a woman's full reproductive life, or to predict the vagaries of population momentum, particularly in view of the rapidly growing number of young males and females. Nor is the prediction of new fertility technology or prolife legislation a facile matter. There are causes for limited optimism—particularly the aforementioned population *implosion*—but even more reason to be concerned: greenhouse conditions for fertility, intimating not stabilization, but continued growth, ever-escalating wars against nature, and a global population at the end of the next century surpassing fifteen billion. Such futuristic numbers are woven of mathematical paradox, even metaphysics, that evoke a new nausea, the possibility that we will be unable to effect planetary balance.

In the epilogue, entitled "Global Truce," to effectively counteract this dismal picture, unambiguously born out in most parts of the world, I consider the alternative future, one still within our grasp.

Americans spend three times more in one year on Halloween costumes than they do on family planning; immeasurably more money on eye shadow and deodorant than on protecting endangered species. Our priorities are self-destructive. In the spirit of alternative personal approaches to the global predicament, one must reflect on the economic and philosoph- ical bases for any number of crucial endeavors, many of which are described or intimated throughout this work: greatly enhanced family planning and ecological bilateral aid and donor assistance (according to the recent Japanese model of largesse—a single $125 billion gift to the Third World); a strategy to airlift urgent conservation assistance to at least eighteen biodiversity "hot spots" on the planet; the reformulation of GNP into an ENP (ecological net profits) accountability procedure for regions and whole nations; rethinking political boundaries into ecological ones, a definition of both biodiversity prospecting, as it has been labelled; and most fittingly, the discovery of the New World—not new continents to be plundered, but a familiar planet to be revered. Revivifying ancient moral principles of individual responsibility and restraint, our guides in this eth- ical renaissance, this new age of discovery, are not merely indigenous peo- ple, women, and children, but spiritual, political, and corporate leaders of the Valdez, and NGO (aka Rio) Summit generation with vision and com- passion who have seized upon our best, most caring, and rational capabil- ities, the basis for ethical self-governance, and proceeded to act according- ly. Jain economics is cited as one crucial corollary of this revolution.

Such transformations will not be possible if the root causes—demo- graphic pressure and imprudent consumption—are not viewed with the appropriate sobriety and wisdom.

The strategic developments suggested in this work are all viewed as practical requirements for any true resuscitation of the natural environ- ment, in which I include a natural human population, where children are loved and cared for, and their parents may find joy and dignity in their lives. Realistic curbs on overpopulation are only so good as our corre- sponding contemplation of, and behavior toward nature (an equation that encompasses our treatment of one another). Both are battle fronts; both family planning and ecological sustainability factor equally in our scaling back humanity's unprecedented aggression against the Creation. We are no longer speaking about "utopia," per se, but about ensuring a biological future. What is *best* may be beyond humanity's reach, at pre- sent. But what is *good* may be possible.

The pattern of these two endeavors I offer in the spirit of "a modest proposal" (the phrase first intoned by Gorbachev in the early days of Glasnost): a global truce that would cut short this melancholy war which is destroying Earth and all her precious progeny.

~1~

The Balance of Nature

THERE ARE FIFTY-TWO Antarctic avian species, eight of which breed on the continent, eleven on the peninsula, the rest along the many sub-Antarctic islands, like Marion. Measurements of bird biomass on Marion Island some years ago revealed the presence of sixty-four million pounds of fresh guano, five hundred tons of dropped feathers, three hundred fifty tons of dead birds, and two hundred tons of eggs. Biology is multitudinous in the frigid southern seas.

Amid tens of millions of square kilometers of high altitude aridity, Antarctica enshrines a viable system of fertility, of population balance, which includes 340 known Antarctic plant species, even two seed-bearing angiosperms on the ice. There are eighty-five species of moss, two hundred different lichens, in addition to the smaller forms of life: untold species of bacteria, yeast, diatoms, and foraminifera. Mites roam the interiors of seal nostrils, yellow *Xanthoria* lichens wedge themselves into minute crannies of the remote TransAntarctic Mountain walls, while cyanobacteria have been found living inside Dry Valley rocks, heating the interiors to a toasty seventy degrees, despite exterior blizzards. At Mount Faraway in the Theron Mountains of Western Princess Martha Land, as well as at the remote Vostock Station, at an altitude of thirteen thousand feet, six pairs of skuas have been seen. A single skua made it to the South Pole itself. Such legendary tenacity transcends the individual birds and suggests something stellar about evolutionary biology in Antarctica: trillions upon trillions of neurons sensitized to sea and salt, wind and ice, maintaining genetic equipoise and population stability in what is the driest, highest, harshest region on the planet. Countless marine organisms in this southern ocean go into suspended animation throughout the winter, revealing yet another facet of Antarctica's perfectly adapted populations.

Not surprisingly, the sheer pageant of biological numbers in Antarctica—trillions of krill, hundreds of millions of other creatures—follows a pattern of triumphant speciation, a condition of population equality and sharing, of free biological socialism, that appears basic to the success of life everywhere on the planet. What is perhaps most astonishing about the various plant and animal communities in Antarctica is that they are not *more* numerous. Given the vast underpinnings of the food base—phytoplankton and krill—one can only admire and envy whatever built-in fertility checks have been ordained there. Certain coral reefs along Australia's Great Barrier, for instance, contain as many as twenty thousand species of fish, far more than are known to exist in the Antarctic Ocean. Any sizeable portion of tropical rain forest still standing will quickly dwarf all of Antarctica, not for mammals or even birds, but insects. Yet, the effective principles of population stability are undeviating in those other regions, as well. And though the hand of humanity has been heavy upon reefs and rain forests, tainting biological evidence which might otherwise provide a clear window on the workings of evolution, certain explicit population patterns have become perceptible.

While it is known that on average three hundred species go extinct every million years or so, the pertinacity and refinement of plant and animal evolution indicates that nearly all populations on Earth have achieved an exquisite, self-regulatory equilibrium providing them the means to preserve the vitality of their species. At least in the absence of man. In other words, they will ordinarily control their numbers. Toward that resolute goal, nature performs a constant series of numeric gymnastics, maintaining high amplitudes—where populations surge in size—and equally impressive troughs—where their numbers subsequently collapse, though not all the way. Sometimes self-regulation is blatant, at other times subtle. In the stark terms of science, numbers, per se, mean little to the planet. Eight million multicellular creatures dwell within a square inch of salt pan. In two pinches of soil substrate in Norway, one investigator found over ten thousand separate groups of microbes.[1] That's not individuals, but different *types* of individuals! In approximately one pound of fertile soil anywhere on the planet, there are likely to be four hundred billion algae, five hundred million fungi, five hundred million protozoa, and ten million bacteria.[2] Eighteen thousand different species of beetle have been postulated for just one hectare of Panamanian rain forest. According to Edward O. Wilson, something like a billion billion insects are alive at any given moment, weighing more than all of humanity combined.[3] Abundant microbes thrive on the bare sands of the Namibian desert, where summer temperatures exceed 170 degrees. Meanwhile, a single human being possesses an internal population of some three hundred trillion cells, give or take 2.5 million, at any given second. We harbor some seven million follicle mites in our eyelashes, and approximately twenty-four billion bacteria in each armpit. Billions of yeasts, bacteria and viruses crawl over our forehead, while some one hundred billion cells inhabit our brain. Each of these worlds within worlds indicates a population that is perfectly poised, a mysterious and essential ecosystem.

Some populations are not so poised, however, driven by strategies whose overall design we may never want to understand. A *Polycythemia vera* cancer cell, for example, found within some luckless human beings, can generate nearly seventeen trillion descendants in six weeks, with an aggressive weight of twenty pounds strung together by fibrous tissues. From the perspective of the host, such metastasis implies an overpopulated cellular region, to put it mildly, though it comprises less than 6 percent of the total organism, a rate of numeric increase far less than certain economies, slums, countries, and the human race in general. However, from the vantage of the cancer, whose motto is perpetual growth, there is nothing overpopulated about this sequence of events. Only the host knows for sure.

Within the arena of overpopulation, there are other radical view-points and stabilization (i.e., death of the host) techniques, as well. Take the Norwegian and Alaskan lemmings who may multiply five hundred times their normal group size every three or four years. To put that in proper context, think in terms of the megacity Calcutta with an added increment of street-dwellers equivalent to the total number of current humans on the planet, or nearly 5.8 billion. For the lemmings, this is a very temporary kind of hell, which precipitates a nonviable sociology, namely, famine. Their hormones release a distress call which tells them they are too many, that they must spread out in search of new sources of sedge and seedling and shoot. Invariably, many come upon water. They try to swim to the other side, dog-paddling for up to fifteen minutes. That's the limit of their endurance. If the waves are higher than six inches, they will drown, and many do. They are true environmental refugees, a condition increasingly familiar to *Homo sapiens.* The lemmings' little corpses provide superb fertilizer for the northern grasslands which benefit from a new crop of seeds and berries, the mainstay of caribou herds, which in turn provide other predators their dinner (or trophies). Enough lemmings perpetually survive this crisis to begin the cycle of regeneration all over again, which pleases yet other predators. The first two laws of thermodynamics propel these cyclical disasters and rebirths. The Law of the Conservation of Matter/Energy suggests that the recycling of corpses is inherent to the complexity and species interdependency of the biosphere. The Entropy Law provides that excess cannot persist, that imbalance must ultimately be stabilized, one way or another.

What is true for lemmings is, of course, true for insects, be they moths, gnats, cicada, or locusts. Population sizes of the lasiocampid moth are radically convulsed on average once in forty years, their high range an astonishing ten thousand times the low range. Ninety percent of all locusts on Earth flew to Morocco in 1988 to satisfy what appeared to scientists to be a collective hunger. Their journey over land, mountain, desert, and ocean was marked by what seemed to be an enormous-looking dust cloud extending several miles in all directions. Morocco could not feed the billions of locusts. Many of the insects died, some survived. What impelled so many creatures to their predictable death? An unquestioning orientation toward homeostasis? Mass migrations, death, and resurrection are all pieces of the boom and bust puzzle.

By comparison, the United Nations Population Fund estimates that there are currently one hundred million human transnational migrants, some refugees, some temporary workers. In addition, hundreds of millions of domestic human migrants have fled to urban centers where the effects of boom and bust can be tracked in terms of crime, crowding, pollution, and infant, child, and maternal mortality.

Unlike human urban slum dwellers (about whom there is some debate with regard to the character of their immune system: is it strengthened, war-hardened by harsh conditions, or does it break down more readily? Epidemiological and fertility data from slums around the world is inconsistent), starlings, howler monkeys, and hummingbirds appear to maintain population balance by taking an inventory of their numbers every day, presumably to avoid the kinds of cyclical disasters previously mentioned. Worms and tadpoles are able to secrete growth inhibitors. Among the lynx populations of the Northwest Territories, boom and bust patterns occurred in eight-to-ten-year cycles, the feline ranging in population from four to eighty thousand. Sometimes, ecological overshoot can plummet the population below its threshold for recovery. Such an event can account for local extinction. On St. Matthew Island in the Bering Sea, colonizer reindeer devoured the island's plant life. Their base population of two thousand exceeded the island's carrying capacity. Within three years the herd was virtually wiped out.

Until recently, human beings were very much a part of this biological system of checks and balances which seems to hold firm for all organisms. Four primary inclemencies kept *Homo sapiens* in relative population calm: high infant mortality, war, famine, and disease, all contributing to a meager life expectancy. The Black Plague (*Pasteurella pestis*) was transmitted from the Tibetan Silk Route to a harbor at Sicily in 1347. Rodents account for 50 percent of all mammals, and it was the friendly rat, carrier of the rat flea (*Xenopsylla cheopis*) that caused such demolition. At least 30 percent of the human population died out—half of all people between Iceland and India. Boom and bust need not operate according to food scarcities and resulting famine. Disease, acting upon a host, or dense network of hosts, plays a similar role in the maintenance of populations. Not unlike the moths and the lemmings, Europeans witnessed a spectacular revival of their populations within a century of the Plague, exceeding their pre-Plague numbers. What is quite different about human beings from their furry Arctic or Antarctic cousins is the distorted duration between our amplitudes and troughs, our booms and our busts. Through a series of seemingly unrelated technological and scientific breakthroughs, we would appear to have extricated ourselves from the normal biological rules governing all populations, engineering an enduring "grace" period that has enabled us to keep growing unhaltingly.

One could cite bipedal posture, extended periods of child development and maternal nurturance, stable food-gathering base camps, fire (and the resulting extension of our biological clock and accelerated growth of neurons in the brain), and a host of other paleontological distinctions that marked *Homo sapiens* as somehow destined to be different. Certainly the advent of agriculture itself was the beginning of our recent break-away. More recently still, a rapid succession of mechanical inventions—most notably the multiplication of energy and heat capacity—added appreciable fuel to our food, privacy and insulation pyramids, and thus the population boom.

Yet, until very recently, most human communities beyond the pale of industrialization continued to comply with the unstated rules of boom and bust, usually by chance, as in the case of the above-mentioned primal causes—high infant mortality, war, famine, and disease—though sometimes by contraceptive choice or cultural lifestyle. Mbuti Pygmies, traditional Bengalis, the cave-dwelling Tasaday of Mindinao, and Tibetans, each took culturally ordained steps to limit their numbers through a variety of techniques: basic abstinence for three years following a birth; the application of various kinds of natural secretions or animal dung to the vagina (much in the manner of modern foams); and rites of polyandry, whereby a woman limited her fertility by marrying several husbands. In fact, several thousand traditional contraceptives are known throughout the world. Several human population groups were able to maintain, or to be currently maintaining, zero population growth (ZPG), which refers to a total fertility rate (TFR) of approximately two children per woman or less.

In America, in what is today northern New Mexico's Pecos Valley, some two thousand Indians lived in relative harmony according to what today would be described as an "ecologically sustainable" lifestyle. They, too, achieved what can be extrapolated as a zero population growth society. The Pecos fashioned an imposing four-story quadrangular pueblo with 660 rooms and countless kivas surrounding a majestic courtyard, amid the broad expanse of the Sangre de Cristo Mountains in the mid-1400s. For at least a century, this city, built upon a rocky ridge, thrived on local agriculture, never exceeding the semi-arid land's respectable carrying capacity.[4]

Similarly, near what is Fresno, California, twenty thousand Yokut hunter/gatherers lived in a single city of sod and thatch huts beside what was an enormous lake, three hundred years ago. It was the largest known hunter/gathering assemblage in the world, an ecologically sustainable megacity. The Yokut traded with other tribes across the High Sierra, exchanging grass, herbs, beads, and vegetables for obsidian, moccasins, clay, and fire drills. They ate wasps, skunk, deer, mussels, and clams, as well as the sweetest blackberries in North America. Their meat-eating culture was achievable only because of their relatively small number.

Further North, along San Francisco Bay, the Ohlone Indians lived in a similarly undeviating paradise for nearly two thousand years. The life expectancy of these indigenous peoples was probably less than half that of today's average American (could they have known, or minded, the years they were missing?) though not appreciably lower than denizens of the modern African nation, Guinea Bissau, where the average life expectancy still hovers around the age of forty.

In some countries today there is currently a negative population growth. In Singapore, for example, the government, worried that its population of 3.1 million "is not growing fast enough" has taken to the promulgation of inventive dating incentives for the high percentage of single citizens.[5]

But, in spite of the zero population, or negative population trends within certain countries, regions, and tribes, our species as a whole is characterized at present by a problematic global total fertility rate average of 3.2, which translated into over ninety-seven million newborns in 1992, the highest annual number for human births in history. According to the Population Reference Bureau in Washington, world population growth in both 1995 and 1996 was 1.5, which translates into a doubling time for the existing 5.8 billion people on the planet of approximately forty-seven years. In many developing countries, where over 80 percent of all human growth is occurring, the TFR equates with nearly four children per couple. Those towns, cities, regions, and countries with such TFRs may double their population in as few as seventeen years (an amateurish rate of increase by comparison with lemmings or moths, but extremely serious given the unique nature of human impact on the environment). Like economic inflation, such rapid population growth diminishes the perceived value and "quality of life package" of every living organism. As competition for life-sustaining resources escalates, more and more of nature is deemed a resource. The exploitation of a resource transforms subject into object, transmogrifying beauty, nuance, uniqueness, and that which is necessarily and biologically separate from ourselves, into a mere utility. Utilitarianism has had its share of economic and ethical advocates, but in truth, it perverts the world. A child is no blessing when its generation is inadvertently mobilized in fitful opposition to its surroundings, seeking to exploit, to combat, in other words, the very "nature" which has given birth to it in the first place. Ironically, explosive human population growth was triggered by a convergence of factors that all suggested an amplification of utility and value—namely, decreasing infant mortality, increased longevity, and greater prosperity, the result of new immunizations, enhanced energy extraction, and the Green Revolution. This strictly human ambiguity has continued to obscure the moral and biological implications of our vastly overpopulated species.

Unlike lemmings, who live and die and are reborn in a strictly defined territory—"their" territory—humanity is blessed with at least the appearance of no bounds. Human food choices have drastically narrowed as our population has increased. While monoculture can be attributed to global market forces, its fast-growing, energy-intensive, cash-crop mentality is actually a response to demographic pressure. But food acquisition, which—along with sexual partners and a breeding site—defines the total orbit of all other species, has relatively less importance among *Homo sapiens*. Our state of boundlessness has engendered a rare delusion of reprieve from natural codes. It has meant that we are not only global carnivores, but globally territorial. No other single population (other than those which inhabit us, or have affixed themselves to our comings and goings) has so flaunted its biological and sexual prominence.

Evidence overwhelmingly suggests that even when our numbers were not so distorted, other species which came into contact with our forebears did so at their own extreme peril. The movement of Siberian hunters who descended upon North and South America some twelve thousand years ago coincided with the rapid extinction of 80 percent of all mammal and avian genera that had thrived during the preceding Pleistocene. Considering the widespread remains of stone weaponry and charcoal fire pits that marked this sudden human migration, which conquered at the apparent rate of sixteen kilometers a year, such massive extinction must be more than mere coincidence.[6]

The same carnage can be traced everywhere early man wandered, from New Zealand, where the earliest indigenous peoples wiped out large numbers of native avian species, to Polynesia, the lowlands of Europe, and Scandinavia, where man has had a negative ecological presence on the mountains there since the earliest Stone Age, according to recent studies.[7]

Furthering this view of innate human aggression, Raymond Dart quantified the high frequency of bone injuries sustained by our ancestors, from the *Australopithecines* to fourth-glacial *Homo sapiens,* typically during the hunt. Dart's description of this "blood-lust differentiator, this predaceous habit, this mark of Cain that separates man dietetically from his anthropoidal relatives and allies him rather with the deadliest of Carnivora" suggests that in *Homo sapiens,* overpopulation has more to do with ecological impact than mere numbers. This supposition accords well with what we now know about ourselves.[8]

Indeed, overpopulation is not, in and of itself, a transgression against nature. The inflated community of lemmings, in its frenzy to feed itself, does not destroy the Arctic. Quite to the contrary, its multiplicity of corpses nurtures the soil there, providing a veritable gourmet's feast for other organisms (what the nineteenth-century Japanese, in describing human corpses, first called "night soil"). A colony of driver-ants, made up of perhaps twenty million workers, devour everything before them, mile after mile, when they move out. According to Wilson, they are "a heavy burden for the ecosystem to bear," reducing its biomass and altering even the "proportions of species." But they have been getting away with it for many millions of years without noticeably altering the planet.[9] Similarly, in recent years, the Crown of Thorns starfish near Guam have been devastating the coral reefs at the rate of one kilometer per month, a syndrome which marine biologist Dr. Richard Chesher attributes to the cumulative pressure upon the starfish from human activities. But the only known species to actually change the whole planet, to interfere with nature, is *Homo sapiens.* That interference is overwhelmingly troublesome: first, because it existed when the total human population on Earth was under a million; secondly, because those same aggressive convictions and habits of mind persist today, empowered by an unimaginably more deadly technology than stone hatchets and spears; thirdly, because we are more than likely to exceed ten billion people, a current projection which I take to be rather optimistic; and finally, because we are quickly reducing the entire planet to what biologists call a "simple ecosystem." That is, one dominated by very few primary species. Simple ecosystems are a total anomaly in nature. Nor is there any guarantee that a planet-wide biologic simplicity could support complex organisms like human beings.

THIS BRINGS ME back to the biodiverse Antarctic, where human beings grasping after "resources," first served warning to that primeval landmass in the year 1786.[10] That is when the first sealing expedition arrived at South Georgia Island, eleven years after Captain James Cook reported sighting abundant fur seals in the region. By 1791, at least 102 ships were conducting massacres of the many seal species there. Others, like the southern elephant seal and the abundant crabeaters, were heavily impacted. A two-ton elephant seal, once "rendered," could produce two barrels of oil. Of the thirty to forty million Antarctic seals, most are crabeaters, one of the more abundant mammals on Earth. Brown, fawn, and blonde-colored, they scatter out, three to four seals per square kilometer of ice, lounging much of the time like sultans, unhurried, not about to expend precious energy fleeing from the harpoon or the spear. It is believed that the crabeaters collectively consume over sixty million tons of krill each year. The vast krill populations seem to withstand such mass destruction without so much as flinching. For the seals, however, the same cannot be said. One species in particular, the Kerguelen fur seal was virtually wiped out. Today, at places like South Georgia Island, it is making a comeback after several recent international treaties provided policing mechanisms for its reestablishment.

But, for tens of millions of years their only predator had been the killer whales that hunted along the polynyas (openings in the ice), rushing and circling, pummelling the bergs with their tails, until they had managed to dislodge a seal. With the arrival of this new and ungainly species, man, the seals, and the whales themselves, were taken by surprise overnight. The Norwegians came up with a harpoon-canon winch technique for killing whales which they introduced to the Antarctic in 1904, establishing the first sordid shore-based whale processing industry there. Subsequently, two-thirds of all baleens were exterminated. Despite International Whaling Commission rulings, at least two countries continue to kill many thousands of minckes every year.

Antarctic Treaty nations agreed in 1961 to maintain Antarctica as an international preserve, unowned, unmilitarized, a bastion of pure research. But today, more than three dozen countries are vying for strategic presence in this splendid wilderness. The seemingly diminutive human populations hover precisely about those scarce ice-free nesting sites (a mere three hundred miles of possibilities, out of more than eighteen thousand miles of ice-locked coastline) where millions of

Antarctic birds and mammals also congregate. The small contingent of human newcomers—a species not remotely suited, biologically speaking, to the southern continent—has brought with it a host of lethal chemicals and pollutants, the indirect fall-out from human demographic pressure. By that causal link I refer to the complex political, economic, cultural, and technological wellsprings of human overpopulation, whose most blatant, or least pretty, expression is its cumulative ecological damage.

McMurdo Sound, the embayment adjacent to the major American base, is virtually dead, according to one senior marine biologist with the National Science Foundation.[11] Human activities in Antarctica have unleashed a steady stream of polyethylene particles, polystyrene foam, trace metals, and radioactivity (the Americans once illegally installed a nuclear power plant at McMurdo before it leaked and had to be scrapped, along with tons of contaminated soil). Bombs have been exploded on the ice, toxic waste has been buried or strewn, all manner of noxious discharges have flowed from leaking fifty gallon drums, and an entire penguin rookery was killed by the dogs at Esperanza. At most of the bases, road building and construction has disrupted the fragile ecosystems. Dust and foot traffic has weakened lichen communities (the redwoods of Antarctica); sea-borne and air pollutants from ever-increasing numbers of ecotourist ships have infiltrated the wilderness. Garbage is randomly tossed from those ships, or by land-based personnel, or burned in open pits, the smoke penetrating microbial communities and wreaking the same biological disruptions that would occur in a laboratory setting. Thousands of tourists, managers, scientists, and bureaucrats land by ship and by air, and go off tromping over delicate Tortula, Bryum algens, and *Grimmia antarctici*, the dark, heavy clumps of moss and grass. As late as 1964, the seals were still being slaughtered. U.S. and French servicemen actually blew up bird rookeries in the course of various construction projects, "to see penguins fly," as one worker is alleged to have put it. Antarctic seamen have tossed hundreds of thousands of live penguins into ship furnaces for fuel, or eaten them. But an even more sinister syndrome has been unleashed. Since 1970, the global greenhouse effect has begun to reduce the amount of sea ice during winter months, which in turn has devastated the population size of krill, as well as Chinstrap and Adelie penguins, according to scientists William Fraser and Wayne Trivelpiece, both biologists at Montana State University. In fact, on King George Island, the number of Chinstrap have plummeted by 35 percent, the Adelies, 40 percent. At the same time, the Japanese and Russians are killing five hundred thousand metric tons of krill each year, 1 percent of the total krill ecosystem. According to Langdon Quetin and Robin Ross, biologists at the University of California at Santa Barbara, that amount represents a significant proportion of the crustaceans, considering many are egg-carrying females. [12]

I fasted one Christmas night at an Antarctic base on the Western Peninsula where penguin steaks were being served up. (At least two vegetarian scientists in Antarctica, one from Poland, the other from India, have started greenhouses at their respective bases). The next morning, I scrambled amid garbage dumps strewn in the midst of rookeries, and watched penguins struggle to extricate themselves from wire mesh. A few of the Adelie lay dead in an effluent stream produced by the station. I saw seals frolicking in oil streaks, others fleeing from military vehicles by land. At Paradise Bay, an albatross nested in the charred ruins of a former station that had been burned down by a disgruntled scientist suffering from what in northern polar regions the Eskimos call *pibloktoq,* or Arctic hysteria, the total disorientation that has been known to result from long winter darkness. At yet another human Antarctic settlement, I once lay on the guano-covered rocks near to a rookery and beheld the sorry spectacle of low-flying helicopters taunting the birds for sport. In their panic, adult penguins were separated from their young. The stampede managed to crush a large number of eggs. Everyday, since the turn of the century, similar conflicts have been played out.

High concentrations of DDE and PCB have been recorded in Wilson's petrels, in skuas, cormorants, penguins, and the Weddell Seal. These latter marvels of creation have been discretely observed breeding under the ice. They are able to dive nearly a quarter mile down, remaining there for at least seventy-three minutes before resurfacing. How they cope with the pressure of the deep, of bodily gas exchange, is as yet a mystery. Antarctic seals, like many other mammals, will absorb their own fetuses under times of stress to prevent nonviable births. But it may well be that population dynamics in certain parts of Antarctica have already been skewed. Certainly in the crucial, biodiverse regions of the many bases this is so.

Such negative ecological impact in a place as otherwise remote from human population centers as Antarctica, conveys two salient facts about *Homo sapiens,* consistent with our species' history, but colossally dangerous at this point in time. First, we have demonstrated the power and willingness to lay waste whole populations, not just those that happen to be in our immediate path or conveniently placed for purposes of our dinner.

Second, we degrade or ruin significant portions of habitat, thus inhibiting future generations of a particular organism or complex of organisms. By severing its basis for fertility, we deny a species the opportunity to revive itself, a condition that can only lead to its extinction. That a very small number of organisms (relatively speaking) should incur such devastation in so short a timeframe is much like the workings of a disease pathogen, with one significant exception: no disease on record, not even the Black Plague, has yet driven multiple species to extinction. The dinosaurs died out gracefully, over a period of tens of millions of years, not a mere few centuries. Today, at least 83 percent of all bird species—the descendents of the dinosaurs—have become endangered, in only a few hundred years, due to human aggression and the complicity, knowing or unknowing, of development and economic culture.

Humanity is self-interested. It has always reacted extraterritorially to pressure, moving out during interglacials, claiming new territory, prizing foodstuffs, ensuring surplus, strategizing in the face of perceived threats. This is why Thomas Jefferson initiated the Louisiana Purchase, at a time when population density for most of the United States was a mere ten persons per square mile; to prevent, in his words, "the exterminating havoc of one quarter of the globe" from infecting America. He was referring to immigration from Europe, not Latin America.[13] In a similar vein, the same year Argentina delivered a pregnant woman to Antarctica, Brazil launched four hundred huge developments in the Amazon so as, in then President Medici's words, "to give men without land a land with men."

Hunger, sex, fear, greed, wrath, and curiosity have guided our wants and our migrations. These aspects of the human world have been aggravated as our numbers—and all they imply—have increased. Had the population not escalated so, there is no reason to assume that humanity would not have remained in balance, much like the penguins: elegant survivors, stable, seemingly content, subject to biological normalcy without the need or desire or even the possibility of managing or attempting to overpower nature. This more tranquil picture does not so much as reject the evidence of our carnivorous past, but absorbs it more gracefully, given our diminutive population size thousands of years ago. The counterargument to such nostalgia is the paradoxical possibility that with fewer humans, per capita income, and thus consumption and fossil fuel extraction, might have been even more unrestrained. Singapore is a case in point. Even poor, relatively small-sized nations, such as the Cote d'Ivoire and Cameroon, have shown enormous levels of energy consumption and

CO_2 generation, while many oil-rich countries, like Kuwait, the UAR, Iraq, and Qatar, have absolutely no wildlife protection.

The penguins and seals of Antarctica are still thriving, though that could all change instantly if ozone depletion should alter the genetic viability of phytoplankton upon which the krill, and thus the penguins and seals, depend. Phytoplankton is known to be vulnerable to ultraviolet-B radiation. While the overall rate of chlorofluorocarbon (CFC) production has dropped by nearly 50 percent in the last five years, humanity produced some nineteen billion pounds of CFCs worldwide between 1978 and 1988. The damage from that assault is still rising, literally, and will be reaching the stratosphere to wreak its cannibalistic havoc on the ozone molecule early in the next century. Already, small pockets of the air column over Antarctica have shown depletion exceeding ninety percent during the late spring months. Over parts of Europe and Canada, the ozone layer has thinned in winter by as much as 20 percent. In India, the number of CFC-based refrigerators is projected to reach eighty million units by the year 2010, up from six million in 1989.[14] China, meanwhile, with its gigantic economic boom and 1.23 billion people, is producing nearly ten million refrigerators a year. A recent survey showed that half of all government officials in that country did not know what ozone or CFCs were. This is not surprising, however. In China, some 60 percent of all workers in environmental areas have not even graduated from high-school.[15]

The penguins and seals have another substantial threat, namely, global warming, resulting from the liberation of ice-locked methane in the Antarctic itself and the trapping of CO_2 and other anthropogenic effluent burdens, together threatening to melt portions of the Western Peninsula where penguins and marine mammals live and breed. Already, satellite data has revealed icebergs the size of Rhode Island have broken off from the Antarctic continent. Human induced carbon emissions will double in the next generation, from the current level of seven billion to eight billion tons a year.[16] With a high enough CO_2 regime, far beyond present levels, but not inconsistent with, say, ten billion or more human fossil fuel consumers, the Antarctic land mass might eventually be returned to its condition of sixty million years ago, prior to the great chill, when the continent teemed not with seals and penguins but amphibians and reptiles and luxuriant native vegetation probably more akin to that of present-day South America. If that were to happen, every coastal city and plain would be flooded. For that matter, much of Antarctica would be flooded as well. The salinity and temperature of the oceans would change, enacting a corresponding impact on untold numbers of marine species.

Population dynamics are thus explicitly linked to environment. A stable environment will normally engender stable populations, and vice versa. This is known as *scale,* and it never varies. Human scale, for example, has ensured that most door handles and beds always remain approximately the size of a human hand and a human body, respectively. The same can be said of most animals' nests and lairs. Whether the smallest known organism, the mycoplasmas virus, or the largest, a giant sequoia—with as much as forty thousand board feet of life—all individuals and species conform to scale, a genetic and population average, the result of boom and bust vitality. Only a disease, such as a population of cancer cells, falls out of scale, booming perilously, and eventually committing suicide by killing its host. In this respect, the cancer cell has declared unthinking war upon its carrier, willing to sacrifice itself for the temporary satisfactions of explosive growth. To psychoanalyze the motives of the cancer cell is to stare down the naked territorial imperative face to face.

But the case can be made that along with the cancer cell, human beings have also declared war, and are also now out of scale. The pattern in our population first intimated itself during the transitional Mesolithic: the aforementioned Siberian hunters descending like army ants, eight thousand year old petroglyphs from South Africa depicting the earliest known battle scenes. By the reign of Sargon of Akkad (c. 2872 B.C.) the evidence of widespread aggression is unambiguous. Chroniclers tell us that Sargon "turned (the village of) Kazalla into dust and heaps of ruins; he destroyed even the resting places of birds." "And they utterly destroyed all that was in the city, both man and woman, young and old, and ox, and sheep, and ass, with the edge of the sword," wailed the author of the book of Joshua (6:21). A few thousand years later, Winston Churchill wrote to his wife in August, 1914, "Everything tends toward catastrophe & collapse. I am interested, geared up and happy. Is it not horrible to be built like that? The preparations have a hideous fascination for me. I pray to God to forgive me for such fearful moods of levity." Thirty years later, along the Merderet River in Normandy, in June of 1944, "The slaughter once started could not be stopped. . . . Having slaughtered every German in sight, they ran on into the barns of the French farmhouses where they killed the hogs, cows and sheep. The orgy ended when the last beast was dead."[17]

The world has seen its share of perturbations, of course, that make even the fiercest of warlords seem petty and amateurish: asteroids, periodic glaciation, the fires caused by an estimated six million lightning blasts striking the planet's surface every second, hurricanes, and volcanos. Such disasters of varying scope have moved evolution forward over a period of 3.9 billion years. In the early Cambrian period, 540 million years ago, the speed of evolution suddenly leapt forward as the planet's oxygen saturation reached 21 percent, where it is, more or less to this day. With oxygen came an ozone layer, and with ozone, a veritable Big Bang of biodiversity. Two hundred million years later, at the end of the Paleozoic era, a disaster of unknown origins swept the planet, eliminating approximately 96 percent of all marine animals. Yet, from the ranks of those hangers-on emerged the first fledgling dinosaurs. One hundred eighty million years later the dinosaurs disappeared, just as rain forests were everywhere proliferating. Out of this succession arose the first shrews and eventually lemurs, distant ancestors of *Homo sapiens.*

Five great extinction spasms have occurred on the planet, that we know of. Not one of these catastrophes has been triggered as the result of some biologic malfunction, or disorder, let alone a single species. But that is precisely the explanation for the crisis we all now find ourselves confronted with. This perplexing, senseless tragedy must be viewed in clear, unwavering terms. There is no turning away from it: we are each contributing to the sixth pattern of extinction on Earth, the first one, apparently, in sixty-five million years. The devastation is the direct result of our total population dynamic (TPD). By that I refer to the whole social, political, cultural, and religious array of causes and consequences of World War III, a war whose symptoms have engulfed every cell, gene, and ecosystem throughout the world, and whose chemical traces are to be found on the ocean floor and in the high stratosphere. The effects of this TPD are detectable in every mammary gland and pair of testes, in the optic nerves of Argentine cattle and in the mercury-infested rivers of the Amazon, in hospital beds of smog-laden Denver and across the hungry, diseased, debt-ridden, and desertified swathe of sub-Saharan Africa.

Because the planet has spent billions of years adding, not subtracting species, we can safely assume without debating its teleological whys or wherefores that biodiversity has a crucial purpose in both the short- and long-term scheme of things here on Earth. Against this criterion of planetary scale and TPD, it is clear that our species is desperately overpopulated. Those who have the means and can afford the time to read these words, will no doubt suffer psychologically on account of their species' ungainliness in nature, but will be among the least likely to experience the real human fall-out, the physical ordeal of overpopulation. The true beneficiaries of that burden are poor, discouraged, hungry, illiterate, oppressed, and often sick. And there are several billion such people, a figure rapidly escalating.

Homo sapiens had achieved an astonishing size of four hundred million at the time of the first outbreak of plague, in 1347. Yet, by 1500, we were a global swarm of seven hundred million. By 1850, our throngs had topped one billion. Thus, while our transgressive nature has not changed in thousands of years, the multibillion explosion of our actual numbers is a very recent phenomenon. It has yet to reach its amplitude, and it would be premature to speculate on the coming ecological trough. Those who have carefully read between the lines of history, ventured apocalyptic extrapolations, and had the courage to predict future calamity have done so at the risk of public damnation by those prominent "exceptionalists" who see only blue sky and can not imagine that human ingenuity and advanced technology will not solve everything. Yet a reading of history suggests that, if anything, Thomas Malthus and Paul Ehrlich were generous in their predictions and even understated the extent of coming suffering.

Given the persistence and scope of our malice and hedonism, it would be the worst form of stupidity and complicity to simply ignore what is happening to us, and what we in turn are doing to the Earth. As E. O. Wilson rightly describes, we have but one planet and one experiment. We'd better get it right.

It is impossible to know whether the physical world could sustain ten, or fifteen, or twenty billion people, under any conditions of human behavior. If, for example, our descendants chose to eat fast-growing species of sustainably produced fruits and vegetables, to remain totally passive, nonconsumerist, utilizing solar energy in conjunction with a hydrogen-fuel cell economy for their basic needs, not traveling, harming no living beings, confined essentially to their garden cubicles across designated desert regions of the planet where the convergence of human densities and wild biodiversity were least in conflict, there might be a case for a vastly larger human population, but how vast one cannot say. One investigator has theorized that if technology could convert all food sources to liquid, step up the efficiency of marine photosynthesizers, limit all energy use to that which was solely productive of food (even recycling and cannibalizing liquid human cadavers), then our species might attain a theoretical number of sixty thousand million million, which merely highlights the frailties of theoretical demographics, for that quanity would translate into a planetary density of 120 people per square meter.[18] At various times, the U.N. Food and Agriculture Organization in Rome and the Vatican have suggested that the Earth could feed forty billion people at her dinner table, or nearly forty Chinas. (It should be pointed out that scientists with the Pontifical Academy, however, have recently rejected the Pope's calculations and called for population stabilization, in tune with most other ecologists).

What should be clear, however, is that at a population size of forty, even twenty billion, we will no longer be the conventionally defined species known as *Homo sapiens*, endowed with the preconditions allowing for a humanity, but rather, some far more malicious, unpredictable, and emotionally bereft creature, stressed to the point of utter, relentless self-destruction. That is my prediction, and that is the awesome and terrifying lesson of population dynamics and evolution here on Earth, whether in Antarctica, or a place like China.

At night, when I lie awake meditating on these ponderous matters, I want to believe that there is still time to counterbalance this paralyzing suzerainty of which I am a part. For my children's sake . . . *for the children,* there are compelling reasons for doing so. And in that platitude of long-standing respectability rests, perhaps, the most painful paradox of all: that all those toddlers, however adorable, must be, in part, held back, somehow consciously curtailed from being; that the actual *size* of the coming generations, to whom we would devote our love and attention, our dreams, hopes, and fervent prayers, must be considerably less numerous than the present one.

~2~

A Paradox of Souls: China

THE LAST DAYS OF THE ONE-CHILD POLICY

Hope eternal for a stabilized, well-cared-for human population is the one unconditional maxim that motivates and sustains the often harsh, unappreciated world of family planning, and nowhere more so than in China. Throughout my travels there, many family planning cadres pleaded with me to keep smiling. To manifest positive thinking. Otherwise, they said, people will lose heart and give up. Of course they're right. And there are some justifiable reasons for limited optimism. It is estimated, for example, that all of the population programs worldwide have thus far prevented some four hundred million people from being born, considerably more than half of them in China. The social, medical, economic, and ecological implications of this number for the next century, if family planning assistance continues, are that four billion fewer consumers and despoilers are expected, a population size equivalent to the total human population of the 1970s.[1]

Moreover, the use of contraceptives by (married) couples (contraceptive prevalence rate, or CPR) has risen dramatically throughout the world. In China, according to one estimate the rate was 73 percent in 1990, and an extraordinarily high 83 percent in 1997. By contrast, CPR in the United States averages 68 percent. Throughout the rest of the developing world, approximately 44 percent of all couples are protected against childbearing. Such gains have been made in the past twenty years. With increasing government support and carefully targeted social mobilization, future strides might even be more rapid and dramatic. Or they might not.

In the late 1980s, a global study by the United Nations Population Fund (formerly, U.N. Fund for Population Activities [UNFPA]) discerned several fundamental conclusions that could be drawn from years of family planning experience. For example, the more types of contraceptives offered, the higher the rate of acceptance by men and women ("acceptors"). Thirty-five countries were studied and it was shown that those with only two types of contraceptives available (i.e., sterilization and the IUD) were less than half as successful as those where five or more options were present (the so-called *cafeteria* style). In addition, according to a recent unpublished UNFPA document, when women had the right to choose their own form of birth control, 91 percent continued to use it, versus a persistence rate of only 28 percent among those women who were not free to choose. Such lessons have entered the mainstream of family planning policy recommendations, with varying degrees of success, in over 140 countries. One particularly distressing indication of the need for enhanced contraceptive prevalence is born out by the fact that a woman who may herself desire no more than two children, will require nine to ten abortions in her lifetime to accomplish that goal, in the absence of contraceptive availability.[2]

While such data and percentage points may appear far removed from the glaring abyss of ozone depletion and the blowing up of penguin rookeries, in fact they are completely relatable. From the total population dynamic (TPD), or ecological perspective, our ill graces add up. Every individual, like every vote, counts. This is a platitude of particular gravity in geographically confining nations. In China, it is equally true, but much more difficult to grasp.

And thus, for reasons having to do with the unprecedented size of the world's current population of children, and the immense number of child-bearing females, many would argue that the decade of the 1990s is the crucial one for reversing human fertility rates before a planetary baby-boom drags down our species and condemns most other species as well. There is little time left for concerted action, the scope of which is daunting.

This is especially true in China, where the TPD, as I have earlier described it, has presently unleashed two opposing impulses—economic gain and escalating fertility—that together defy the classic "demographic transition model." Demographic transition holds that high infant mortality and a high fertility rate will inevitably shift, with economic advantage, to low infant mortality and slightly declining fertility. As economic prosperity continues to advance, the working class is said to rise up in purchasing power, to be able to spend more money on health care and less time in the home, and to be less inclined to have more children. Hence, in the third and final phase of demographic transition, both infant mortality and fertility will drop rapidly to a stable, fertility replacement level. In China, however, infant mortality and the fertility rate dropped without a corresponding per capita rise in the country's economic performance, though the standard of living was better than in most developing countries. Now, with the new-found scent of riches and the return of Hong Kong, infant mortality remains extremely low, but the fertility rate is rising—despite a high CPR. The standard of living will continue to increase for some, but at the expense of tragic ecological consequences, and a broad gap between those who benefit from economic good times and those who do not. In the meantime, the population remains guided by a nearly hormonal sociology which reads: times are good, have more babies. This is a hugely problematic scenario.[3]

"To get rich is glorious," said Deng Xiaoping in 1978, oddly echoing a sentiment of Mao Zedong thirty years earlier. In 1993, the Chinese Communist Party, about to be utterly dropped, officially endorsed profit. Such economic policy inconsistencies reflect a similar ambivalence with respect to the Chinese party line concerning fertility. Mao frequently changed his mind about the population issue. Initially, he denounced birth control, arguing that the solution to more and more people was, simply put, "production." Karl Marx had first theorized this concept, in opposition to Thomas Malthus, who more rightly perceived that in the end, the earth's resources were frighteningly finite, no matter how energetic or inventive people might prove themselves in the future. People,

insisted Mao, were not a problem. And the more people, the more production. He was widely quoted as declaring, "of all things in the world
people are the most precious." That was at a time when the life expectancy in China was thirty-five years and infant mortality was raging between
two and three hundred per thousand live births.

It is worthwhile pausing for a moment and considering deeply what a
world with a human life expectancy of thirty-five would be like. This was
essentially the *average* human condition prior to the twentieth century—
the circumstances into which an estimated eighty billion *Homo sapiens*
have been born. Collectively, they have left their mark, and it has been a
controversial one. Individually, a minute smattering of Beethovens has
incurred a trail of joy and triumph. But well over 79.99 billion of our forebears have simply vanished without a trace, having lived short and inexplicable existences. In spite of the overwhelming pattern of early death,
however, nearly all of human development, art, accomplishment, and culture has evolved and prospered under a half-life regime. To have many children was to combat this narrow life-expectancy. "It is not uncommon, I
have been frequently told, in the Highlands of Scotland for a mother who
has borned twenty children not to have two alive," wrote Adam Smith in
1776 (*Inquiry into the Nature and Causes of the Wealth of Nations*).

China, not unlike the rest of humanity, has never deviated from its
pursuit of more time: time to fulfill the meaning of life, the connection to
nature, or, in the case of some cultures, the duty to ancestors. In 1990,
average human life expectancy in China was sixty-nine years, and the
mean infant mortality rate (IMR) per thousand births, was fourteen in the
cities, and between twenty-two and fifty-one in rural sectors.[4] In the 1950s
mothers who had lots of children in China (and in France) were awarded
medals honoring them as heroes. Within a year or two, following declining per captia figures, evidence of much malnutrition in the hinterlands,
and a desperately sagging industrial base, Mao's thinking became slightly
more "sophisticated." He decided that China was heading toward economic disaster. No more medals were given out. Excess children were
viewed as an impediment to efficient production. In fact, rampant pregnancy was considered criminal.

Communism was quick to embrace Deng's free market exhortation.
Within a decade of the country's economic liberalization—throughout
the 1980s—there were at least 225 thousand privately run companies in
the densely populated coastal provinces[5] and the GNP bounded from

$120 to $427 billion. Today, the acquisition of washers and dryers, refrigerators, television sets, and a host of other household goods is soaring and production is expected to double before the year 2000. Businessmen from throughout the world have been flocking for several years to the spring trade fairs in Guandong. In 1980, manufactured exports were worth nine billion dollars to China; by 1989, thirty-seven billion dollars. Deng intended to raise China's gross domestic product (GDP) from its current $330 (a wildly fluctuating average, depending on the province) to $1,000 per person by the year 2000, thus tripling the size of the economy. Coupled with its current enormous foreign trade surplus, China promises to be the economic superpower of the twenty-first century, and the largest consumer economy the world has ever seen.

This fanfare of the common man can be observed in the sheer flow of new goods; in the row-after-row of town enterprises, joint-enterprise production facilities churning out plastics, household goods, toys, chemicals, tractors, forklifts, steel, tampons, and concrete. The new onslaught has the look of freeway gridlock—not of bicycles but new automobiles, all moving slowly past one high-rise development after another. This purchasing euphoria can be deciphered among the crowds around the counters of any store in nearly every city and town throughout the nation's twenty-seven provinces and three municipalities. This is the first impulse, a production frenzy that will, in turn, chew up the environment in one way or another.

There is a second, related trend, an opposite one in terms of demographic predictability. Corresponding to these otherwise celebratory, consumer-driven developments are the agitations of a new runaway population boom that everyone thought, just a few years ago, had been contained. It hadn't, other than in a few urban regions like Shanghai, where migration and ecological demolition are posing their own too recognizable turmoils.[6] It is, of course, true that China has made remarkable strides toward curbing its human size, more than any other country in history. The total fertility rate (TFR) dropped in China from over 6.0 in 1960, to 2.5 today, a 60 percent decrease. Compare that with a 47 percent decline in Mexico, 38 percent in Indonesia, and a 31 percent drop across India over the same time period. Put in a different, more spectacular context, it took the United States fifty-eight years (1842–1900) to diminish its TFR from 6.0 to 3.5. In China, the same decline required all of seven years (1968–75). Such phasing out of high fertility required twelve years in South Korea, fifteen years in Thailand, and twenty-seven years in Sri

Lanka and Indonesia, countries otherwise hailed by the international family planning community.

But China's base population is gigantic, and because the country's TFR has been stuck for a decade and is now stubbornly rising once again, like an army of living ghosts returning to haunt a nation (a perfectly comprehensible Confucionist image), there is justified concern that economic and agricultural gains will be nullified by all the new mouths to feed each day, each month, each coming year. Based upon the size of the regional populations, and incoming data from a number of researchers, it appears that since 1983 the number of couples having a second child in China has gone from 10 percent to possibly as high as 50 percent. And that is because new exclusions to the one-child policy are becoming so universal in China, that the policy itself is essentially bankrupt. And thus, despite its earlier successes, China is now confronted by a colossal dilemma. According to a recent official (CPIRC) "China Population Research," study by Chen Shengli, if China's existing TFR of 2.5 continues, the country will number 2.5 *billion* by the year 2090; a TFR of 2.3 would mean 2.2 billion in the year 2090. A TFR of 2.0 (the country's official figure) would balance out at 1.5 billion. Such are the perils of decimal points. The bombshell facing China is the unlikelihood of attaining a TFR of 2.0, particularly given the fact that the existing 2.5 TFR is now up from 2.3, a figure that had been inert for a decade, and during which time there was every compulsion and incentive in the world to bring the TFR further down. But that didn't happen. And now, in the final years of this century, as the economy overheats and that TFR should most assuredly be going down, it is continuing to edge upward, in spite of official denials and a much-touted Chinese government "satisfaction" with the fertility status quo. Whatever the decimal factor, China is rewriting the demographic textbooks through its defiance of all traditional theories. Population psychologist Virginia Abernethy has long argued that wealth can translate into a false sense of fertility confidence. The more money, the more children. She quotes from Cuban demographers S. Diaz, Briquets, and L. Perez writing about their own country: "The fertility rises in almost every age group suggest that couples viewed the future as more promising and felt they could now afford more children."[7]

There are well over one hundred million married Chinese women of childbearing age as of the late 1990s. Their preferred family size appears to be two or three, depending on the region.[8] These couples are increasing

China's current growth rate of 1.4 percent, with an annual tally exceeding the total population of Australia.[9] That's a net increase of between sixteen and eighteen million new mouths to feed every year (some Chinese scientists are claiming twenty million), sixty-four thousand births and seventeen thousand deaths every day, making for a net daily increase of nearly forty-seven thousand.[10] During the 1990s, China will have added to itself the equivalent of the number of people in Great Britain, France, and Italy combined, or over 160 million. The huge irony is that China's annual birthrate is now what it was in 1973, when the countrywide TFR was 4.5.

China's population is well over 1.2 billion, or 22 percent of the planet. The data are derivative of the official count. But it is probably higher than that. For example, in addition to the married couples, there are over two hundred million unmarried women and girls of childbearing age in the country. The teenagers are not statistically considered fertility risks, as they are in many other countries, despite solid Chinese information describing their vulnerability. CPRs are not counted among unmarried individuals. Yet, a recent Shanghai poll showed that one out of five women was pregnant at the time of her first marriage.[11] As China's economy glistens, one can expect more and more young girls to become pregnant, and to come seeking help. In the short term, even presuming a mammoth and unprecedented chastity, one hundred million married eligible mothers, with an average country fertility rate of 2.5, suggests that China will exceed 1.3 billion by the year 2000, and attain a number between 1.6 and 1.7 billion by the year 2050. Chinese ecologists have long believed that the country's maximal carrying capacity is between six and seven hundred million people.[12] At nearly double that capacity, currently, with thirty million newborns a year expected during the coming generation, China is living on borrowed time.[13]

One afternoon in Beijing over tea, Madame Peng Peiyun, the warm, jovial, full-bodied force behind China's State Family Planning Commission, with its fifty million paid and unpaid workers, confided in me that further declines in the birthrate, in her opinion, will be very difficult to achieve. She candidly told me that if dramatic new targets are not met, the country could hit a population of two billion sometime late in the next century (a figure contradicted by every other "official" statement). But with the majority of Chinese couples having between two and three and in some cases four children per couple a population of two billion is more than plausible, even if Chinese environmentalists say such a scenario would be a "disaster."[14]

Beijing's allocation for family planning is less than half of one percent of the government's total budget, or 1.3 billion U.S. That figure is expected to double in coming years. Family planning receives an additional $4.7 billion from all other sources, be they donor, provincial, factory, or joint-venture contributions. That combined total averages out to about five dollars per person countrywide. In the U.S., sixteen dollars per person is the estimated cost for family planning, but that does not include the additional thousands of dollars per person borne by the health care system for prenatal to postnatal care, which in China are costs accommodated by the Ministry of Health. Still, says Madame Peng, "It is not enough."

Taicang County, just north of Shanghai, with a population of 420 thousand, has achieved the lowest total fertility rate (TFR) in the whole country, 1.1. This was, and in most respects remains the epicenter of the one-child policy, the famed Chinese gold-standard of fertility control, now, according to authorities in Beijing, in abeyance. Experts have long worried themselves over the *exceptions* to the one-child policy. "Exceptions" were primarily effected for those living in rural areas, or members of officially designated minorities. Until recently, eighteen of the country's provinces were "exception" provinces. The definitions of "urban," "town enterprise," and "rural" are currently in great flux within Chinese circles. Where there is still predominant agriculture going on, the area is considered essentially rural. By that definition, "rural areas" comprise between 70 percent and 83 percent of the country, which implies that the one-child policy was not in fact a country-wide phenomenon, and exerted a very limited impact. Yet, these conclusions were only owned up to by the government as of late 1997. "For manual work you need manpower," Madame Peng explained to me, going on to cite this age-old platitude as the primary reason for excluding rural farmers from the one-child policy.

According to one demographic report, over 87 percent of all births in the country are rural, and as of 1986, in one national survey fewer than 18 percent of all fertile women had complied with the one-child policy. There have been countless suggestions offered by the country's experts as to how couples might have improved compliance with the one-child policy. Ping Tu, for example, an associate professor at the Institute of Population Research at Peking University, points out that in some provinces, like Shaanxi (one of the poorest in the country), women do not even consider using contraceptives until the birth of their first child.

He argued, therefore, that rather than emphasizing just one child, what was actually required was a policy of spacing, and of delaying that first birth. This has become the international model for family planning in countless other countries.[15]

From a high-rise in Taicang's early morning, staring South toward Shanghai, there is a maze of construction enveloped in a pall of smokes that conceals 130 thousand women of childbearing age, one hundred thousand couples. Taicang comes recommended on the basis of a district-wide birthrate of 9.14 children per thousand in 1991, the very best in China. Liu An Ru, the cheerful local Family Planning Commission Chairman, escorted me to the city's Fertility Museum where condoms and the dangerously outmoded Chinese-made steel ring IUDs still in use are behind glass, as well as photographs of deformed monsters, two-headed, protoplasmic blobs, the apparent offspring of incestuous matches which local authorities make much of, by way of a warning.

Sex education begins at the age of fifteen in the twenty-eight Taicang district schools. Secondary (middle) school enrollment is allegedly among the highest in the world here, and I was told 100 percent paid for by the government. (Throughout China, 97 percent of the children get primary education; 70 percent, on average go to middle school, or junior high school; 30 percent go on to high school; but thus far only 2 percent go to college, a level half that of some other developing countries.) This town and district (called by the same name, Taicang) embody the goal of international family planning. Get students enrolled at the secondary level, especially those of the female gender, and your population problems will be, if not solved, at least slowed. That is the conventional wisdom. Taicang has taken it to heart. There is a training course for premarital couples, as well as for grandparents who are schooled in the latest techniques of looking after grandchildren while the parents are off "getting rich." The great irony about "getting rich" in China is that rising per capita income has actually encouraged parents to have more children, not fewer. To revisit Virginia Abernethy's insights, such trends completely fly in the face of classic demographic transition theory, namely, the more family and personal income, the fewer the children. Given China's pursuit of economic stardom, this single unsettling truth about prosperity spells the last days of the one-child policy, and a lurking mine-field of other demographic probabilities.

What about the fertility rate for those thirty thousand unwed girls of childbearing age? I asked Liu An Ru. No problem, he was quick to respond.

What about abortion? No specific data on abortion, he said, other than to remind me with some pride that abortion, as well as sterilization, were legalized in China in 1953. But then he added the assessment that there is very little abortion in the whole county because most people are responsible for their own contraception. Later on, another official in the area indicated that there "may be" 0.6 abortions for every 1 birth. If that's true, of course, it implies a veritable abortion industry.[16] The preferred mode of contraception in Taicang for 67 percent of all "eligible" women is the IUD; condoms and pills are used by 20 percent of married couples, while sterilization accounts for 13 percent of overall birth control. Married couples obtain pills, IUD insertions, or sterilizations for free. High-school students can get over-the-counter pills and condoms at local retail stores. But IUD insertions are available only after the woman has been married and had her first child. Doctors do not encourage the IUD until child number one comes along, which tends in much of China to happen immediately. Afterward, parents do not seem to want another, at least in Taicang, where six thousand Family Planning Association volunteers are out pounding the pavement every day still disseminating the benefits of contraceptive use, knocking on doors, and counseling parents. There is approximately one family planning association member for every twenty to twenty-five couples, the highest concentration of family planners per capita in the world. Elsewhere in China, the ratio varies, from between one planner in three hundred people, to one planner in twenty-seven hundred.[17]

Forty years ago Taicang's locals got their water from the river. These days, the river is black, but the people have managed to construct water purification systems and pumps. I go out to a small suburb of Taicang, the village of Ludu, along one of those joint-enterprise roads. Interspersed among fields of wheat, cotton, rice, peanuts, garlic, and sesame, are small businesses with fancy bronze gates and expansive driveways. A black Mercedes 450 SL with Japanese businessmen exits from one of the factories. Only a few years ago, this was an agricultural commune, farmed by Ludu's 780 occupants. Now, the farmers are in business for themselves, paying into an old age fund, which is a whole new experiment for China. A home costs between three to four thousand dollars in Ludu. As yet there is no central heating in the homes, though there are occasional electric shower stalls. There is no garbage collection. Instead, the people make their own compost, spreading it in the fields as they have done for millennia. Rag-pickers from Taicang a few miles away come to recycle the plastic and cans. One sees tent enclaves of such garbage along the main highway out of Shanghai.

As I am served a lunch of fresh vegetables in one of the homes (my breath visible in the air), my pockets stuffed by generous locals with peanut candies manufactured across the street, the mayor proudly explains how one local architect is now making eight thousand yuan a year, nearly twenty thousand dollars. Most residents are earning two thousand yuan a year, five hundred dollars, far higher than the national GNP level of $370. The first private automobile was purchased here in 1986. Now there are many more. According to one local, everyone "feels much better" thanks to Deng Xaioping's open door policy.

The drop in Taicang's fertility, like that in many urban regions across coastal China, occurred several years before this entrepreneurial fever infected the country. In fact, a fertility plateau was attained even before the one-child policy had been announced in 1979, leading UNFPA officials to wonder why Beijing ever instituted the stringent measure in the first place.[18] The answer is a complex one whose diagnosis summons the extraordinary contradictions and difficulties which the human species as a whole must confront in the coming months and years.

The origins of the policy go back at least to 1954, when Mao began to sense that while people were precious, too many precious people could be disastrous. Various birth control conferences were convened and the Ministry of Public Health began its antipopulation boom campaign in August 1956. A year later, fearful of his country's ability to feed itself, convinced in his own mind that Chinese love-making had reached a state of "total anarchy," Mao feared that the Chinese people were heading toward "extinction."[19] Amazingly, having attained this point of view, Mao reversed his position a year later, and adopted once again the sweet, simple notion that more people on the farm meant more food. At that time, the secretary of the Communist Youth League was quoted as saying, "The force of six hundred million liberated people is tens of thousands of times stronger than a nuclear explosion. Such a force is capable of creating wonders which our enemies cannot even imagine."[20] Thus commenced the fervent government mobilization of China's productive energies, a three-year misguided missile, the "Great Leap Forward," which only succeeded in undermining the country's energy and agricultural sectors—never to be repeated, promises Beijing—with resulting famine that took thirty million lives. It was a true ecological "trough," one of the worst human tragedies ever, quickly followed by a population boom, as one might predict. In fact, within just a few years, the birthrate doubled, from the low twenties to over forty per thousand, while the death rate plunged from forty-five to approximately ten per thousand. China in the late 1950s and early 1960s had the biological look of the Arctic grasslands, home to the lemmings.[21] Premier Zhou Enlai called for a new campaign to control births. What had been, up until 1971, a three child limit, was now altered to two children. In one year, 1975, seventeen million women had IUDs inserted. It was an all-time global record. Nor should it be forgotten that the Chinese female's body was the nearly singular battlefield upon which this patriotic premise of population control was waged by the Beijing authorities.[22]

In 1979, presented with staggering computer demographic projections which showed more population-driven economic crisis in store for the country, Deng Xiaoping consulted with his closest aides, meditated on the future, and in April of that year, when spring was in the air of Beijing, made his decision. The Office of Population Theory Research of the Beijing College of Economics had come up with its published "Population Theory" two years before, in which it had been concluded, "Human reproduction, like the production of goods and services in a planned economy, must not remain in a state of anarchy."[23] It was a firm call for direct state intervention into the behavior of individuals, for the good of the nation. Convinced that China's population must be restricted to 1.2 billion by the year 2000, Deng called for fertility to be reduced below the replacement level, meaning less than 2.2 children per couple. It was decided that the only way to get a 2.2 TFR was to insist on a TFR of 1, given the many uncontrollable variables of a diverse population. This was a remarkable moment in history, if you think about it. Here was a government schooled on the dissemination of all things Chinese, of China at the center of the Earth, suddenly resolving to dramatically hold back the number of Chinese. It was perhaps the truest insight into the Chinese economic personality. The externally imposed Communist ideology had been peeled back, just slightly. Underneath lay the previous capitalistic China, naked and unblushing and scared. The equation had been worked out by an inner circle of academicians on computers.

One of those scientists, Dr. Tian Xueyuan, director of the Population Research Institute of the Chinese Academy of Social Sciences in Beijing, described for me the momentum of the final analyses. It came down to two very obvious projections tabulated far into the future: that of a two-child scenario, versus a one-child. What Tian and two colleagues discovered was that China's population in the year 2050, if computed according to the one-child norm, would equal no more than China's population in the year 2015, if driven by a two-child norm. The implications were terrifying in every respect, thirty-five years of lost economic time. What was even more unsettling was the fact that China still had—and most assuredly has today—the overwhelmingly difficult task of even attaining fertility replacement, the two-child norm, let alone the vastly more distant one-child ceiling. Tian's findings were published in the *People's Daily* in 1977. That newspaper enjoyed a circulation of four million readers. No one could ignore the fact that if population continued to inflate, it would only undo all of China's hard-won progress to date. Per capita income, the true value of the yuan, and the country's ability to feed itself, would be greatly compromised—more famine. China would not seek help from outside donors. Communism had to go it alone. Fertility momentum was driving the country toward catastrophe.

Deng's policy went into effect. On September 26, 1980, an open letter was issued to the Communist Party membership and cadres of the youth league urging them to set the example by having no more than one child each. In September of 1982 in a report of the Twelfth National People's Party, China determined to keep its population within the limits of 1.2 billion by the end of the century. That became the magic number of family planning. But the country's leaders knew very well that a one-child policy would not be taken lightly down on the farm, for its implications were at odds with several thousand years of Chinese Confucianist tradition.

For probably 50 percent of all farmers whose first child had been, or was to be, a girl, Beijing's new edict would eliminate their chance to bring a son into this world; a male who could help generate an income on the farm and look after the parents in their old age, the customary practice in a nation almost entirely lacking social security. There was some security, depending on the wealth of the commune. But, in truth, it was unpredictable, and at best impoverished. Under the so-called "five-guarantee scheme" of rural old age security, every one of China's more than seven hundred thousand villages must provide "grain, fabric, medicine, old-age care, and burial" for any residents requiring it, a nebulous wish-list that has not ensured much confidence in those who would forsake the solidity of a son.[24]

When reporter Sheryl WuDunn returned to her ancestral village in China she met a forty-five-year-old, recently married gentleman who wanted his first child but felt pressure from his wealthier neighbors to wait until he'd made more money. In five years, said WuDunn, the village of Pan Shi (population of four hundred) had seen 80 percent of its farming occupants acquire televisions. However, the poorest residents were in deep trouble. One couple had lost eleven children and their land, and were evidently being sustained by cousins on a diet consisting primarily of "rice porridge with salted fish and a bit of vegetables." The village itself was not apparently contributing much, if any, old age security to the poor.[25]

The one-child policy collided with a number of pre-Communist Chinese mores that had governed the country since antiquity. Considering the fact that most women in agrarian societies do much, or most of the work (a fact being exploited now in the technological sectors of the Pacific Rim), the persistent male-dominated pattern of belief which holds that the woman provides less than the male is perversely erroneous. But that distinct bias, with its corresponding false dependency on the male child has firm roots in China, and in a custom which traditionally prompted the young bride to leave her family and live with her in-laws, a condition endemic within India, as well. The habits of mind favoring males date all the way back to that amorphous, mythopoetic period in early China, where poetry, law, and the workings of the government seem to have been fused, all firmly prejudicial toward women. Ancestor worship, an obligation that was incumbent upon every socioeconomic class throughout the country, whether kingly or indigent, was the duty of the eldest son.[26] According to the The Classic of Filial Piety, The Doctrine of the Mean, The Great Learning, and various works of the revered Mencius and Confucius, without the male heir, the ancestors themselves die out. The son ensures the immortality of his parents. While the Communists completely overhauled this system of preferential ethics, it still prevails throughout rural China. In one survey of ten villages spread across ten provinces, over 45 percent of couples questioned showed a desire for three or more children, a throwback, says demographer Li Jingneng, to China's long-standing notion that filial piety was best served by perpetuating the clan; that the greatest sin against one's parents was lack of posterity.[27] This bias against women shows its tragic face in many guises. For example, of the more than seventy million estimated malnourished individuals throughout the country, health workers know that the vast majority of them are female.[28]

"Having sons is what women come into the world for," said one woman, trapped in an age-old syndrome of oppression and exhausted female compliance that neither Mao nor Deng could erase. "What's the point of it all if you don't have a son? It's what we live for."[29] Under the Woman's Rights Protection Law in China, women have the right to give birth to a child under quality conditions, but not with fertility freedom. The Marriage Law of 1980 makes it the responsibility of every couple in China to practice family planning, but the real thrust and burden of the law devolves to women.

Not surprisingly, the same Confucianist sentiment is at work in China's much emulated neighbor, South Korea, with its remarkably low total fertility rate (TFR =1.7) and rapidly escalating per capita income. Korea is a good example of what the Chinese would like to see occur on the Mainland (the Taicang model), though of course in much grander style, and with less ecological turmoil. But while women in South Korea have been hailed as "the backbone of industrialization," Korean tradition relegates them to second-class citizens, subordinate to their father, their husband, and finally to their son. Their salaries and benefits in the workplace stagnate far below that of their male counterparts.[30]

In 1979, the year the one-child policy went into effect, there were nearly eight million induced abortions, over thirteen million IUD insertions, and seven million sterilizations throughout China. Women of childbearing age who'd already had one child were encouraged to be fitted with IUDs. That was the law. Infanticide was rumored to be on the rise everywhere as a result. Many couples whose first child was a girl chose to either not report her birth, or give her up for foreign adoption, or, possibly, kill her. The data is unclear. Most believe that cases of infanticide were rare. Others are not so sure. According to *Washington Post* correspondent Michael Weisskopf reporting in January 1985, doctors in Inner Mongolia routinely killed second children (by horrible means) under pressure of the one-child policy. Other reports of lethal injections continue to surface.[31]

Adoptions—almost entirely of girls—more than doubled after the one-child policy. Gender-specific abortion is illegal in China, yet there seem to be few other explanations—other than infanticide—for a sex ratio indicating at least five to six hundred thousand girls that were officially "missing" each year in the mid-1980s.[32] Because the country manufactures nearly ten thousand ultrasound-B scanners a year, it is argued that the gender abortion theory seems somewhat plausible. But there is little data to support it from any of the provinces. In fact, the Ministry of Public Health and the State Family Planning Commission have made it illegal to even tell parents the sex of the fetus.[33]

In 1981, China's population was the first in history to exceed one billion, up from 583 million at the time of China's first census in 1953. The number "one billion" sent chills throughout China's scientific community. Demographers and economists within China had not been prepared for a figure of one billion, but rather, were looking toward nine hundred million. The corrected data meant that the per capita economic figures dropped instantly by 10 percent. Frightened, the country now feebly clung to a family planning vision that would hold back growth at 1.2 billion, and then shrink the country's population toward an ecologically sustainable size, with each family size being approximately 1.5. This was no bland doctrine or far-off volition, but an urgent calling, much akin to the sense of a military invasion or civil war. The leadership knew it had to take up antinatalist arms to defend itself. By the mid-1980s, following a massive mobilization of the family planning system, there were indications throughout much of the country that TFRs had indeed dropped to 2.1. This was an ephemeral characterization, however.

Resistance to the one-child policy was widespread enough that allowances had to be made throughout rural China almost from the beginning, exceptions to the law that have harbored a de facto two-child policy. In 1983, 2 percent of all Chinese, twenty-one million people, were sterilized, 80 percent of them women. A year later, the government eased off, slightly, by issuing a directive that exhorted family planners to display "an attitude characterized by the heart of a dear mother, the advice of a grandmother, and the love of a sister."[34]

Back in the 1980s, just as this tender leniency was purporting to infiltrate national policy, a new set of disincentives were simultaneously introduced for those couples having more than one child, thus generating conflicting signals and revealing just how difficult it is to coherently dictate personal sexual habits to over a billion people, no matter how honorable or perceptive one's intentions.[35] For the impenitent mother of three children, 80 percent of her family's income would be taken away under the new punitive measures. However, if the mother "willingly" submitted to sterilization, only 50 percent of her income would be withheld. Multiple offenders risked losing everything—dwelling, food rations, even their license to work. One official in the Ministry of Agriculture explained to the press that temporary coercive measures were actually a "philanthropic and wise policy"; that from the wider point of view, it was imperative that China act responsibly to curb its population explosion. Farmers, he said, were impervious to logic. They had to be forced to control their family size for their own good.[36]

Other conflicting signals from Beijing in the mid-1980s further bewildered those charged with carrying out the one-child policy, namely, a lowered age for legal marriage, and the decollectivization of the farming communes. These were blatant collision courses that immediately increased birthrates throughout the country by making it impossibly tempting for farmers to employ as much labor as they could, namely, their own children, plural. In some areas, land was actually allocated according to the number of laborers working for a family, without delineating whether those laborers were family members or not. The contradictions cascaded.

In Liaoning province in 1984 and 1985, second births were authorized when the first child was a girl.[37] Eighteen provinces now have formal allowances for two children. In actual fact, family planning in China is an enigma. It varies considerably according to the province and local conditions. In economic boom times, Beijing's primary authority is its military manpower, as well as its ability to engage in international economic commitments, gaining most-favored nation status for low-tariff export of goods, and so forth. Otherwise, domestic policy in China is a labyrinthine confederacy that is driven not so much by laws as by individuals.

In the last emperor's childhood home, a beautiful forested estate within Beijing looking out upon a semifrozen lake, I sat one Saturday morning beneath a large Ming Dynasty landscape painting and spoke with Dr. Qian (pronounced Chen) Xinzhong. It was the last day of the Year of the Cock celebrations. Outside, in the cold wind, hundreds of Beijingers browsed through an outdoor vegetable market, buying and selling pears, apples, squash, broccoli, cauliflower, various mushrooms, tomatoes, garlic, onions, potatoes, lettuce, and cabbage, much of it grown in countless little greenhouses throughout the city. Comrade Qian, his white hair cropped handsomely, forehead gleaming, his bearing and bonework reminiscent of nobility, had recently published his book, *Renkouxinpian*, meaning "new look into the population problem," in which he spelled out the history and future of China's demographic situation. In the early 1980s, when Chinese population control was at its fervent height, Qian—along with Indira Gandhi—was handed the first United Nations Population Award for his "outstanding contribution to the awareness of population questions and to their solutions." His solution, temporary in nature he repeatedly stressed, was tactful, but firm compliance with the one-child policy, though allowing for eleven special exceptions. U.N. Secretary General Javier Perez de Cuellar cited his own "deep appreciation" of both Qian and Gandhi for having mobilized their respective countries against the greatest threat facing humanity. For its praise of Qian Xinzhong, UNFPA was bitterly criticized by many inside the Reagan Administration, which would go on to derail any American support of UNFPA a few years later based on the allegation that UNFPA had ignored Chinese human rights abuses in its pursuit of lowering fertility in the country.

But as one senior UNFPA representative in Beijing told me, "the Chinese need us." His goal, and that of a sadly underfunded UNFPA in general, has been to work diplomatically behind the scenes to assist the country on a compassionate path toward population stabilization. In China this has not been easy, partly because of the many critics on the outside who appear incredibly insensitive to the bigger picture. When China presented its deeply felt concerns about a global population crisis at the Mexico City conference in 1984, the United States response was one of marked antagonism. According to Reagan officials, fertility rates had a "neutral" impact. It was not the fault of reproductive behavior that socioeconomic conditions were intolerable in some countries, but of badly conceived governments. There could be no dialogue on the issue, in other words. The Reagan position was emboldened by a report from the National Academy of Sciences issued by the Working Group on Population Growth and Economic Development that insisted that population growth posed no crisis. China, along with Indonesia and India, embittered and incredulous, went its own way, pursuing its own deeply considered policies with a steadiness of hand and purpose, though with no encouragement from the country club Republicans in America, who instead insisted that there was no population problem. Until the Democrats came back into power, American leadership was looked upon by China, and by much of the Third World, as sadly uninformed. Today, U.S. Congressmen would naively like to apply the same incoherent, failing American population ethics to China, where there is one-third the amount of good arable land and five times as many people as in the U.S.

Clad elegantly for winter, proud of his one grandchild, the elderly Qian radiated a career of devotion to the ideal of population stability. Qian adopted two of his four children, the offspring of a beloved colleague who died young. In 1964 he became minister of public health. During the Cultural Revolution he was prosecuted as a member of the old guard. By

1970, he had been "rehabilitated" and had resumed his post, which he kept throughout the decade of the 1970s, a period when those who resisted compulsory family planning were considered selfish "counter-revolutionaries." From 1982 to 1984 Qian was the State Family Planning Commissioner. Though he himself takes little credit, many see him as one of the leading architects of the one-child policy and its most clairvoyant executor.

When Qian took office, there were nearly nine hundred million people in his country. The rural TFR, accounting for 80 percent of the nation, was a staggering 5+. In the cities, three children per couple was normal. There was, according to Qian, an air of desperation in Beijing, as if the whole country was heading toward the Apocalypse Mao himself had feared, some unimaginable ecological disaster induced by three billion Chinese. Actually, it was quite imaginable. A mere century before, such a disaster had befallen China, confirming the worst fears of Thomas Malthus's first edition of *Principles of Population*. Between civil war and famine conditions, an estimated seventy million Chinese died between 1850 and 1880, following the Taiping Rebellion of Hung Hsiu-ch'uan, who considered himself the younger brother of Christ, and whose utopian blueprint for communal life and agriculture was adopted by Mao himself. Yet by 1901, following the disastrous fallout of the Taiping Rebellion, China's population had rebounded to a seething 426 million. By Qian's time, it had more than doubled. The Cultural Revolution had totally abandoned any pretense of population control. Now, food production was not keeping pace, arable land was exhausted, forests were disappearing, pollution was smothering the cities, increasing numbers of malnourished rural poor were voicing discontent. These were all clear harbingers of a Chinese doomsday. At the same time, critics throughout the world were beginning to wonder what happened to all the giant panda bears, and to express concern that China's uncontrolled utilization of coal was contributing an undue amount of carbon emissions to the planet's upper atmosphere. Other developing countries with persistent hunger problems were concerned that China's population might unleash a competitive famine, usurping control of food aid and diverting the flow of scarce Africa-bound grain supplies from the Western powers.

Qian's ministry set about to rapidly raise consciousness. It masterminded such slogans as, "Promote vigorously the policy of one couple, one child, and control strictly and stringently two babies per couple, and strictly prevent one couple, three babies." Even granting a different elocution in Chinese, I told him I did not think it quite rolled off the tongue.[38] But Qian did more than promote crafty slogans. Recognizing the inevitable dissatisfaction with the one-child policy in many rural areas, he went to the people.

"I held a discussion with farmers and their wives and posed the following offer to them," he told me. "You are twenty-five years old now and we (Beijing) are asking you to have just one baby. But when you are fifty, you will be allowed two grandchildren. What do you think? And they all answered, 'No problem! If in the year 2000 our children can have more freedom, then we're willing to make some sacrifice now.' I realized from that discussion that our policies must be explained clearly and simply to the people," Qian explained.

Following his deeply moving encounters with villagers throughout the Chinese heartland, Qian returned to Beijing, where he and his many colleagues set about to implement a number of (some would say self-contradictory) exclusions from the one-child rule, carried away by a sense of destiny, or compassion, or both, I imagine. But he also knew what he was doing. The "exceptions" were actually cultural incentives, spawned by a sense of social justice, fairness, and realism. Of course, it was a gamble, knowing the power of decimal points the way he did.

As of 1974, all contraceptives were made free to married couples in China. Special "contraceptive stations" for distribution were created in every province, organized and managed by the local family planning committees. Later on, the Ministry of Chemical Industries and the State Pharmaceutical Administration got involved to upgrade and increase the flow of contraceptive supplies. At the same time, much in the bare-footed doctor manner, local cadres, fortified with supplies, would go from house to house giving them out and checking to see that IUDs were working properly.[39]

Qian proposed legitimizing eleven exceptions to the one-child policy, which emphasized fairness for the country's fifty-five official ethnic groups, for the handicapped, for mountain people, and for poor fishermen.

In 1984, the Chinese public perceived that a major policy shift had occurred, spawned by a Central Committee Document known as "No.7." The rumor spread that Beijing was easing up, exceptions to the rule were proliferating, and the crisis had gone away. Everyone, it seemed, was now allowed to have two or more children.[40] The Family Planning Commission was not able to put a cap on the rumor mill, or not quickly enough. China's population growth rate lurched from 11.2 to 14.8 per thousand in one year. That one hiccup in the system will translate, according to Qian, into one hundred million more Chinese in the year 2050. Such is the power of population momentum.

Professor Ma Yin Chu, president of Beijing University, had stated his own forward views back in the 1950s. They were ignored. According to Qian, had the eminent professor been listened to, there would be two hundred million fewer Chinese today. Qian would not go so far as to name the true brainchild behind the one-child policy. But he stated with self-effacing animation that he and his cohorts had "successfully prevented the birth of 260 million people" in spite of many setbacks.

Qian knows his history. He is now convinced that the slightest easing up on population control policy will translate into a hundred million more newborns before you know what's hit you, a sudden cluster the size of Mexico's population, in other words. Qian introduced both practical and hard science to family planning to prevent this. It was the only way, he believed, that society would take this numbers game seriously. Coming from the medical field, he was the first to acknowledge China's need for Western technology in the birth control arena. Pride was useless. What was required, he alleged, were better surgical techniques and plenty of contraceptives. Today, China has over forty contraceptive factories, more than half of them upgraded by UNFPA, and produces nearly a billion condoms, several billion pills, twenty-two million IUDs, and three hundred million vaginal foam suppositories every year.[41]

There is no question that China's proven ability to deliver health services to most of its residents is among the most remarkable in the world. But there are recognizable areas where improvement is crucial if China is to more effectively wrestle with its fast-growing population. UNFPA in Beijing estimates that by shifting from the old SSR (stainless steel ring) IUD to the far more effective Copper T 220C and 380A, as they're called, that within a decade "35.6 million induced abortions, 1.4 million spontaneous abortions, 18.4 million births, and 16,300 maternal deaths" would be prevented. In addition, the technological change alone could lower China's TFR significantly after just two or three years, by one tenth of one percent. These are remarkable findings.[42]

In broadly considering China's past and future, the recommendations of UNFPA, and those of Dr. Qian, together seem to point in a viable direction. To my way of viewing him, Qian embodies the full paradox of compassion tempered by unflinching realism. He knows that the nature of finitude is ruthless in a land teeming with over 1.2 billion people. China is only a microcosm of the whole earth, its environmental constraints emblematic of the larger problem. Any choices made in Beijing will effect nearly every plant and animal species in the country, and be felt in countless ways elsewhere in the world. Qian and his colleagues thought deeply about the one-child policy, ever mindful of the larger sphere.

If one is to speak of empathy, remember that not only individuals, but the world, too, needs empathy. Similarly, if the world is to be unburdened, individuals themselves, one by one, must also be freed so that they can walk more softly, and in fewer numbers. How do you apply yourself, given such delicate and harrowing ideals, asked Qian? He'd outlined his response. Most couples (the exceptions delineated) should concern themselves with bringing up no more than one child, a child that is loved, fawned over, disciplined, and given every advantage. Adoption, by his own example, is an additional, much needed option.

But how does one ensure a preference for an ideal family size of one child, given the trends toward two and three children? For their part, UNFPA has stressed other coefficients of the family planning future in China that deemphasize targets, that reject coercion of any kind, but which are urgently focused on enhancing the overall quality of family planning, as well as maternal and child health care, especially in poorly served rural areas. In addition to their emphasis on new technologies and wide-ranging contraceptive methods (at least five), they also emphasize the need for work by women outside of their homes so as to delay or diminish the mother's desire for more children. In addition, UNFPA is supporting population research in some twenty-two universities in China, developing teaching materials for young students, and integrating literacy and income generation projects with family planning. UNFPA stresses the need for psychological support of the woman, and has introduced the idea of "interpersonal counseling" for those grassroots family planners who go from door to door throughout the country. There is nothing particularly new about such recommendations. They have been part of the working vocabulary in the fertility realm for forty years. The real issue is continuing to keep that vocabulary in focus.

"I myself participated in the formulation of the one-baby policy and when the policy was implemented, at that moment I felt encouraged, I was hopeful," Qian said quietly, reminiscing on a long and remarkable career.

I had asked him what he was doing on the very day that the one-child policy went public in China. Did he go out for a long reflective walk through town, pick up groceries, visit his grandchild, sit around and listen to the radio? Did he open a bottle of wine and get drunk, or take his wife to a movie? What were his thoughts? And I kept trying to place this smiling grandfather, his hands in the air, wrinkled and fine, gesturing with a deeply understated conviction, beside the entire population of the United States. That was the amount of human life he and his associates would actually prevent from coming into existence. The spiritual dimension of this achievement is, like all feats of the imagination, intangible, intimated, an endless deferral whose consequences we will never know. On another, more palpable level, we can well appreciate the significance and its causes and effects, much as with the invention of the zero, long ago, in India. A negation, like nonviolence, or nonintervention, or nonproliferation. This one man, part of an idealistic team, had done something profoundly important. Mikhail Gorbachev liberated a similar number of people throughout Central Europe, a great achievement that is proving to be slightly marred only by the expected vicissitudes of human nature. But Qian liberated the unborn, a perfect act of conscience. Conceived in ecological terms, he was like a great general who preempted a battle that was going to be waged by another 260 million consumers against the planet.

Finally, he stated, in an even, though unmeasured voice, "It was only through implementing the one-child policy that we could, in a real sense, check the population growth in China. So when it was put forward I thought it was very necessary and I was very much encouraged. Many developing countries are not able to address the problem of overpopulation squarely and therefore I cannot be too optimistic about the future of the world."

Nor was Qian all that optimistic about China, either. "Due to various blunders . . . the one-child policy will have to continue for another ten to twenty years because we have not reached our targets." He was referring to Beijing's goal of checking China's population at 1.2 billion by the year 2000. It did not happen because of what Qian sees as the unfortunate easing up on the one-child policy. By late 1997, the Chinese had quietly absolved themselves of the 1.2 billion goal. It had become officially a 1.3 billion goal. Consider the implication of such a muted shift: in a matter of three years, without the slightest fanfare, the Chinese accepted one hundred million more people, just like that. And as far as the one-child policy, most observers agree that it is finished. At a population conference in Beijing in mid-October 1997, Chinese officials conceded that the one-child policy was obsolete; that various imbalances would somehow magically be reconciled, enormous demographic gulfs and loopholes filled in by new emergent trends. Qian didn't see it that way. Yet it was his own belief in various "exclusions" at the very beginning of the policy (a way of short-circuiting a Confucianist civil war) that had come back to haunt the whole agenda.

WHEN I FIRST visited China, in 1978, there was a very hard and introverted edge about her. No other people seemed quite so aware of their population and environmental predicament back then. There was tacit alarm and grave uncertainty. A year later, the one-child policy was unleashed. In the last fifteen years, like no other country in history, China has learned to live with more than a billion people. This is a vast experiment. No other government, with the exception of India, can really know what China is dealing with. No one would want to. The Chinese are, by and large, enormously sympathetic, radiant people. It is easy to admire, to be enamored of, to love them—horrific events, particularly China's attempted conquest of Tibet, notwithstanding. But this love, so to speak, founders in the demographic den of iniquity, where the sheer colossus of China and all her numbers pose a paralyzing burden on Chinese environment, and thus, on the very nature of what it means to be Chinese.

Every smiling, photogenic baby dressed in colorful silken pantaloons, bobbling across the sun-bright courtyards of the not-so-Forbidden City, or riding herd on their parents' shoulders through bicycle-laden back-alleys, will steal your heart. Every scene of Grandpa kneeling on a street corner to tie his grandchild's shoelaces, or families out for their leisurely late afternoon stroll together, sucking on penny candies, fawning over their kids, is poetry in motion. These age-old value-laden images conjure a familiar China that is now caught between a crossfire of biology and dreams. Whatever its family planning successes to date, China is in no position to rest on her laurels.

CHINESE ECOLOGY AND ECONOMICS

THROUGHOUT CHINA ONE hears it aired in countless guises that as the country changes from a labor to a technology intensive economy, increasing wealth will supercede the population crisis; that no human being who generates income is too many. The so-called human deficit will simply disappear as per capita income has risen to a comfortable level. What about rural China, I asked repeatedly, where poverty is still widespread, the economic benefits of those few major cities in the country having generated little trickle-down prosperity? Even that is changing, I was assured.

The International Monetary Fund in May of 1993 calculated that China had become the world's third largest economy, after the U.S. and Japan, with a nearly two-trillion-dollar purchasing power. According to one estimate (the China State Statistical Bureau), Chinese urban affluence is now on a par with most other Southeast Asian consumption, including that of the Thai and Malaysians.[43]

Yet, at present, more than 80 percent of the nation's workforce earns a per capita income of three hundred dollars per year or less, while a third of the country is bringing in even less than that—in some remote areas as little as eighty dollars per year. At least 664 counties are below the Chinese poverty line, or 20 percent of the nation. Yet, even in a region like Anwang, where villagers earn on average fifteen dollars per month, there is no less striving after wealth and improvement. New roads are being built, new terracing for high yielding soy and corn hewn from the mountain slopes, new sources of electricity installed so that the people can mill their own corn with machines at night and make noodles for sale by day. Cisterns are being built and innoculations administered to the livestock to improve their health and number.[44]

What on the surface would appear to be the benign (or at least acceptable) aspirations of a developing country, a national preference for a modicum of comfort (*xiaokang shuiping*) and monetary gain consistent with the economic priorities of the rest of the world, in actual fact is taking a decisive toll on Chinese ecology. Professor Li Jingneng, the director of the Institute of Population and Development Research at Nankai University in Tianjin, points out several crucial ecological problems associated with China's fast-burgeoning population/economy. The country currently possesses some one hundred milion hectares of arable land (11 percent of the nation's total land area), which places China twenty-forth in the world for arable land availability, less than a quarter of an acre per person, a decline of nearly 50 percent in per capita cultivated land since 1949. This contrasts with some two acres per person in the United States. At an average density of 1100 people per square kilometer and growing, the country is now (in agricultural terms) at least eight times more populated than America. Keep in mind that "arable land" typically refers to total or partial cultivation. It may mean enclosed grasslands which are alternately plowed. But in China, arable land refers to intensively farmed soils. Loss of grasslands constitutes yet an additional factor of overall deterioration. There is no apparent land left in the country that can be converted for purposes of agriculture. China thus finds itself with approximately 7 percent of all farmland on Earth, but nearly 22 percent of the human population.[45] At least 70 percent of China's population is directly dependent on the agricultural sector.

Where there is agriculture, the existence and interdependent web of most species larger than insects and rodents is vastly diminished or eliminated entirely. The remaining 30 percent of the Chinese population depends directly on industry and urban life, which once again tends to vanquish most preexisting wildlife. Estimates on plant and animal life in China indicate approximately thirty thousand types of bryophytes, pteridophytes, and seed plants; twenty-one hundred species of mammals, avians, reptiles, and amphibians; twenty-one hundred species of fish; and some one million invertebrate types. If these NEPA (China's National Environmental Protection Agency) figures approach even vague accuracy, then China hosts representatives of nearly 10 percent of all known fish species, 10 percent of all avians, mammals, reptiles, and amphibians, and (remarkably) 95 percent of all known invertebrates, making it one of the most biodiverse nonrain forest nations in the world. While few all-China surveys have been carried out, and little in the way of comprehensive analysis, it is believed that 257 animal and 354 plant species are currently headed toward extinction, short of draconian life-saving measures. These species include the Chinese rhinoceros, the wild horse, wild elephant, mandarin duck, leaf and golden monkey, high-nosed antelope, panda, snow leopard, Chinese dolphin, and alligator. Probably nothing can save the Chinese tiger from extinction. The country exports tens of thousands of cartons of tiger bone tablets and bottles of tiger wine every year.

Investigations in the northeastern province of Ambdo, in Tibet, where population has increased five times in the last twenty years, have shown that vast regions of grasslands (as extensive as many European countries) are being rapidly degraded, or destroyed. Between the incoming Chinese colonists and Tibetans themselves, who are repopulating after their tragic decimation by Chinese troops during the 1950s (at least six million Tibetans killed), nearly every major species has been listed internationally as endangered.[46] The IUCN in Switzerland (International Union for the Conservation of Nature and Natural Resources) and the World Resources Institute in Washington, D.C., report at least thirty-one animal and bird species endangered in Tibet. Wild yaks have been machine-gunned for their meat by the Chinese in the Himalayas. Other threatened species include the snow leopard, the Asiatic black bear and grey wolf, the wild Bactrian camel and black-necked crane, Cabot's tragopan and the Sichuan partridge, the Tibetan macaque and brown-chested jungle flycatcher.[47]

At the same time, hunters from abroad have been invited to Tibet to kill wildlife for fees—thirteen thousand dollars for a white-lipped deer, twenty-three thousand dollars for an Argali sheep. The Ministry of Forestry is charged with enforcing the 1988 Wildlife Protection Act but evidently has no authority to curb the sale of pelts. A delegation from the International Campaign for Tibet's Human Rights found baby snow leopard furs for sale in various markets, some as inexpensive as thirty dollars each.[48]

As reported in 1988 by CITES (Convention on International Trade in Endangered Species of Wild Flora and Fauna), China has exported thousands of live primates, nearly one hundred thousand cat skins, and nearly seventy thousand reptile skins every year during the past decade. The Chinese diet in some parts of the country comprises a number of endangered species. Man-Han banquets have been known to include bear's paw, camel's hump, white crane, even elephant trunk, as well as the highly endangered clouded leopard.[49]

Agriculture, industry, and commerce, to say nothing of animal experimentation, factory farming, and the countless other ways in which animals and whole ecosystems are exploited, taken together suggest a colossal substitution imposed by one species upon all others. As China's population grows, the substitution continues to intensify in other ways, further adding to the human hegemony of net primary production (NPP), the amount of natural photosynthetic vegetation on the planet which has been co-opted and usurped by human intervention. The current global NPP is estimated to be between 45 and 50 percent. Every year China converts some four thousand square miles of additional land into urban or rural development—new cities, new factories, new housing developments. At least 87 percent of the country lacks most foliage beyond that which could be described as agricultural. Another 120 thousand square kilometers are now desert, twice the amount since the time of China's independence.[50]

The rate of deforestation in China stands at some 1.2 percent per year of the remaining stands of forest, largely on account of the need for cooking and heating fuel, where inexpensive coal is not available. Most remaining woods in the northeast provinces of Jeilongjiang and Jilin, and much of the forest in the southwest province of Yunnan, for example, have been hacked to oblivion. The species that have been lost as a result have not been quantified or qualified but the amount of burned board feet and destroyed hectares each year in China are biologically devastating, one would surmise. The forests of Guanxi province will likely disappear by 2010 or so. Forest cover in Sichuan has been reduced from 20 percent cover in 1960 to less than 13 percent in 1994.

The forces at work in China are symptomatic of human economic growth. Norman Myers has suggested that at the beginning of the agricultural revolution some ten thousand years ago, the Earth was covered with sixty-two million square kilometers of forests, half the ice-free land area of the planet. Presently, at most, forty million square kilometers of forest remain.

As the forests are depleted and agricultural intensity increases in a continuous effort to provide edibles for a rapidly expanding population, the finitude of China's agricultural lands becomes more and more apparent. China's grain production peaked in 1984 and has been declining since then.[51] At the same time, eighty-seven million hectares of grassland are degenerated each year, another five million hectares becoming desert.[52] As China's massive population wrestles with its declining food yields, at least five billion tons of precious topsoil are washed away annually. One third of all cultivated land in China is severely eroded and eroding. Deforestation is one-and-a-half times faster than the rate of reforestation, despite some very impressive strides by the Ministry of Forests. Throughout the country, mature forests will have vanished completely within six years. The total loss of forest to date is estimated at one hundred million cubic meters.

Coupled with China's population impact on its forests (and consequently upon its already scarce amounts of rainfall) is the burden of ground-based and atmospheric pollution from coal, a regional prelude to the country's substantial contribution to the global "greenhouse effect." Seventy-five percent of China's energy comes from coal, of which 85 percent is burned without any pollution controls. China produces and consumes more coal than any other country in the world, 25 percent of the world's total. This is easy for China to do: the resource is relatively inexpensive, and the country is endowed with some 50 percent of all known coal reserves.

I was told by Dr. Qu Geping, former head of NEPA, the country's Environmental Protection Agency, that China plans to increase coal consumption by three times in the next twenty to thirty years. In a very rough correspondence, that energy escalation is defined as a 14 percent economic increase. It will also coincide with a quadrupling of the present number of Chinese-made automobiles. Taken together, these two energy-consuming impositions will utterly undo any carbon emission controls implemented in the West. The pollution fall-out rate in Los Angeles during the 1950s per square kilometer per month was approximately 7.7 tons—the worst it has ever been, equivalent to the level of Mexico City today. But in China levels have surpassed one hundred tons! According to Dr. Qu, hydro—small or large—is not being perceived as an answer to China's energy problems. Nevertheless, the ecologically hideous Three Gorges project of the upper Yangtze River is well underway, its in-country critics all but muted.

In other ecological sectors, sixteen hundred billion gallons of sewage enter China's coastal waters every year. Most of it flows untreated. Many of China's cities are experiencing massive drinking water deficits. Groundwater levels throughout China are dropping, in some areas as much as one meter per year. Excessive pumping has literally lowered Shanghai. As of 1988, analysis of China's rivers, ground water, air, and coastal zones yielded extremely high levels of contamination. At the same time, irrigation expansion is necessarily shrinking. Many existing irrigation channels in the country are badly choked with silt.[53]

And the problems proliferate. Some 60 percent of all Chinese factories built during the 1950s are ecologically "backward" (as they are in every developing country, and wherever Communism once prevailed). During the ten years of the Cultural Revolution in the 1960s and 1970s, environmental issues were bypassed almost entirely in favor of growth.

There are 173 Chinese cities with populations exceeding 350 thousand. An effort is underway to "eliminate the difference between workers and peasants, and between the city and the countryside."[54] It is part of Qu's "synchronous development" concept. This homogenization is intended to accomplish two things: first, to increase the numbers of workers in so-called township enterprises, industries that can earn more profit than traditional labor-intensive agriculture; and second, to build up such enterprises out in the country for disenfranchised agricultural workers so that they will not necessarily come to the big cities looking for work, but can remain in their own home regions and find alternative employment. It has been estimated that as many as 40 percent of the country's eight hundred million farmers will, by the end of the century, have to work in other industrial sectors across rural China. That will probably mean a greatly increased environmental burden; the Chinese human population appropriating more and more vegetative cover and net primary production areas. This is the crux of China's ecological dilemma: in stark terms, too many people industrially or agriculturally overtaking every last corner of the country.

In Shenyang, the capital of Liaoning province in southern Manchuria (the northeast), 6.5 million people have created one of the country's worst environmental mires. There are insufficient sewage processing facilities, the central river has been pronounced dead by local ecologists for several years, thirty-two meters of groundwater have been lost, new industrial suburban satellite communities of between two hundred thousand and four hundred thousand are springing up in sensitive watershed areas, there is no overall protective plan, and the World Bank ranks Shenyang as one of Asia's seven most polluted cities. According to environmental consultant Jeff Girsh, who, with a team of others, studied Shenyang in an effort to help the local government plan for future development, air and water pollution in that city makes Beijing look downright desirable, by comparison. As China's "homogenization" evolves, little Shenyangs and Shanghais, like cancer cells, will spring up throughout China. With between 160 and 200 million more people every decade wanting more and more prosperity, there would appear to be no other alternative. As of the mid-1990s, 24 new cities and 921 new towns were being built every year in China. From 1949 to 1979 Chinese housing encroached upon 709 million square meters of land, previously rural, but in just the last decade it has covered that much again. But the real crisis of land conversion and deterioration in China is coming about as a result of the transfer of pollutants and population to rural industrial complexes. It is not so much a decentralizing phenomenon, say the Chinese, as one of rural urbanization, so huge is the population.[55]

Satellite data taken over regions like Shanghai already reveal the distressing trend toward what I would call total human appropriation regions (THARs). They resemble the so-called Dead Zones in the ocean, where human effluents of one form or another have destroyed most or all marina biota. There are now industrial regions in China whose air is so polluted that even aerial reconnaissance fails to yield a resolved picture for months each year. These cities, such as Benxi, with a population of over one million, have simply vanished beneath a sea of unrelenting air pollution. Curbing the ill-effects of urban appropriation is not easily systematized in China since each province has its own specific population agendas and growing socioeconomic disparities to contend with. Furthermore, each province is empowered to generate its own pollution-control laws, making it next to impossible to engender unified ecological standards throughout the thirty government regions. Part of the problem is China's stated lack of hard cash to implement expensive pollution clean-up devices, relying instead upon good will of the masses, and reasonable compromises that do not reverse sorely needed economic gains.

While over two hundred environmental standards *have* been set in place the population bomb continues to outstrip ecological restoration. China's corporate sector will be hard pressed to situate industries away from population centers, as much as the government would like to encourage it to do so. Inevitably, the pollution burden will be divided between outlying populations, and wilderness areas themselves. But the more difficult question persists: where will the needed pollution control and management funds come from? Despite the country's breakneck economic growth, it has not yet lifted the overall per capita income beyond $370. Hence, a centralized vision of environmental legislation and controls, and the appropriate targeting of budget line items, is the only hope, as in most other countries. That means choosing priorities.

"We are still poor. We cannot afford to set very high standards for environmental protection. We have to do everything according to our practical limits," Qu quietly explains. Nevertheless, to China's great credit and despite its poverty, for the period 1990–95 approximately one hundred billion yuan (roughly seventeen billion dollars) or 0.7–0.85 percent of the GNP was allocated toward environmental protection. In the evolution of U.S. budgets, such proportions of the GNP were not environmentally expended until after per capita income had exceeded approximately two thousand dollars. But, according to Qu, much more money is needed. The Chinese estimate that they require at least ten times their current spending allocations to really get a handle on existing industrial pollution, and prevent new despoliation during this decade, and that's with *good* management. But the payoff, theoretically, should come. According to one study, 15 percent of China's GNP is actually lost because of internalized costs associated with environmental damage.[56] Such "inaccessible" and internalized costs are by no means unique to poor, developing countries, of course. Thousands of recently ascertained toxic waste dumps throughout the United States implicate a supposedly enlightened economy and offer few guarantees that money will ever be set aside for reclamation. Qu addresses society's lack of ecological financing in general terms: "Our policy of balanced development . . . will achieve the unification of economic benefit, social benefit and environmental benefit. It is a positive policy which stresses prevention rather than cure."[57] Interestingly, this is precisely the system upon which Chinese medicine is predicated. China now has the highest life expectancy and one of the lowest infant mortality rates of any developing country. Its health care system, in many respects, is second to none.

The overwhelming causes and consequences of China's many ecological woes were not systematically addressed until 1988, when China's National Environmental Protection Agency was founded. Its director, the untiring Dr. Qu, felt from the beginning that government, working through the people, could harmoniously balance environmental impact. It was Qu who first applied the policy of "polluter pays" in China. But he took the notion a step further by stating that "whoever causes pollution shall be reponsible for its elimination." But Dr. Qu's most ardent vision has hinged upon his insistence that environmental quality requires enhanced management, not heavy financial inputs. Having gone to Africa and seen communities that were starving amid clean air and tranquility, Qu told me that he has vowed to steer China toward a more realistic approach, and that has meant eliminating the pollution of poverty, as he called it. He does not accept the ultimatum that "growth must be stopped, or civilization will be destroyed." To the contrary, he believes that the more highly developed and technological a culture, the more means it has to control environmental pollution. Unfortunately, it reads much like the logic held by those who would argue that in China the more wealth, the less severe the population crisis. If China's extraordinary economic zeal can be taxed to help cover the costs of management, Qu's crusade may succeed. In the meantime, he insists, man must not "give up eating for fear of choking"; that "natural ecosystems are not ideal ones; (but) only through rational remaking by mankind can they be idealized." In a country staring at a horizon of two billion people, the ideal of wilderness, that romance of nature, has been necessarily redefined according to human need. The impending tragedy for China is that it is one country that still possesses, according to the World Resources Institute, over 22 percent of its land mass in a wilderness state (or nearly 211 million hectares), unlike, say India or Indonesia, which have 0.0 (zero) wilderness. (A good working definition of such wilderness, provided by the World Resources Institute in Washington, is of a parcel of land at least four thousand square kilometers in extent that is totally undefiled—no power lines, roads, railroad tracks, buildings, homes, pipelines, landing strips, no mark of humanity whatsoever.) Thus, from the point of view of wilderness habitat—with all that that implies for unimpeded animal corridors, biodiversity, moral, equitable, aesthetic, and genetic viability of nonhuman populations— China, like Antarctica, has much more to lose from rapid development than any other region on Earth.[58] Because its biological heritage is so complex, and its remaining wilderness so uniquely extensive, population and economic issues in China are at the forefront of global ecological concern.

Qu insists that the ideal of "back to nature" is simply not possible anymore. In this respect, he views China as a laboratory of realism. "Requirements (i.e., environmental standards) can only be raised when the economy is developed," he repeats. Ironically, he adds that those countries capable of affording environmental protection do not pursue it, while those unable to afford it (i.e., China) do. It is therefore not merely the price tag, he argues, but the "philosophical system" that will effect ecological change. But one need only look to China's post-Communist family planning experience to appreciate the frailty of any such philosophy.

A policy of "control" that is intended to facilitate a "rational" approach to development is simply not predictable, when the population itself is out of control. Against the inevitable economic tidal-wave of opportunism in China's immediate future, "rational" is not easily translated, either. It suffers from the tragic and ineluctable ambiguity of China's desire to achieve a state of well-being for its people. But how do you harmonize 1.2 billion economic aspirants with a finite and rapidly deteriorating environment? Foreign investors have signed contracts pledging over sixty billion dollars for purposes of selling everything from hamburgers and candy to plastics and shampoo.[59] That has been the preferred choice of Chinese strategies to deal with her problems: capitalization and development. Chinese vessels put in at over 150 countries around the world. China is the eleventh largest trader in the world, but the majority of Chinese are still very poor. Within six years the government hopes to more than triple the per capita GNP. In the year 2000, two billion tons of coal, four hundred million tons of petrol, and fifty billion cubic meters of natural gas will all be needed to supply the required two hundred billion kilowatt-hours of a 1.3 billion population.[60] As of 1981, China was consuming five times more energy than Japan, 95 percent of which consists of low-grade coal. Yet, the energy efficiency in China is considerably lower than in developed countries. Because about a third of all production capacity is still untapped, the coming few years of rapid industrialization suggest an enormous increase in environmental degradation. According to Amory Lovins, "If China keeps burning coal and little else, the world could face an ecological disaster. It will ruin the climate for everybody."[61]

China's new wild-west economy symbolizes the state of the world, the state of human desires and basic biologic urgings. What well over a billion Chinese do with their ancient biological heritage in the coming fifty years will coincide with the economic/ecological curve of every developing country where population is the critical factor. In developed countries with essentially zero population growth, economic prosperity will increasingly translate into environmental concern, erratic protection, continually declining wildlife populations, and ever more stringent laws applied to environmentally sound technologies and engineering. But such efforts will not necessarily trickle down to the poor nations of the world trying to achieve a developed standard of living. Eighty percent of the world's population, in other words, is reinventing the wheel beginning with the dirtiest industries. And because the developed nations are finding themselves entrapped by global recession and, in some cases, unimaginable national debt, their largesse and willingness to cede anything to the poor is diminishing. Nobody is giving China free environmental clean-up technologies. China, like every other country, needs hard dollars and seems willing to do anything to get them. In its quest for greenbacks, China now exports more goods to the U.S. than Malaysia, Thailand, Indonesia, and the Philippines combined. In all of those countries, China's impact is already lowering the value and dollar price of manufactured exports, which translates into added degradation of those other countries' remaining natural areas.[62]

The pulse of China's runaway economy is best sensed in Shanghai, a city of horrendous dimensions. From atop the seventy-story super-chic Jin Jiang Hotel, the city resembles a hazy, surreal, entangled exoskeleton the size of a huge crater on the surface of Venus, hemorrhaging bilious fluids and caustic vapors. Its minions stream, its traffic chokes, the construction zones everywhere grate with the bashing of hammer-toting men and women salvaging pieces of steel girding from vanquished concrete blocks, hammering, unloading, digging, breaking down old buildings by hand, reerecting huge scaffoldings in the manner of the painter Brueghel's memorable icon of human confusion, *The Tower of Babel.* The renovation of Shanghai's waterfront summons images of Tokyo or Dresden after the bombings of World War II, and the sci-fi milieu of *Blade Runner.* It is a concrete metastasis that has erupted in all directions, pustular and fierce. The horizons around Shanghai are a pall of congested, smoke-saturated color.

Jiangsu province, intersected by Highway 204 which leads out of Shanghai, is China's fastest growing area. It witnessed a 26 percent gross domestic product (GDP) rate of increase during the early 1990s. Shanghai, Taicang County to the immediate north, the Pudong New Area, and all of Jiangsu province are the epicenter of the New Economy in China, where more than 50 percent of industrial production is deriving from joint ventures, and private business. The average worker in most plants is being paid between thirty-four and fifty cents an hour versus $3.50 in South Korea. This explains the influx of foreign corporations wanting to exploit the incredibly low labor wages. China's economy, spearheaded by epicenters like Shanghai, is on its way toward achieving the per capita income of other industrializing nations on the Pacific Rim. When it does, it may well be "larger than all industrialized countries in the world combined. It would be a bit like the rise of Japan, except that China has nuclear weapons and nearly ten times the population."[63]

In fact, in fifty years the Japanese population will be but 5 percent of China's. At that time the Japanese will be an old (literally aged) population, while China's population will be young, of a military age. And while Beijing denies it, there are reports that at least some of China's nuclear armaments in Tibet are aimed at India. The Chinese, after all, helped build Pakistan's own ballistic missile capability, a very real threat to India. China currently pays over three million full-time troops, in addition to six hundred thousand members of the People's Armed Police. Chinese spending is believed to be roughly three times the amount of money allocated by Beijing for the State Family Planning Commission, the National Environmental Protection Agency and the Ministry of Forestry combined. Why, one wonders?

On May 21, 1992, China conducted a nuclear test of 660 thousand tons of TNT at the Lop Nor testing range in the northwest of the country.

It was the most powerful nuclear explosion on earth in ten years. It served to remind both Pakistan and India—neighboring nuclear powers with gigantic problems of their own—that in Asia, nothing is predictable.

Against this bewildering backdrop, several crucial questions arise, though no easy answers. What should U.S. foreign policy toward China emphasize? Economics, ecology, human rights, or family planning? How can these arenas be sensibly combined? One thing is clear: America must fervently support China's State Family Planning efforts through much more generous assistance, while encouraging U.S. foreign investment to impose the same ecological imperatives on its factories, coventures, and products that would be required within U.S. borders.

Increasingly independent, though never separated from the truth of Beijing's military force, what can Chinese provincial leaders do to maintain family planning vigilance and strive for ecological sustainability within their own regions? The country's visionaries—people like Dr. Qu Geping, Dr. Qian Xinzhong, and Madame Peng Peiyun—have each provided viable, if fragile blueprints for action.

~3~

The Ecology of Pain: India

SAMVARTAKA, CLOUD OF DOOMSDAY

In a determined effort to counterbalance China's military presence in Asia, Prime Minister Indira Gandhi began stockpiling plutonium and building up a nuclear capability during the early years of her regime.[1] India's concerns encompassed not just China, against whom she'd fought a limited one month war in 1962 (and would later engage in border skirmishes up through 1987), but also Pakistan, her long-time adversary. In 1971 the Indo–Pakistani War (which culminated in the independence of Bangladesh, formerly East Pakistan) resulted in a death toll exceeding three million people, leaving tens of millions of Bengalis ever more destitute, destroying untold numbers of wildlife, and forcing at least nine million others into exile in India, a nation scarcely recovered from a famine which had seen at least one million die the year before.[2]

When I investigated the Indo–Pakistani War, interviewing numerous refugees in Calcutta, obtaining testimonies from eyewitnesses, a picture of widespread rape, cannibalism, and ecological mayhem emerged, the vengeful particulars of a sordid and complex disaster. Meanwhile, up in Dacca, postwar famine was taking its own additional toll. I watched members of the Anjuman-e-Mahifidul Islamic organization collecting as many as four hundred unclaimed corpses off the streets every day. In Tongee, a refugee camp outside Dacca, I worked with other volunteers in the handing out of foodstuffs to thousands of doomed and dying environmental refugees. Newly formed Bangladesh was confronted with a population of nearly ninety million, 60 percent of whom were malnourished, many starving. I saw human corpses festering beneath scavenging dogs that dragged at the entrails. Human life expectancy was optimistically believed to be forty-three; per capita income about one hundred dollars. Meanwhile, ten thousand babies were being born every day in Bangladesh. The military dictatorship was trying to clean up the streets. They would grab "squatters," toss them into the back of trucks, and drive them off to camps. Most would starve to death, like the ones at Tongee. There was a woman in the camps that I remember, young, exquisitely beautiful, dying, who smiled bountifully at me. There was radiance amid Armageddon, some impossible joie de vivre from the depths of melancholy, nihilism tinged with humanity. She has remained for me a symbol of the Indian subcontinent.

Further south, maintaining the offensive following its war with Pakistan, India then detonated its first nuclear weapon beneath the ordinarily tranquil deserts of Rajasthan in 1974, hastening the development of an infuriated Pakistan's own secret nuclear program. Throughout the 1970s and 1980s, India and Pakistan remained enemies, their northern combat troops exchanging bazooka fire in the Karakoram range.

Countless Kashmiri Muslims would like to see Pakistan invade Kashmir and rid this enchanted Himalayan sanctuary of its "Indian overlords" once and for all. A vocal contingent of Kashmiri Muslims see in their quest for liberation a just cause for a *jihad,* or holy war, such as was waged in what is Bangladesh. And in an interview with the press, the so-called "father of the Pakistani atomic bomb," Dr. Abdul Qadeer Khan, had—according to Seymour Hersh, writing in *The New Yorker*—stated that "if driven to the wall there will be no option left" but the use of nuclear weapons, a sentiment underscored by Pakistan's High Commissioner to India Riaz Khokar, who has described Pakistan's "insecurity" as the result of his country's "fear of India."[3]

Since its independence in 1947, population in Pakistan has increased fourfold, from 32.5 million to more than 138 million.[4] Women are expected to procreate and raise children, the preferred family size (PFS) norm being 4.9 children. The official TFR, as of late 1997, was 5.6. Those few college educated Pakistani appear willing to have four, not 4.9 children. Family planners believe that strong international support of fertility control might enable Pakistan to check its population at around 335 million sometime in the middle of the next century. But because official government policy is so anti-Hindu and—despite some changes—still essentially pronatalist, it appears more likely that the country will exceed 550 million sometime in the twenty-first century. That same pronatalist, anti-Indian sentiment was echoed by a former chief minister in Kashmir who stated, "We should reject the government's family planning program. This is aimed at further reducing the Muslim population in Kashmir. Every Kashmiri Muslim should have four wives to produce at least one dozen children."[5]

As Pakistan races toward half-a-billion people sometime late in the next century, her archrival India—"the world's proving ground for birth control"[6]—is fast approaching one billion. Approximately 11 percent, or one hundred million, are Muslim. The vast majority are Hindu, with a small percentage of Sikh, Jain, Zorastrian, Christian, and a large minority of tribals or *adivasis* (566 individual tribes). There were, as of 1980, an estimated 3743 so-called backward castes, 2378 Hindu subcastes, and 1086 scheduled castes in India, adding up to the most fragmented cultural puzzle in human history. The country speaks somewhere between 500 and 1652 dialects and languages depending on the survey.[7] India is not one country, socially speaking. It never has been. Every ethnic and religious group throughout India typically sees strength in numbers, as they try to gain political autonomy or economic guarantees of some kind. And as in every other nation, these ethnic groups, pressured into becoming neighbors in the same land, have inherited stark political boundaries, some—like those in Kashmir—still internally disputed. Slightly less than one third the geographical size of China, India's human size will probably overtake that of China's in the middle of the next century. Already, India's population is twice the *density* of China's. As of mid-1998, nearly 990 million people inhabit India's 870 million acres (1.1 million square miles). Bound together by the besieged Himalayas, these two countries—India and China—will comprise as much as one third of the mid-twenty-first century's human population. In fact, many see India hitting 2.5 billion by the end of that century. This fact of human numbers is the most important statement that can be made of India, a country whose demographic and ecological instability—like that of China—poses tragic consequences for the planet.

Regardless of her many boundaries, socioeconomic distinctions, and a dizzying number of languages, customs, and gods, the Indian subcontinent as a whole knows only one war, and it is being fought inadvertently, though at times deliberately, against nature, a masterpiece of nature that is crying out.[8]

In the beginning, those cries were less audible, the pain less evident. The forests were enchanted, an ideal, the abode of Lord Siva, also known as the Wild God, Rudra, the Ultimate Yogi. They were a source of inspiration, a sanctuary for worship, absolution, and repose. Because Siva was believed to protect all wanderers in even the harshest wilderness, Indians long ago traveled fearlessly, building an ancient network of roads through nearly every forest in the country. In this time of innocence, the Wild God inadvertently invited domestication, the emergence of cities. Even twenty-five hundred years ago, there were as many as forty thousand villages in the country, connected to one another by these roads. People routinely wandered into nearby woods seeking communion with monks and sages, who dwelled under the tropical and temperate canopies. It was inevitable that the forests should come under intense worship, scrutiny, and finally, pressure. Indians learned how best to exploit the wood. Ancient dietary manuals hailed the fruit as being the essential foodstuff; recommended green trees for fashioning farming utensils; advised upon the vast pharmacopoeia to be hewn from the tropics. The cultivation of orchards was considered in and of itself a form of meditation.[9]

Because the size of the human population was still relatively miniscule, whatever damage was wrought could be reasonably absorbed by the natural environment. From this (as yet *sacred*) pragmatism arose what has been described as the foremost tradition in India, namely, *Pancavati,* meaning "five groves." The word surfaces in virtually every known Indian language and refers to five kinds of sacred trees: the Indian *banyan,* associated with bearing human progeny; the *peepal,* abode of Lord Visnu, every part of it ready-made for utilization; the *asoka,* which eases suffering, provides relief for certain gynecological problems, as well as *ghee* (fat) for numerous food dishes; the *bela,* said to possess the most curative fruit in the land, more nutritional, even, than mango; and the *harada,* a sure cure for every ailment. Subsidiary to these five were a profusion of other plants and shrubs and trees, all part of the spiritual, vegetative hegemony. Communities throughout India tended to substitute and introduce local species into the sacred grove . . . coconut, banana, basil, myrobalan, jackfruit, sal, neem, keekar, babool, Sami, tamal, sandal, blackberry, and so on. All were sanctified, all subject to consumption, but never total consumption. The clearing of forests was forbidden, a sin (*adharma*) against the body of god. The original Sanskrit term for forest was *aranya*, meaning literally, "no war."[10]

Indian scientists of the sixth century B.C. were purported to have known nearly 875 thousand species. A century later, Aristotle and his compatriots were aware of fewer than five hundred.[11] This profound knowledge of Indian biology was advanced in order to safeguard nature, not to foster its compromise. Yet, familiarity with the sacred fueled all manner of ecological violation. The inevitability of this contradiction was implicit in what the writer V. S. Naipaul has labelled "a wounded civilization." That which was spiritual became profitable, particularly as population increased. The bounty of nature inspired human excess. Ironically, and fittingly, the analogy of simultaneous creation and destruction is inherent to the personality of many of India's ancient deities, a clear enough commentary on the human psyche.

Thousands of years ago, most of our ancestors had not yet caught this fever of consumerism. Our needs, curiosity, and pleasures were met without having to degrade and alter nature's rhythms. There is a clear threshold of violation that is reached either by an individual's excessive behavior—as when one person burns down an entire forest—or by the inevitable mass destruction that results when a population as a whole exceeds in its myriad demands the carrying capacity of its territory. The formula by which we can tell when we've destroyed something is not hidden from us, nor does it imply any kind of science. By degrees, destruction has been clearly marked throughout time and anybody could always read it and understand it.

Typically, so-called ecological overshoot resulted when a population found itself marooned atop an exhausted food base or plot of terrain. Like other species in nature, whether starfish or wildebeest, that population then moved on to the next file or tract of land. When the new niche was exhausted, our ancestors shifted to yet another locale. Locales, until recent times, were seemingly expendable by human standards, because regions were always large enough to absorb injury. And when the ecological stress upon whole regions was noticed, our ancestors simply migrated, searching out new pales and dominions. Thus emerged a style of life known in northeastern India as *jhuming*, or "shifting cultivation." Every year in India, five million hectares are processed by this ten-thousand-year-old method of migratory agriculture. Once the human tribe moved on, the burned out fields were left fallow, or at least that was the ecological recompense prior to a population boom.

When, in the 1940s, anthropologist Furer–Haimendorf visited Nishi villages in what is today India's northeastern-most and least-populated state, Arunachal Pradesh, the tribal people lived on mountain ridges in the jungle, descending into the valleys for catching game. Population was (even relative to today) totally sparse. ". . . feuds and revenge killings then undoubtedly acted as a check on the growth of the population. This check has now been removed," writes Furer–Haimendorf, "and the availability of medical services has limited the effect of epidemics, which on occasions took a heavy toll. An increase in the Nishi population is hence inevitable."[12] Adding to this, the building of a motorable road has encouraged the abandonment of former remote ridge-side communities and the reestablishing of population centers in the broad valleys. Ploughs and bullocks have been introduced for tilling the land, which has suddenly become valuable. Intensive utilization for rice-growing purposes has meant the "transformation of the natural environment" and the steady decline in fallow periods. Moreover, "with the increasing population growth, land is gradually becoming an object of conflict . . . whereas previously men used to quarrel about women and mithan (cattle) most disputes now arise from competition for land."[13]

There are some sixty-five million Indian indigenous peoples like those throughout Arunachal Pradesh, and hundreds of millions of untouchables. They have high birth rates and their infant mortality rates are declining. In essence, they are a population boom within a population boom, much like China's own minorities. Attempts by the government to translocate the tribals out of parklands have been ineffective, by and large. More at issue is the tribal way of life, that—under conditions of overpopulation—is tragically in opposition to essential forest ecology. It means that more livestock will munch on more leaves; more people will cut more wood for basic necessities, and there will be less and less primary forest for native species.

Where there is no competition—the condition of humanity many thousands of years ago, and vestigially in a few remaining outposts (as among India's last remaining Todas of the Nilgiri mountains in Tamil

Nadu State)—humankind knows how to be benign and live well.[14] It is not wishful thinking to want to be like those people. Indeed, the whole realm of sustainability, what many today think of as a kind of scientific and ethical "method" essential to our survival, derives simply from the wisdom of some of our ancestors. Not all of them, however. It is known for a fact that many traditional, so to speak "land-based" groups were environmental terrorists in their time. But it is equally true that countless peoples have been, and presently are "poor," yet leading relatively happy, productive, and sustainable lives. The test of sustainability has been proven, and contested, in numerous ways. For example, recent data from Belize indicates that the harvesting of medicinal plants from tropical forest plots can yield more dollar value in the regional market than agricultural produce or lumber from those same plots.[15]

But two caveats quickly emerge: first, there is a limit to the regional market for medicinal plants. The moment that market is necessarily expanded, new destructive forces descend on the source of supply.[16] And second, as the larger market economy imposes certain conditions of cost and extraction, the increased temptation to exploit the land more intensively for profit forces the harvesters to confront difficult ecological choices that may conflict with the dynamics of the group decision-making process, in the case of a commons, or with personal greed, or insecurity, in the case of private holdings. Among many fishermen in the southern state of Kerala, these various factors have been devastating. Short-term profit motivations, an indiscriminate harvesting of the marine ecosystem, has led to a syndrome whereby "it actually pays to bring ruin to the commons" in the minds of Kerala's new breed of capitalists.[17] In addition to this community, and personal dilemma, even where otherwise subtle biodiverse products in India have witnessed a new economic appreciation, exploitation by local populations has been totally unsustainable.[18]

There are still a few purely regional economies throughout the world. Such harvesters and farmers are people living directly off the land and isolated, unconnected to any larger human systems of exploitation. In India, until recently, at any rate, one of the last was on the Andaman and Nicobar Islands, where the Jarawa and Onge people had managed to remain fairly well isolated from all outsiders, at least until the late 1970s. Their small portion of rain forest was essentially untouched, from what can now be ascertained. Among such communities, there was a sufficiently complete break in human links affording a micropopulation the opportunity to sustain itself in a pure state, as in a clean-room laboratory. There are few natural clean rooms left. But we know enough about them, in principle, to endeavor to apply the reasoning of their preservation to larger population areas, though with a host of difficulties. But the clean rooms are vanishing rapidly. In the last fifteen years, colonists from the Indian mainland, searching for jobs, dreaming of paradise, have virtually driven the Jarawa and Onge to extinction. As of mid-November 1992, there were eighty Onge and thirty-one Jarawa, the émigré population having swollen to over 277 thousand, up from 30,971 in 1951, an annual growth rate during the past decade of 4.7 percent, even double that for the rest of the country.

India's immediate neighbor to the northeast, Bhutan, an ancient Buddhist nation with a per capita income on a par with India's, and a population 650 times smaller, is "poor" by most official world statistics. The International Human Suffering Index, for example, equates Bhutan with sub-Saharan Burkina Faso.[19] When American Ambassador to India John Kenneth Galbraith visited Bhutan in the late 1960s, he had to do so by yak, and it took nearly a week to reach the capital. There were no roads, no landing strips, no phones, virtually no electricity, hardly a wheel to be found in the country. When I went to Bhutan in the mid-1970s, the whole country resembled one alpine ski resort—without the skilifts, tourists, tour buses, or knowledge of such things. Bhutan may be the only country in the world where sustainable development on a national level is still underway where much greed has been curbed, the commons revered, and a nationwide ecological sensibility embraced and codified. "Small is Beautiful" is the King's motto. Ecotourism has been limited to no more than five thousand visitors a year (up from twelve hundred when I first journeyed there) though usually less than three thousand foreigners make it to Bhutan, at a cost of $250 per day. Most (though not all) large energy and development projects have been derailed before they've ever gotten started. Over 60 percent of the country is still completely cloaked in primary forest. The largest city in the country, Thimpu, contains a mere twenty thousand people. Whatever the explanation for the nation's wisdom—its petite, Buddhist population of 1.3 million, a religious aversion to harming plants and animals, a magnificent Himalayan isolation—one thing is instantly clear to anyone who visits the country: Bhutan may be poor by Western standards, but it is one of the richest of nations with respect to quality of life and purity of spirit. However, all is not paradisiacal in Bhutan, either. Recent population pressures from non-Drukpa (non-Bhutanese) immigrants, primarily Indian and Nepalese, along the southern border with India, have resulted in armed clashes posing the threat of ethnic civil war. One more clean room is succumbing to agitation just as we begin to know about it.

India's rural poverty, which accounts for nearly 77 percent of the country or well over half-a-million villages, is reminiscent of Bhutan's own modest per capita economy. More than half of all Indians are below the *garibi rekha* or poverty line.[20] But the spirit of India, no matter what else one alleges about the country, is as mesmerizing as it is troubling. I have been returning there for nearly thirty years, enamored of its people, landscapes, and passions. Such feelings render any supposed insights into India's population crisis oddly suspect, and I will be the first to admit it. While there can be no romancing the extreme direness of much that is Indian, it would be an equally insensitive and ignorant blunder to overlook India's beguiling capacity and mind-boggling range of traditions. India represents a very clearly discriminating population which, in spite of high illiteracy, harbors capabilities grossly underestimated by almost everyone, Indians included. But the contradictions abound, and they assault perception. One former minister in the government likens contemporary India to "Nazi Germany," with respect to its violence—violence in the form of oppression of women, children, of the environment, and of all animal life.

Poverty in India is defined by outsiders. On the inside it is something other than mere poverty, more like *pain* that dictates, and separates the haves from the have-nots.[21] Because so much of Indian *nature* is in pain, there are few human residents that can elude entirely, or at the minimum fail to recognize, the thraldom of suffering. But that pan-Indian recognition itself has not proven particularly susceptible to improvement or even empathy under the law, as most rural women in the country might tell you. Or, as one Agency for International Development (A.I.D.) official in New Delhi put it, "India is in a time warp." The Hindi word most apt for this sentiment is *kal,* which means both yesterday and tomorrow, and tends to summarize the Indian approach to getting anything done. Perhaps the most noteworthy example of a social anachronism—one which many Indians condemn, but just as many uphold—is the continuing designation and prejudice attached to an untouchable class (*harijans,* or *shudras,* also known as OBCs—"other backward classes.") They still predominate throughout the country (60 percent of the populous, as noted by the Indian Mandel Commission). Such people typically are forced to live on the margins of village life, and must walk extra miles to find water because the local village will not allow them to share it. The untouchables are barred from all jobs other than what they were "born to do," from marrying out of their realm, and are rarely ever represented in government. (There have been a few recent noteworthy exceptions.) Such class designations reflect an ancient hierarchy, sociopathic, blind, that is part religion, part expediency. Like the gypsies and orphans of the country, who also condemned, the untouchables are considered by many to be the dregs of India, and yet they are its life's blood.[22]

India may have begun much like the Andaman Islands or Bhutan, as a sort of spiritual clean room. In the hallowed late afternoon quiet of a white marble temple or along Kerala's graceful backwaters, I have watched locals peacefully attuned to a life force that insinuates the most delicate nuances amid flurry. That silence within chaos is a uniquely Indian oxymoron, an introspective bustle. You feel its dramatic energies in the innocent, blessed glances of the working people, who cannot, will not hold back a smile at the slightest provocation, in spite of adversity. One experiences it among the indomitable children who gaily converge at the entrance to nearly any doorstoop where one is assured of being invited in. The country intimates contagious affection and is easily capable of bringing out the best in a person. India also summons the past. Twenty-five hundred years ago the country must have been extraordinarily graceful, majestic, intoxicating. But like today, it must also have been seething. How else to explain the fact that two of India's premier religious leaders, the twenty-fourth Jain Tirthankara, Mahavira, and Siddhartha Buddha, both born during the sixth century B.C. into royal families (the latter, in the jungles of southern Nepal), were to renounce all of their possessions, become celibate, and spend their lives wandering throughout the Indian countryside analyzing the sources of despair and seeking through a comprehensive philosophy of nonviolence (*ahimsa*) to remedy a rampant problem? The conclusions they reached (what the ancients knew to be an umbrella concept loosely thought of as *enlightenment*) were nothing short of family planning, ecological sustainability, and a deep, abiding reverence for all living beings that was consistently transmuted into action. Whether Jain, Buddhist, or Hindu, the soul was believed to transmigrate upon death into other living incarnations on its journey toward *moksha,* or *nirvana,* or *atma*—liberation, nonbeing, the world soul or self. This was to become the goal of religious life, one's *karma,* the feedback of one's actions, stipulating the conditions under which a person would return in the next life. A ceaseless series of reincarnations (*samsara*, the biological equivalent of cybernetics) ultimately led to release from this painful world. But in the meantime, each rebirth took the form of some other organism—a cricket, an elephant—and thus, the human soul was intimately related to all other life forms. The Hindu God Vishnu, preserver, was identified with the eagle, the boar, the fish, and the turtle; the swan was associated with Brahma, the creator; the Brahminy kite was linked to Durga, goddess of fortune. Even the princely rat figures as the mount of Ganesh, the god of wisdom whose head is that of an elephant.[23]

By the third century B.C., following Alexander the Great's retreat from India[24] and Chandragupta's consolidation of the Mauryan Empire, South Asia is believed to have contained some fifty million people. Population pressure was already being intensely felt, and nature rampantly exploited.

By the time the East India Company first dropped anchor at Surat in 1607, Mughal rule had fully transformed a country of spirit into one of coveted matter. In Surat's teeming bazaars one could purchase everything from leopard skins and peacock feathers to albino elephants and slave girls. Emperor Jahangir, who kept a nature diary, boasted of having personally killed nearly fourteen thousand animals between 1580 and 1616 while the Emperor Aurangzeb employed his entire armies—when they weren't killing people—in the flushing out of game.[25] In a National Museum of New Delhi miniature,[26] a paradise scene from eighteenth-century India depicts a lotus pond with crocodile and ducks, peacocks in the trees, and a tiger couple at the water's edge. The scene is punctuated by the central fact of four hunters—scantily clad females with sword, and bow and arrow, and rifle. They have not the slightest compassion in their hearts. One of the women, seated in a tranquil yogic position, takes aim with her gun, seconds away from killing the tigers. The whites of the women's eyes shine with menacing calm. Yet this was the same nature accorded inviolate status in India's most revered texts.[27]

But the Mughal impact on nature was amateurish next to the incoming British (and to a slightly lesser extent in the south, the Portuguese) who devastated whole species and cleared the forests in order to grow tea and coffee and a host of other concocted export products. However one might profile the range of indigenous expoitation that had gone on for thousands of years, it now all appeared rather sustainable, by comparison with the new foreign plunder.

In Kerala, for example, virtually the entire coast was cleared of its natural vegetation and replaced with coconuts, once the Portuguese discovered the superior quality of coir over wood for cordage, caulking, and ship rigging. The wide diversity of animals that inhabited the costal thickets were exterminated, while birdlife that could, migrated inland. In addition to the astounding loss of wildlife, the soil too suffered increased erosion as a result of the superficial root structure specific to the coconut tree.[28] Throughout the Western Ghats—that range of southern hills that parallel India's west coast for sixteen hundred kilometers, from the mouth of the River Tapti in Maharashtra, to the southernmost tip of Tamil Nadu—populations of the Malabar giant squirrels, lion-tailed macaque, and the Nilgiri langur were at once threatened as their forest homes were converted to tea and cardamom plantations by the foreign conquerors. Even hundreds of years ago, the fragmentation of ecosystems began to sever one genetic group from another.

Today, the crossword puzzle of India's biological heritage is impossible to recognize. More than 90 percent of the pieces are missing, and what's there is surrounded by roads, fences, and human scavengers, men and women born into a world where they themselves are instantly ecological victims.

On top of India's existing labyrinth of roads, railways and factories were introduced to accommodate Britain's greed. Following the Indian Mutiny of 1857, the British Crown took over from the East India Company in the running of the country, which it managed like an aggressive corporation. By the 1860s, according to a local conservationist, the British were shooting any animal that moved. Local Indian hunters who had not previously thought to kill off all the wildlife, now did so systematically for profit, given Britain's insatiable demand for feathers, skins, exotic foods, and forest products.[29] British forestry meant maximum extraction for the British. Neither India's environment, nor Indians were part of that equation.

To examine the old archival pen-and-ink drawings featuring the bored young British hunters in India with their local guides standing over the corpses of tigers is to glimpse the nauseating fate of empire. Adding her own show of support, in 1961, a year before India went to war with China, Queen Elizabeth took part in a tiger hunt at Ranthambhore, today a beleaguered national park. A photograph shows the Queen standing with other "dignitaries" beside the corpse of a large tiger her party had bagged.[30]

Whatever contradictory gains were made by those few British who cared about wildlife, India's independence and a population of nearly four hundred million, overwhelmed the existing sanctuaries with a people's desperate hunger for land. A new National Parks Act was initiated in 1955, during the same period when the Indian cheetah went extinct, yet as of 1965 only twenty-six hundred square miles of the country had been granted sanctuary status. More land than that had been preserved a century before in the United States, where the population was a small fraction of India's. What this meant was that by the time India—under Indira Gandhi—had truly taken its biodiversity loss seriously, with the commencement of Project Tiger in 1973, the damage was nearly irreversible.[31]

Indian wildlife and habitat loss poses heartbreaking choices for a country headed toward doubling, possibly tripling its population size in the coming century. Approximately 4 percent of India is protected (on a par with the global average). That land is divided into more than seventy national parks and 370 wildlife sanctuaries. However, every one of these allegedly protected areas is falling prey to the surrounding human tumult. As a result, nearly every ecosystem and a huge number of species are in trouble, though opinions differ greatly as to the actual total number of species in India.[32]

Along with their primeval habitats, India's tigers and rhinos, turtles and crocodiles, elephants and even India's national bird, the peacock, are all being driven to *ecological virtual reality*, to mere memory and forlorn fantasy, by poachers, the countless hunters working on behalf of breeders and international zoological collections, but mostly by the systematic encroachment of human beings.

At the same time, the cow and the buffalo, reverence for which Mahatma Gandhi described as the core of any vegetarian Hindusim, are today being massively butchered for their steaks under cruel and deplorable conditions, along with goats, chickens, sheep, camels, and every other domestic creature.

This animal peril is the direct outcome of the ever decreasing availability of space and natural resources. Since 1951, India's energy use has increased thirty-seven times per capita. The fact that 80 percent of all Indians are living in varying conditions of impoverishment, with little or no access to safe water, sanitation, or quality medical attention, has meant that whatever consumption does occur, takes place in a highly concentrated manner, relying on primary resources.

Adding to the desperate character of that equation is the fact that the majority of gains of the Green Revolution are over, in India. Indian agriculture, based principally on cereal crops like maize, wheat, rice, bajra, and a host of coarse grains known as *jowar,* is now rapidly in decline, yet the requirements for foodgrains are going to increase from 146 to an estimated 238 million tons per year in the coming decade.[33] As of 1985, half of India's 3.5 million square kilometers, which is equivalent to 329 milion hectares or approximately 1.35 percent of the earth's terrestrial share, was already being deemed "wasteland," and as much as 260 million hectares additionally moisture-stressed.[34] What this all means is that food production is no longer guaranteed, nor self-sufficient, while the marginalization of small plots and the growing inequities of food distribution have exacerbated a growing nutritional illiteracy. Per capita availability of pulses, grams of protein, and edible oils have all been decreasing steadily. Not surprisingly, 85 percent of all Indians have substandard diets. The National Institute of Health and Family Welfare states that 65 percent of all children in India are malnourished. Considering the fact that more than half the country is under the age of fourteen, and that another sixty-five million newborns will have to be fed, somehow, by the end of this century (at an untenable cost to the country of sixteen thousand rupees per infant) such data is ill-boding, to put it mildly.[35]

This glimpse of widespread famine on the horizon is further strained by the fact that there is a widely recognized sex bias with respect to food consumption within the Indian family, as there is in China. Women inevitably receive much less food than men, even accounting for weight differentials. This nutritional oppression impacts mental capacity and personal motivation, further aggravating an existing crisis of illiteracy among women, 75 percent of whom cannot read a newspaper. Illiteracy varies from state to state across India. In 1921, less than two percent of all Indian women were literate. More than seventy years later, the all-country average is still less than 25 percent, and not quite double that for men.

These trends—and others—have utterly invalidated earlier predictions about the country with respect to food consumption. For example, the U.N. Food and Agriculture Organization published a study in 1982 suggesting that Indian agriculture could feed 2.6 billion people. But that was before a subsequent investigation which showed that at least a third of the country's arable land was "completely unproductive." Later, it was argued that the Indo–Gangetic plains by themselves could easily feed 1.8 billion people (the World Bank stabilization figure) assuming "the Indian diet remains essentially vegetarian as it is today."[36] That too has proven to rest upon vastly erroneous assumptions. According to the Anthropological Survey of India headed by Dr. Kumar Suresh Singh, it was found that 88 per cent of India's communities—of all Indians—eat meat, which can mean anything from field rats and baby crocodiles, to civet cats, jackals, and tigers.[37] In addition, at least one sixth of the Gangetic plains are now periodically devastated by floods as a result of watershed destruction in the Himalayas, where sown areas are frequently three times the recommended amount, population density per hectare may exceed ten persons and ten cattle, while nearly half of all springs have gone dry. Eight thousand square miles of Indian arable land are lost in the form of topsoil erosion every year, six billion tons, double that of the U.S.[38] (But, again, remember that India has one-third the territory of the U.S.) At the same time, all of the associated problems of intensive irrigation have come back to haunt the country. Virtually no new irrigation expansion is possible in India, and more than a third of existing channels are clogged with silt, with leakage, or have added to the existing alkaline wastelands. Two of the country's largest states, Uttar Pradesh and Bihar—the breadbelts of the Gangetic plains—find more than half of their residents well below the poverty line, which does not argue for the kind of sound environmental tendering that would ensure fallow periods, forest cycles, proper irrigation, and agricultural restraint—all of the key presumptions of due diligence of the aforementioned FAO report.[39]

The Ganges, like India's thirteen other major rivers, is severely polluted. Nearly a billion and a half litres of untreated sewage are cast into the 1,580 mile long "Ganga" every day, though many experts involved in the Ganga Action Plan have been trying to intercept it. Eighty percent of all hospital patients in India are victims of environmental pollution, most water-borne.[40] Many victims catch their viral diarrhea, typhoid, and infectious hepatitis by drinking holy water (*charanamrita*) at the countless temples, where disastrously high levels of fecal coliform bacteria—levels eighteen times higher than the Bureau of Indian Standards—have been consistently recorded.[41] Nearly 60 percent of all Indians are without access to safe water. Water tables in some parts of the country have fallen by one hundred feet. In Haryana and Punjab, key agricultural states, aquifers are nearly exhausted.

Many other Indians live in atrociously polluted cities, or in the vicinity of unregulated heavy industry. New Delhi is considered to have possibly the worst air pollution in the world for many months each year. The sheer ubiquity of the two-wheelers (called "fart-farts" locally) which contribute 65 percent of air pollution in the city, is nearly impossible to control for emissions.[42] An astounding half of all adult residents in fifty villages surrounding the State of Orissa's Talcher Thermal Power Station have tuberculosis. Ash from the power station contains nearly 63 percent silica.[43] Along with TB, the villagers of Talcher are suffering from a host of additional infections. Women particularly are vulnerable, as they may spend 80 percent of their lives indoors, exposed to what is the equivalent of a constant low inversion of smoke and other chemical pollutants.

Along with declining agricultural yields, and swelling pollution regimes, other woes benight India's swarming numbers. As many as 115 million Indian children who should be in school are not. Rather, they are working under adverse industrial conditions with little respite offered by the government. The 1986 Child Labor (Prohibition and Regulation) Act offers them no protection from hazardous conditions, or from the frequent beatings and sexual abuse of their employers. Nor are children allowed to form unions to protect themselves, under a 1926 law. The situation represents a colossal area of human rights abuse, which some foreign parliamentarians have tried to stop through the power of boycotting imports of Indian products made by children. But little has changed. India's child labor force is equivalent to one of the ten largest national populations in the world. The work conditions have engendered a painful breeding ground of serious health maladies from chronic bronchitis to stunted growth. The children routinely handle toxic chemicals like potassium chlorate and zinc oxides, starting at three in the morning and going until evening. Girls outnumber the boys three to one. There is no such thing as holidays for them and no government policing. Children from the age of three years old are employed making matches and fireworks and carpets because of their alleged nimble fingers. Older children labor in stone quarries in Kerala, slate factories in Andhra and Madhya Pradesh, in deep mines in Meghalaya; they work in road project trenches, manage handlooms in Kashmir, or spend their young lives handrolling Indian cigarettes (Bidi) in nearly every town and city. They work electroplating and hand presses, as well as glass furnaces that put out seven hundred degrees of heat. They are, along with women, India's most exposed and oppressed class, their diseases expressed in tragically high infant and child mortality statistics.[44]

The oppression of people and of biological habitat follow identical patterns. All human ecological exploitation backfires. What I have called the THAR effect, or total human appropriation of a region, results from industry, agriculture, irrigation, and the countless other urban, suburban, or rural ways by which humans overintrude. But there is no greater, nor more visible area of maleffect, no more devastating loss to India than that of her forests, the substance and background of so much of the country's religious landscape, the source of water catchment and subsequent food self-sufficiency, of fuel and fodder supply, the basis of employment for tens of millions, the roof overhead, the floor underfoot. The realm of most terrestrial biodiversity. All are fast disappearing.

While the "official" forest cover hovers around 19 percent, the former minister of environment and forests, Maneka Gandhi (widow of the late Sanjay Gandhi, daughter-in-law of the late Prime Minister Indira Gandhi, and one of India's truly radiant and empathetic beacons) indicated otherwise to me.[45] At her home one evening she explained how she had studied the satellite images and discovered that, at best, India retained 9 percent, not 19 percent, of its forest. And even that 9 percent figure came bolstered by the presence on satellite of sugar cane crops. Satellites do not distinguish between forest and mature sugar cane stands, which are quite high. Furthermore, the sugar cane, unlike the forest, admits to virtually no biological community, while inviting the heavy burden of soil-destructive pesticides.

India currently spawns twenty million newborns every year. With a total fertility rate (TFR) of 4.1, an average life expectancy of sixty, a GNP per capita of $160, and a total population doubling time of thirty-six years, this population is poised to totally decimate India's few remaining forests, whether the existing cover is 9 percent or 19 percent, in very few remaining years.

According to Mrs. Gandhi, in India there is little accountability. The law states you cannot cut down a tree unless it's dead. So what the people do is to set fire to trees, or debark them, and then when it has died they "legally" cut it down and take it away. "If you look at the trees anywhere in India," she says, "you'll note that they have very few branches."

India's tree-planting efforts are "a total sham," Gandhi reiterates, pointing out that her former Ministry of Environment and Forests is allocated less money than any other ministry in India. Up until 1981 the ministry itself was set within a beautiful grove of forest, and then the Asian

Games committee convinced the Government to build huge high-rise structures and tear down all the trees. Gandhi replanted ten thousand seedlings that are now coming up. She supervised the planting. They are her legacy. Two years after coming into office, she says, corrupt officials threatened by her views, her attempt to legislate a host of new animal rights legislation, her concerns over unregulated industrial pollution, and her efforts to revamp forestry programs managed to get her booted out of office. She believes the election was rigged.

India does not utilize its remaining forests as a revenue source—as they do in places like Malaysia and Indonesia—but as a community resource. This "think globally, act locally" concept raises certain, seemingly insoluable ethical questions. Economists have long wondered how to morally address trade-off possibilities between different consuming groups. But if "consumer sovereignty" is deemed politically obligatory—as it usually is in peace time, and as a community resource suggests—then, as economist A. K. Bhattacharyya has described, "the gains or losses suffered by any population set times 1 cannot be set off against the losses or gains of another population set times 2." This is why the north/south dialectic remains utterly unresolved. One man's torment is another's pleasure, but both are politically equal under international law, particularly the GATT which has seldom acknowledged environmental considerations as valid terms of denial or bias between trading partners.[46]

Pressure on the forests of India comes not so much from "consumption," as from subsistence. In the West, it is consumption that kills. In India, it is the lack of consumables, a paucity exacerbated every day, as nearly fifty-five thousand newborns come into existence. And everyday at least four hundred million Indians carry wood out of the forests in bundles on their heads to provide fuel, food, housing, and fodder. The law allows for one large bundle per day, as much as you can carry. And this translates into about 190 million tons of fuelwood per year, at India's present population.[47] If Indians could afford oil—or, if the forests were somehow rendered off-limits to Indians (an impossibility), then the price of a barrel of oil might jump to a hundred dollars worldwide, a point hammered home at the Rio Summit when India's former minister of environment and forests, Kamal Nath, insisted that the northern economic bloc recognize that its continued franchise would be undone if the south should fail to conserve its own resources. "And hence, it is in the interest as much of the north as of the south that there not be any parsimony in participatory mechanisms designed to give expression to this recognition of the principle of shared responsibility," he argued. To this end, Nath, like nearly every other minister of environment in the developing world, is not simply talking about management, but money, which Nath feels is owed to India. "We are seeking recognition of the principle that since historically, it is the exploitation of the resources of the south which has fuelled environment-damaging development in the north, a small fraction of the prosperity so secured must, as a matter of obligation, be devoted to survival into the future."[48]

The language of "obligations" is an unwelcome one to Western ears. But such intent is more fiercely sabotaged by the cruel truths of self-preservation in India. Trees are what the politicians have to give the people—not money. One headload of wood per person per day. By subsidizing the poor in this way, the government is slowing down the pace of total destruction, but is helpless to prevent it. In Varanasi, an electric crematorium was recently constructed because people cannot afford the nearly one thousand rupee cost for a wood pyre on which to dispose of their dead according to Hindu custom. It used to be that the same funeral pyre cost fifty rupees.[49] This is but one example of the impact increasing population is having on a declining resource base. In India, land is divided into three categories: revenue land, smaller private holdings called *patta*, and existing forest. All are destined for exploitation. As for revenue land (government nonforest lands which account for a vast majority of India) anyone can homestead there (squat). When they have squatted long enough, it becomes by law their private *patta*, at which point they can burn it down, if they should so desire. You see the squatters everywhere in India. There are several million of them in Calcutta and Mumbai, Delhi and Chennai. By law, squatters' rights supersede forest rights. Several cases have been challenged in the courts. The squatters always win. India is a tenacious democracy. But as India is discovering, democracy and ecology are at odds when the population overshoots its carrying capacity. China learned the same lesson from a different political point of view.

While chimney smoke is China's most lasting icon, the smoke from small outdoor cooking fires, whether on city streets, or along roadsides far away in the country, on mountain ridges, in tea plantations, or in jungle swamps, is what most indelibly characterizes India's war zone, its unrelenting contribution to the global greenhouse effect.

India appears to be losing a larger percentage of its forest every year than any other country in the world, or over 3 percent of its total remaining stands, which would translate into 15,000 square kilometers annually. By comparison, Brazil is losing 13,820 square kilometers a year, or 0.4 percent of remaining forest. Ecuador is losing 2.4 percent; Indonesia 0.9 percent, or 10 thousand square kilometers. At this rate, simple calculations suggest that within another ten to fifteen years, the forests of India will be gone, truly gone. In parts of the country, deforestation has reduced annual rainfall from 150 to 75 inches.[50]

Indian grasslands are also disappearing—11 percent, or eleven hundred of the world's species of grasses being rapidly eliminated by the largest cattle population in the world.[51] The country comprises 50 percent of the world's buffaloes, 15 percent of all cows, 15 percent of all goats, and 4 percent of all sheep. Population pressure among these animals in this century has reduced necessary grazing space by ten times, leaving less than twelve million hectares of suitable pasture. As a result of malnurished cattle, milk yields in India are among the lowest in the world, 173 kilograms per cow, versus 3,710 kilograms in Denmark.[52] And thus, the ecological backfire delimits the very calcium content in the bones of children. One sees cases of rickets throughout India. It is the perfect irony: a country with vast numbers of milk-producing bovine, destroys its feeding base, and thus depletes the quality and amount of the milk. The Gangetic Plains has lost nearly all of its grasslands. When grasslands are managed properly, they can grow back quickly. Not so forests and shrub, which are being increasingly denuded by India's goat, sheep, and free grazing cattle populations which—lacking sufficient grassland—extend their grazing behavior toward the shrinking forests, where they would not ordinarily venture for various reasons (tigers and lack of grass).[53] The biodiversity of the grasslands has been completely unsettled, with many open plains-dwelling species losing out to overpopulated livestock. In many regions of India the wolf, the Bengal tiger, and lesser florican, chinkara, partridges, and quails are disappearing, as are the great Indian bustard and blackbuck.[54]

Coastal regions are also mired in the population vortex throughout India. The tourist industry is developing hundreds of hotels along beaches, which means the probable extinction of India's sea turtles and other species. And unlike, say, Mexico, which has finally established a full-time and sizeable constabulary to physically protect nesting turtles, India is far behind in that arena.

The country's coastal waters receive over twenty thousand tons of pesticides and fungicides, and thirty-one thousand tons of detergents every year. Most of the coastal mangroves are gone. A mere seven hundred hectares are left in all of Kerala. India's coral reefs—like those of neighboring Sri Lanka—have also been obliterated. According to studies by India's National Institute of Oceanography, forty thousand tons of coral are mined just from the Gulf of Mannar alone, at India's southern tip. From the Lakshadweep in the west, to the Nicobar Islands in the east, the situation is the same: uncurtailed devastation.

Adding to the country's other water-related woes, Indians have access to only half the fresh water they enjoyed at the time of independence, despite nearly sixteen hundred dams in the country.[55]

In the midst of all this countrywide demolition, perhaps no other environmental battle has captured the attention of Indian ecologists as the fight to save the tiger, a species at risk of extinction whose plight symbolizes that of every other exotic creature in the country. By 1972 there were an estimated 1,827 Indian tigers left, down from nearly fifty thousand at the turn of the century. At the twentieth anniversary of Project Tiger (held in New Delhi during February, 1993) scientists argued with some pride that there were now four thousand Indian tigers.[56] Maneka Gandhi disagrees. "The entire figure is rubbish," she told me days after the august assemblage. "It is based upon data manufactured by a certain so-called tiger specialist who multiplied a base population twenty years ago of three hundred by the number of presumed couples, their likely number of three offspring each two years, year by year, substracting 10 percent for poaching, subtracting 10 percent for other calamities, and thus arrived at a number of four thousand. He's a demographer. Nobody has a clue as to the number of tigers we have and I'm willing to bet it's not over a thousand." She says that police are constantly sweeping down upon various poaching rings, yet, nobody ever goes to jail because the police are so eager to take bribes, instead.

At least 1,175 square kilometers of tiger preserve have been lost just in the last six years to various forms of encroachment. In just one state, Himachal Pradesh, thirty wildlife sanctuaries and two major national parks are now "imperiled." Wildlife authorities are said to "feel helpless in providing full protection to some of the rare species."[57] In other parks, the government has just stopped short of declaring wildlife "industrialized." Poachers have used helicopters to spot tigers within the Corbett Tiger Reserve in Uttar Pradesh. At the Melghat Reserve in Maharashtra, pressure from seventeen thousand villagers forced the government to give up 25 percent of the reserve in favor of small timber production.[58]

Rajasthan's long-contested Sariska National Park, once the private hunting preserve of maharajahs, has yielded $1.5 million a year in revenues, not from ecotourism but from mining the park.[59]

There are some fifteen hundred villages in the existing nineteen tiger parks. There is a nuclear plant proposal in Nagarjunasagar, a hydroelectric project that could destroy Manas, and a dolomite mining project already underway at the Buxa Tiger Reserve, like that in Rajasthan. In 1991, Darlaghat Sanctuary in Himachal Pradesh added a cement plant.

While biological systematists the world over argue over genetic corridors and habitat preservation tactics, the real challenge has become clear: will the Indian government simply denotify (sanction the destruction of) more and more protected areas as adjoining village populations increase?[60]

As bad as it is for the tiger in India, it is far worse for the Asiatic lion, an animal revered in India's ancient Hindu text, the *Atharva Veda,* but which began going noticeably extinct throughout India around 1814. In 1966, six hundred square kilometres of the Gir forest of Gujarat State were declared a lion sanctuary. But the human population pressures were intense by then: by 1971 there were nearly five thousand local *maladharis* (cattle herding families) and nearly seventeen thousand head of cattle, in addition to another forty-eight thousand cattle from other areas which came to Gir for grazing during the monsoon. An estimated 90 percent of the lion's food was appropriated. By 1974, there were 167 lions remaining. The pressures on the felines are doomsdayish.[61] Nature has not provisioned for nearly a billion carnivorous humans to live agreeably side by side with a few big cats.

The same biological contests now affect every species in the country. The elephant is the most visible case in point. There are an estimated twenty thousand wild elephants left in India. Their migration paths have been destroyed, or crisscrossed with electric wires to try and prevent their movement across farmlands. Countless other Indian elephants live and die in shackles.

A much less visible, but nonetheless endangered Indian species is the musk deer, of which a mere two thousand are left. Its pod of musk now commands as much as fifteen thousand rupees, or five years salary for many Indians. Even more endangered are the last few magnificent hangul stags of Kashmir whose sanctuary, the Dachigam Wildlife Preserve on the outskirts of Srinagar, founded in 1951, appears doomed as the result of population pressure in myriad guises. By 1971 the World Wildlife Fund conducted a census which revealed a mere 153 animals left.

Meat-eating poachers (mostly Muslim) in Manipur, between Myan-mar and Nagaland, have virtually wiped out one of three remaining thamin races in the world, a rare circular-antlered deer known locally as sangai, the "deer that looks back at you." As of 1979, aerial surveys showed a mere thirty left.

It required six permanently established armed antipoaching patrols to save the barasinga deer from extinction, and that was inside the Dudhwa National Park in Uttar Pradesh. Such patrols are few. The tragic truth is, India cannot patrol itself.[62]

In Assam, India's sole ape, the jovial hoolock gibbon, along with the golden langur, the clouded leopard, the pigmy hog, wild buffalo, and rhi-noceros, are each being devastated by poachers. [63]

In Kerala's Periyar Wildlife Sanctuary, two hundred forest guards and wardens have proven insufficient to keep poachers away. Elephants are slaughtered for their tusks; the slender loris for its eyes; and lion-tailed macaques are hunted for their skins and their meat, believed by some locals to increase a man's potency, as if that were a problem in India.[64]

In the high Ladakhi Himalayas, only 100 Przevalski black-necked cranes, and 150 Tibetan gazelles remain, in addition to a meager few snow leopards, Tibetan lynx, and Pallas's cat. On occasion the Indian military is called out to protect these animals. But out along the Andaman, Nicobar and Sentinel Islands, far from the military, poachers have had a heyday, sell-ing endangered turtle eggs and rare meats in open marketplaces, whether that of wild boar, chital, or the giant monitor lizards. Nonindigenous hunters deploy large arrays of traps—much like gill nets spread out over hundreds of yards. Many of the local creatures are endangered, and listed under Schedule I of the Wildlife (Protection) Act. Of the islands' 240 species and subspecies of birds, the endemic ones are mostly rare, or already gone.

The precise outcome of these trends may be subject to some specula-tion. But it is only a question of time before Indians discover that they have brutally reduced their once bountiful jewel of creation to a sterile wasteland of simple ecosystems—weeds and desert—bereft of all but human diversity. Such is the imponderable volatility of the country's demographics and the sheer, untempered survival needs, bluntly sought, by so many people.

The prognosis for all animals in the country is grim. When I asked Maneka Gandhi what hope, if any, there might be, she was angrily resolved in her response. "None!" she repeated. Her face had the look of one who had wiped away quite a few tears in the past and had now come to accept—almost with a coldness—certain inevitabilities about India and the way of the world.[65] Though having recently lost her post as minister of environment and forests, in many respects Maneka Gandhi had lost none of her power. Instead of moving whole mountains, her goal now is to save individual lives, to spare as many of the billions of doomed domestic creatures as possible. This is the goal of all conservation biology, namely, the alleviation of pressure on as many other species, and individuals, as possible, in spite of the ponderous recognition that human nature seems utterly incapable of true egalitarian coexistence with other life forms.

Mrs. Gandhi now runs the Sanjay Gandhi Animal Welfare Center in New Delhi. She writes a column, lectures occasionally, but spends most of her time fighting to stop an epidemic of animal cruelty throughout her country. India is by no means unique in this realm, but the animal rights movement hardly has even a foothold in Asia, as yet.

"Animal rights' advocates in India are viewed as the lunatic fringe," says Gandhi. "I don't have anything to be defensive about. I don't respond to critics. I am a very good politician in that I look after people as best I can. I don't believe in animals *or* people. I believe in animals *and* people. Or people and animals. Love doesn't stop. I'm not pessimistic. I'm realistic. In a country like this we shouldn't kid ourselves. But at least one can create an awareness. Then you'll have less people throwing stones. It's a drop in the ocean. But it's something."

Perhaps the first and only moment of national consciousness regarding animal rights occurred during Maneka Gandhi's term as minister. New Delhi filmmaker Himanshu Malhotra's half-hour chronicle of the horrors of the Deonar abattoir in Bombay, a film that was cosponsored by Gandhi, aired one night over India's national network, Doordarshan. This was the first powerful glimpse of animal suffering ever televised in the country.

What the viewer witnessed was the arrival of cattle trucks at the slaughterhouse. The animals had been tied together and loaded on top of each other, four abreast. By the time they arrived to be killed, their bones were broken, they were starving and terrified. Many were diseased. Some had already suffocated or died of heart attacks. Acid was poured into their nostrils and tobacco rubbed into their eyes to make them get out of the trucks. Most could not, would not move. So men dragged them by their tails.

Ironically, the only "law" which seems to be observed throughout most of the slaughterhouses in the country is one concerning the slaughterer's self-pride: he must wait until the animal stands up before killing it. It's a macho thing. The slaughterers persuade the animal to stand by forcing electric or molten iron prods up their anuses. Frantically, the twelve hundred pound animal lurches up one last time, as a group of young people converge upon it with rusty hatchets and saws. They chop and slice and it can take a half hour before the convulsing animal is out of its misery.

The filmmaker, Malhotra, told me of his initial hopes that maybe at long last something would change in India. The film elicited some twenty thousand local protests for a day. Incoming cattle trucks were blockaded. The price of meat soared from thirty to sixty rupees. per pound. But then, just as quickly, the furor died down. The municipal commissioner in Bombay insisted he was too "tied up" to deal with the problems and people accepted that.[66]

I once visited an Indian slaughterhouse, in the middle of the night. Young boys, no older than ten, were there with long blades in a concrete bunker slaughtering dozens of sheep as if it were some kind of sport. The experience was as close as I can imagine to going insane.

There is no enforcement of laws, no stun guns, no interest whatsoever in alleviating pain and suffering. Just brazen, sloppy, horrible killing. Much of the meat is shipped to Arab countries. There are over five thousand butchershops which engage in such slaughter in New Delhi alone, over one million throughout the country. One other law stipulates that cows cannot be killed until they are sixteen years old. But few are the experts in India who know how to tell when a cow is sixteen years old.

With respect to goats, of which an enormous number are devoured by Indians, for every goat bred to be slaughtered, the country actually loses some sixty thousand rupees. because the goats wander around public lands chewing up all the vegetation. It is estimated that 60 percent of Indian wasteland is the result of goats that have been bred to be eaten. The city of New Delhi took out its third loan for sixty-three million dollars in the early 1990s to attempt to replant grass and shrubs in the surrounding Aravali hills. Yet, no corresponding effort to stop breeding goats for slaughter ever occurred.

Authorities blame it all on the Muslims' lust for meat, as well as their religious slaughters, such as the Bakhr Id festival in which thousands, possibly hundreds of thousands of camels, goat, sheep, bullocks, to name but a few of the animal types, are killed, having been starved and left without water for days prior. But there are between six and seven Hindus eating meat for every Muslim. Much of the slaughtered pig, goat, and buffalo meat is going to fast food chains throughout the country.

In Tamil Nadu, Kerala, and West Bengal, cattle droving goes on throughout the night. Young herders run the animals, beating them unmercifully to speed up the journey. The cows are already half-starved by the time they arrive at the killing grounds, where their heads are bashed in with pipes. That's how it's done in the south.

Millions of old cows too emaciated to interest the butchers, wander the streets starving to death. This is what India's supposed worship of the bovine comes down to. Desperate, the animals are forced against their nature to "steal" fruit, vegetables, anything they can find in the bazaars, or the garbage dumps, or along the dusty street surfaces. Venders possess bottles of acid and splash the animals in the face to keep them away.

A huge population of bullocks are used for pulling carts. They are the tourist's notion of a quaint, rural India. Seventy percent of these doomed cart-bearers rapidly develop open, painful sores which often become cancerous. The animals die, typically, within three years, or are subjected to the slaughter routine first. No one has yet thought to design a more humane (let alone economical) yoke, which is the cause of the open sores. Mrs. Gandhi has put out a call for such a design.

The horror stories are endless, whether they pertain to the particularly gruesome slaughter of snakes, crocodiles, or pigs (which are eaten alive in some parts of the country).The fashionable Karakul hat is made of lamb's hair. The ewe (the mother) is forced to have a premature birth. How? She is struck with an iron rod or steel pipe or hammer, as many times as it takes, to induce the birth. The newborn is then skinned alive so as to ensure soft fur. Civet cats are caged in a tiny container and beaten every few days because when they are in pain they secrete musk. The poachers continue inflicting the pain as long as the animal lives. In India they test talcum powder and lipstick by thrusting it down the throats of squirrel monkeys. When the monkey dies the "researchers" figure the dose was too much. I hear amused scorn of a culture of butchers into the night. An inconsolable cry coming from India's muted heartland.

The misperception of a vegetarian India is merely one of many myths. With the exception of the ten million Jains, the one million

Bishnoi, 1,495 Todas, and scattered members of other religions in the country, there is absolutely no consistent respect, let alone reverence, for animals in India, or not anymore. Less than 12 percent of the country is vegetarian. In the realm of medicine and science, India employs intensive duplicative experiments on animals because, if for no other reason, they are so cheap to come by, at least in the past. Five hundred monkeys are killed for every single monkey in any other country. The antivivisection board, started by Mrs. Gandhi, and incorporating the earlier Animal Welfare Board, was discontinued once she was out of office. There appears to be no monitoring or regulation of animal experiments, or of the use of animals in commercial research.

While the existing Prevention of Cruelty to Animals Act of 1960 is a very strong piece of legislation, it remains completely unread and unheard of by most people, including the police. Global treaties like CITES (the Convention on the International Trade of Rare & Endangered Species) make little difference in India. Ivory is technically forbidden but it can still be sold under the law according to a provision allowing for the close-out of earlier inventory. Lacking any substantial body of organized field operatives, the government is virtually powerless to detect, or curtail, the sale of endangered species' parts, even if it were serious about doing so.

Even "man's best friend" is not immune to this carnage. Quite to the contrary. Authorities go after the dogs, the hungry ones, with sweet cajolery, then break their legs with metal tongs, drag them by the hundreds into a tiny room and starve them to death or douse them with water and begin the slow process of mass electrocution which typically can take half a day before the writhing animals expire. There is sadistic pleasure taken in these little holocausts. That has been shown to be the case by at least one film which I have observed. Sometimes the slaughter occurs right out on the street. Nobody seems to mind. The animals are simply clubbed to death. It's all part of the government's supposed rabies control program. Yet the government itself has stated that at least 50 percent of all rabies in the cities of India come from pet dog bites, not communal (stray) dogs. But there has been no effort to persuade dog owners to give their pets antirabies vaccines, a practice which has resulted in zero rabies cases in Spain and Hong Kong, for example. Nor has India undertaken sterilization campaigns for its animals, though it has been quick to do so for its women. In the U.S., canine sterilization costs forty dollars per animal. In India, according to Mrs. Gandhi, the cost is two cents. If the city of

Calcutta were to spend the 1.2 million rupees each year allocated for the indiscriminate killing of dogs on their sterilization and the WHO antirabies vaccine instead, the perceived problem would be solved.

As I sat with Mrs. Gandhi listening to her many tales of tragedy, she dabbed a hankerchief to the flare up of mange on her lip which she had caught from one of the many communal dogs she had rescued and was nursing back to health at her home, and she smiled. At that moment, I recognized hope for India.

"It comes up in fits and spurts," she theorized. "There are thousands of animal rights' groups throughout the country but there are no funds. We don't know what to do. When you don't have money you forget about it. You can be full of zeal when you're eighteen years old. But then by the time you get married and you're twenty-two and your husband says to hell with it you shouldn't waste your time picking up stray cats, that's the end of it. There are plenty of people moaning about the rhinoceros and the tiger because they know there's nothing they can do about it. They're going to go extinct. But I want to show the people the common crow, the dog, the cow, the camel, the goat, the water buffalo, that lives right here and now, is suffering. Wherever you are you must make a difference. That's all one can do."

After enough exposure to these unimaginable cruelties in human nature, an inescapable conclusion surfaces, or at least it does in my own mind: the vague, incalculable hunch that human rights have got to be *overcome,* somehow, conquered. What are our rights—to rape, plunder, kill, destroy, declare war upon all other species? Those are the human rights that have to be abolished if the planet is to survive. Mrs. Gandhi— and many others like her throughout India—wants to see hundreds of animal hospitals established, vast new reforestation programs that are realistic, a ban on the exportation of meat, an end to cruel circuses and zoos, the establishment of training centers for wild animal vets, as well as for members of parliament, where they could see what was really going on in their country. Just to make them aware, to encourage new laws, to step up enforcement of those laws. To train far more antipoaching units and to allocate considerably more money from the annual budget toward environmental protection and restoration.

Short of an ethical revolution in India that coincides with serious efforts to immediately curb the population boom, the country will remain in a state of war. One of the clearest examples of how demographic pressure impacts the habitat and animal life comes from the region surrounding the northern town of Dehra Dun, where Project Tiger was launched. 220 thousand new settlers to the region cleared twenty-seven square miles of forest. Now India produces 1.5 million new settlers every month, and that number is growing. Forest clearance for development means destruction of animal life. But the government of India sees development as its only hope to transcend poverty, even while recognizing the increasing poverty of the environment. The National Land Use Policy of 1988 states as its two priorities, "To meet the consumption needs of a growing population by increasing productivity of the integrated land resource in the country," and "To prevent any further deterioration of the land resource by appropriate preventive measures."[67] But no one has yet divined a way to accomplish this hat trick.[68] Already, the countless development battles have left India devoid of any wilderness, by those criteria established by the World Resources Institute definition of the term (four thousand square kilometers of undefiled land).[69] There is only one remaining five-hundred-square-kilometer section of the country that can be described as truly wild, namely, the Palpur Kund Sanctuary in the State of Madhya Pradesh.

A few years ago when the government of India wanted to try and expand the possible territory for the Gir lions, to its bewilderment was the revelation of what precisely zero wilderness means: there was no other park or region for the lions to be placed in the whole country. Palpur Kund was unacceptable because there were some tigers already in residence. Tigers and lions have only ever been known to get along under captive breeding situations.[70]

Just as the animals and their diverse habitats are slipping away, so too the human population plunges ever deeper into self-inflicted turmoil. This is a reciprocal promise. The per capita gap between the needs of a swelling population and the actual availability of clothing, housing, health, water supply, sanitation, electrical generation, and transportation facilities, is rapidly escalating. Of the 3,245 towns and cities covering nearly seven million acres, only 21, or 0.6 percent have even partial sewage treatment facilities throughout the country.[71] According to the National Institute of Health and Family Welfare, just to maintain the status quo in India, against the backdrop of a runaway population boom, the following additional requirements must be met each year in the late 1990s: as many as 1.2 million additional hospital beds, 190 million meters of cloth, a minimum of three million new dwellings, ten million tons of food, a staggering 127 thousand schools, 373 thousand teachers, and four million jobs. This, of course, does not indicate the extent to which the country is already underserved in each of these domains. Researchers H. Simon and B. Sharma conclude, "If this situation remains unchecked, there will be socio-economic chaos and confusion. People will be caught, at both micro and macro levels, in the vicious circle of poverty, underdevelopment and the wasteful demographic patterns of high fertility associated with high morbidity and mortality."[72]

Infant mortality is already between eighty and ninety-five per thousand, on average. Child mortality (from ages one through five) is a staggering 170–85 per thousand, and most of these latter deaths are believed to be avoidable. What kills the children is typically a combination of respiratory infections, diarrhea, malnutrition, measles, whooping cough, and persistent, unattended fever.[73] Rural deaths are twice that of urban deaths. The annual medical breakdown in India is hard to absorb. Tens of millions of new cases of TB every year (more than half the world's total in India, and over 20 percent now deemed incurable), 3.3 million new cases of leprosy, 14 million new individuals stricken with filariasis, 1.7 new malaria cases, 1.4 additional water-borne diseases, and so on.[74] The first official known HIV positive case appeared in India in 1988. With well over two million prostitutes in a country which does little to temper what typically amounts to the sexual enslavement of young girls and the eager complicity of the male market, the AIDS virus is exploding across the Indian subcontinent.

And so it goes . . . facts, data, trends, calculations, statistics. A picture of human turmoil and ecological entropy. Of internal unrest not appreciably different than the agony in Somalia and the Sudan, Bosnia and Liberia. Except on an infinitely vaster scale, and with only an occasional terrorist bomb blast, assassination, or near nuclear exchange. But this is no civil war and the distinction is an important one. What's happening in India as in China involves the total appropriation of nature, with profoundly negative human consequences. Nobody in particular is at war, though there are persistent ethnic outbreaks of killing, some well-known—as in the Punjab, in Kashmir, Assam, and across Bihar—others little mentioned in the world press. But stand upon any street corner, or in any field of India and chances are, you will not be aware of this remarkable conflict, nor at all convinced of its myriad dimensions, though one cannot fail to perceive a certain battle-weariness in the air. Ecological plunder has entered the mindscape.

To this day there are rat temples in Calcutta where the little creatures are treated like visiting royalty. In Rajasthan, hundreds of desert Bishnoi, a subsect of the Hindus, martyred themselves a few centuries ago protecting the desert's trees and gazelles, and perpetuate a remarkably compassionate and vegetarian way of life, while the Jains—whose entire religious and social orientation has consistently embraced nonviolence—have founded *panjorapor* sanctuaries for animals throughout many parts of the country. Put in context, however, these scarce living traditions of love and decency and common sense are merely remnants, emotional throwbacks to an earlier age when there were literally millions of lay people who followed the spiritual gurus, or teachers. But considering the whole of India's—and Asia's—pain, what could have gone wrong? How to account for such pervasive cruelty and sadness? Simply stated, the abovementioned "literally millions." You see, the God Krishna himself allegedly had 16,108 wives.[75]

SEXUAL PLUNDER

INDIA'S TRANSITION LONG ago from a spiritual to a market economy has resulted quite systematically in the rape of nature and the negation of any "clean room." Furthermore, the socially upheld custom of intense utilization has extended far beyond the forests, the mangroves, the grasslands, the mountains, the coral reefs, and coastal waters to the body of women. Exploitation of India's vast biodiversity has coincided with an ongoing denial and ignorance of the female's cultural plight. The psychopathology of these connections hints at the country's complex ecological and population crisis, a fact of no little significance to family planners who are confronted by stubborn historical biases favoring the male. Today's family planning slogan is, "*Beti ho ya Bete. Bacche Do He Achhe*" (Boy or Girl. Two Is Best). Yet in India (as in China) the working slogan appears to be, "Two Sons Is Best."

As early as the seventh century B.C., the *Dharmasastras*—The Rules of Right Conduct—first codified by the famed lawyer Manu (*The Laws of Manu*), placed women under the control of fathers, husbands, and then their own sons.[76] A girl was to be married prior to puberty, before the likelihood of her being raped, in other words. In more recent times, because the amount of the dowry is lower for younger daughters, early marriages have resulted in India having the highest rate of teenage pre-nancies in the world.[77] The marriage rituals traditionally took two weeks. From the first nuptial arrangements, the mother-in-law was poised to rule the daughter-in-law. This was her only domain of power in her entire life. And thus, women themselves, once victimized over enough generations, served this male-dominated system in the guise of fertility task-masters; the passing down from one generation to the next of male-engineered abuse.

After her marriage (usually to a man outside her village), the young woman joined her husband's clan, moving away from her parents and friends, who might never even see her again. She was thus an economic write-off, as far as her parents were concerned. Parents always wanted to marry her off as young as possible, to cut down on their investment and dowry costs. She had to be a virgin, and totally uneducated, passive, at the mercy of whatever man would have her. It was then the young bride's responsibility to bring males into the world. During her pregnancy she was told to eat little so that the baby wouldn't grow so large in the womb that it couldn't come out. And she was warned against green vegetables which were believed to cause miscarriages. She was also forbidden to drink milk because it was understood that milk makes the "baby stick to the uterus during delivery." When she was ready, the *dai,* a village midwife, would push on the mother's stomach during labor, unaware that this could burst the uterus. Cow dung was applied to stop the bleeding. The umbilical cord was cut with a stone.[78] Once she had delivered sufficiently numerous male children, the mother might secretly opt for some form of birth control for which, in ancient times, there were numerous prescriptions. It was said that "the woman who will drink for three days . . . a decoction of the Kallambha plant and the feet of jungle flies will never have children." Or, "The woman who will eat every day for a fortnight forty Mashas of molasses . . . which is three years old will remain barren for the rest of her life." Animal intestines were used as condoms. Pulpless lemon, certain leaves, the lactic acid from fermenting acacia tips, as well as honey were all placed in the vagina to impede sperm.[79]

One of India's most famed, beloved, and controversial demographers, Ashish Bose, puts it this way: "This country loves children, they simply love them. But probability theory works like this: people do not want large families, they want two sons. But probably, in trying to get two sons, you'll get four daughters first."[80] But among Hindus—the vast majority of

Indians—girls traditionally were considered something of a disaster. "Unless you have two or three sons you can't survive," Bose remarked. "If a fruit hawker gets sick, he'll have no food if even for one day he can't work. But if he has sons, they can shine shoes, sell cigarettes, sit on the street and get money, do something. Girls can't do that. In a country where there is no social security at all, no unemployment insurance, no old age pensions, nothing for the poor people, then what happens? They have to rely on the solidarity of the family. They must have sons. Or your brother's sons, or your nephews." Male preference is additionally predicated on the belief that unless your son lights your funeral pyre at death, you will not go to heaven.

The slow starving to death of girls (female mortality being ten times higher than male mortality among children as late as 1973) merely reflected the Indian consensus among men that the female was useless.[81] In a survey of the abortion clinics of Mumbai, only one male fetus was found to have been terminated out of all the thousands of female fetuses. Twenty-two million girls were "missing" from the 1991 census.

Concurrent with these trends, and perhaps at the root of many of them, Indian male infantile sexuality and fantasy has always viewed young women as objects for sexual gratification, the data on which has begun to surface from many quarters in the country. According to the psychoanalyst Sudhir Kakar, there is "widespread sexual misery" among all classes in India, a country with no equivalent word or expression for "orgasm" in many Indian languages.[82] "In this culture, a strong woman terrifies men. Helplessness has to exist. . . . A woman can be raped. It's very violent. The image of hurting a woman does excite the audience," says Udayan Patel, a psychoanalyst of films in Mumbai.[83] When the 1996 film *The Bandit Queen* premiered in Mumbai, based upon a true story, I witnessed hundreds of men in the audience cheering while the female protagonist was repeatedly raped. Women in the audience, meanwhile, were sitting there silently trembling, shedding tears. They were afraid, and ashamed.

At least 75 percent of all marriages include a female spouse who is a minor. You see the girls carrying their young, often begging for food, not as a ploy, or an organized pastime, but out of desperation. In India, 25 percent of the twelve million girls born each year die by age fifteen. These innocent, elegant sprites take one's breath away, and by indelible means burn their lovely images, one by one, into your heart. All the more so because they are exhausted, gentleness surrounded by inconceivable hatred, by Hindu spirits which have labeled them as unclean, defiled, the cause of all problems in the country, their only hope being the birth of at least two sons in marriage. If the female eventually embarks on a spiritual path, she is likely to become an even greater outcast, deemed crazy. Only her children can give her spiritual salvation. But all too often they are her curse, especially if she is one of many unfortunate widows with only daughters as a legacy. The rampant fertility symbolism that pervades Hindu culture mocks such a woman's actual predicament. If she is bold or modern enough to remarry, according to *The Laws of Manu* she knows that she may be reborn in a jackal's vagina.[84]

The miasma of cults, sects, and superstition confuses sexuality in India, scorning while adoring the pretty female, disgracing her if she perpetuates herself, awarding her only a lifetime of labor and submission if she should be so lucky as to have brought into this world a darling son. Against this backdrop, the Hindus' religious scruples are annoyingly pricked by the vague chatter of the government's so-called "population crisis." But what can it mean to one who is following his *dharma,* or destiny? And for whom abstinence is only an academic, meritorious concept for later in life, when the ascetic stages of spiritual development are applauded?

The great and lasting irony, then, has been India's self-proclaimed worship of nature, and of the female, whose countless deifications continue to exert an emotional, aesthetic, and spiritual hold on the country, as well as its international reputation.[85] Little good such adulation has ever done real women. Despite it being illegal since 1961, the dowry system remains steadfast. A woman who poured scalding soup down two of her newborn daughters' throats and buried them under piles of cow dung— "one of the most widely practiced methods of infanticide in southern India"—described the daunting effect of a ten-thousand-rupee (three-hundred-dollar) dowry. A catastrophe for the family. A survey in the southern State of Tamil Nadu by the Community Services Guild of Chennai found that more than half of the 1,250 women questioned had killed their day-old daughters presumably because they too could not imagine being able to pay for their dowries later on. Thirty-eight percent of the women said they'd do it again if they should happen to give birth to another female. Throughout Tamil Nadu infanticide is occurring— whether among farmers, tribals, or wealthier, educated city folk.[86] In response, the regional government has begun leaving cradles in primary health centers so that parents who might otherwise murder their daughters, can instead anonymously and conveniently drop them off to be raised by the state.[87] This is a country not of laws, but expedients.

Given this extent of sexual, psychological, and cross-genderal dys-functionalism throughout much of India, the challenge to family planners seeking to curb ingrained habits has proven especially onerous. There have been some gains, particularly in the south of India. But where the majority of Indians live, forty-five years of family planning has still not managed to arrest a population momentum that will soon see India becoming the most heavily populated, ecologically bankrupt nation in human history—a country constantly on the edge of widespread religious conflict, its forever shuffling leadership in possession of a nuclear arsenal. There is still reason to be hopeful, nevertheless: to envision the strategies and precise mechanisms that might combat this bleak state of affairs, to marshal sufficient political will and social consciousness so as to hold back the avalanche of future generations from entirely overwhelming an already precariously stressed country. It will require nothing less than the government's admission that the nation is in an ecological state of war. An admission that must be much more than a mere admission. Only then is India likely to begin dispatching the countervaling forces necessary to get the job done.

THE FAMILY WELFARE CONUNDRUM

WHEN RAJIV GANDHI came into office, he was at once confronted with a failing family welfare program. That's what it's called in India. The phrase "family planning" was abolished after an earlier administration's unhappy experience with compulsory sterilizations. Gandhi called upon India's most famous demographer, Ashish Bose, for help and Bose was quick to enlighten the prime minister. "Sir, your officials are misleading you," Bose began. "What they are telling you" Bose said, "is that in a few states and Union Territories the program is doing very well. Which are these regions—Kerala, Goa, Chandigarh, and Tamil Nadu. And they had also admitted that in five or six states the program was not doing quite so well. Places like Bihar, Uttar Pradesh, and Rajasthan." Bose put it all in brutal perspective for the prime minister by reminding him that 40 percent of India's population resides in just four states, the "not quite so well" north-ern Hindi belt, which is besotted with the highest infant mortality (well over one hundred per thousand), the highest TFR (5.4), the youngest marriages (sixteen to seventeen), the fastest growth rates (2.27 percent), the lowest life expectancies (forty-nine for women, fifty-two for men), and the worst contraceptive prevalence rates in the whole country (25 percent versus an all-India average of 43.3 percent). And not surprisingly, the preferred family norms were between five and six children. Birthrates were inert at thirty-five per one thousand. Those four states—Bihar, Madhya Pradesh, Rajasthan, and Uttar Pradesh—Bose nicknamed the BIMARU states. Bimaru means "sick" in Hindi, or "not so well." Bose, who laughs a lot, thus disarming most sobriety, loves to fashion such acronyms. To put Bimaru in global perspective, consider the fact that Uttar Pradesh, benumbed by these demographic facts of life, is by itself one of the largest countries in the world, with a population of over 150 million.

Following the (unresolved) Bhopal disaster, which killed at least twelve thousand people, and injured hundreds of thousands of others, the government of India dissociated itself from the responsible company, Union Carbide, which also happened to be the distributor for 50 percent of all condoms in India. This severely diminished the supply to the Bimaru states.

Condom use is low in India, despite there being two billion condoms in the country's inventory at any given hour, because the focus has always been on terminal methods. Moreover, astonishingly, many Indian men seem to get befuddled (for a variety of reasons) in the presence of a condom. It was learned, for example, that the Chennai branch of the Family Planning Association of India buried tens of thousands of unused condoms in the ground. Why? Little demand. Why little demand? Because many people claimed they did not know how to use them. The local Family Planning unit, rather than risking embarrassment at their lack of success, chose to bury them. According to one scientific consultant in the area, even "bank executives" were in the dark as to their use. Because the quality of Indian condom manufacturing is so inconsistent, there tends to be much tearing. Incipient cracks in the latex are broken when semen—which travels at forty to ninety kilometers per hour during ejaculation (and not just in India)—hits the tip. Thus, say sex consultants in India, there is an uneasiness associated with their use.[88]

If you look at what Indian couples are using for contraception, 75 percent of those are going in for sterilization, and nine out of ten are tubectomies.[89] The problem with sterilization in India, as elsewhere, is that people normally take the procedure *after* the demographic damage has been done, or as they say in Delhi, after the "horses have gotten out of the barn." Furthermore, sterilization figures are dropping. That's why there is a lot of rethinking going on now throughout the country. If India is to ever begin to approach fertility replacement, a TFR of 2.4 in other words (down from its current country-wide rate of 3.5), at least 60 percent of all couples will have to be protected by some form of contraception. However, even that 60 percent is now suspect as a reliable barometer of declining fertility. In the wealthy state of Punjab, a contraceptive prevalence rate of 68 percent has produced a TFR exceeding three children. To make matters worse, Indian officials are concerned that even the current 43 percent contraceptive prevalence rate is slipping. In fact, the number of couples protected in the prime reproductive age group, or fifteen to twenty-nine, is a mere 16 percent, from whence it has not deviated for years. As far as abortion is concerned, Indians—unlike Central Europeans—have never perceived medical termination of pregnancy as a form of contraception. It is legal up to twenty weeks in India, but as few as 10 percent of rural clinics are set up to provide for one. (Ironically, in the United States that figure is 11 percent).

The debate over priorities rages on between spacing, IUDs, terminal methods, and the condom. In a 1988 national survey, half of all couples were shown to have never used contraception or had any contact with family planning personnel, and only 20 percent of women under the age of twenty-five reported using contraceptives. The fertility rate among younger women—the backbone of population increase—is actually rising, based on the overall population momentum, both in rural and in urban regions.[90]

But that's not the only bad news. Apart from rapid and spectacular strides needed in the contraceptive prevalence realm, it is fairly well understood by demographers that India will have to get its birth rate down to twenty-one per thousand from a country-wide average of thirty-one. In addition, the death rate will have to drop to about nine per thousand (some argue six, even five) to provide the needed assurances to couples that they can rest easy, so to speak.

One serious impediment among many to this twenty-five year vision is the ongoing Hindu–Muslim crisis, particularly in the northern areas. The reason is that virtually no politician in the north dares speak of family planning there. If a Hindu should be perceived to be denouncing Islamic population growth, he is labelled a racist, as wanting to inhibit Muslims from achieving greater parity with the Hindu majority. And if a Muslim should expostulate on the subject, he is more likely if anything to inflame pronatalist sentiments among his constituents, a minority. But there is an even deeper meaning to the reticence among those in power: it is a serious lack of political will that has, in some respects, crippled India's confidence in fighting the battle. And that is the troubling legacy of Sanjay Gandhi who, in some respects, was a visionary along Chinese lines.

The roots of Sanjay's vision date back to the beginning of the century. In 1892, 25 percent of the Indian budget was going toward paying off British pensioners, not toward helping India. A series of economic devaluations of the rupee against the British pound, in addition to famine, and the introduction from China of plague-carrying rats in Bombay harbor, created the worst economic depression in India's recent history, just at the moment that Britain and the West were rapidly ascending.[91] Between 1895 and 1905 medical, economic, and ecological conditions were dire enough in India that the country's population actually began to decline from excess mortality in absolute numbers, to below the level of the first census which had been taken in 1872.

Until 1921, this decrease continued, despite a birth rate per one thousand of 48.1. That's because the death rate was 47.2. Malaria, TB, polio, diphtheria–tetanus, and ailments associated with malnutrition and the breakdown of the immune system were the major killers, particularly of children having bacterial pneumonia, measles, and diarrhea. But consider how amazing the numbers are. Nature, somehow aware that there were 260 million carnivorous *Homo sapiens* in a finite space, packed in at eighty-three per square kilometer, ordained an almost imperceptible attrition, a net loss of one per thousand. This was a clear window on how biological determinants prefer to operate in a vacuum (prior to human medical engineering). If those forces had continued, that declining population rate would have manifested an India amounting to fewer than 225 million in 1998. Per capita income, potentially, would be on a par with South Korea's. The matrix of human pain would have been hugely softened, freeing up other energies that could be applied toward conservation and the amelioration of massive domains of suffering. Having subverted nature's manner of resolving demographic pressure, however, India's density in the mid-1990s averages 216 per sqare kilometer (176 for rural, 30,002 for urban). Population increase is now 2.22 percent annually, or approximately eighteen million and counting, more than the whole population of Sri Lanka.[92]

What happened? In the coming decade following the 1921 census, everything changed for India. By 1931 small medical breakthroughs, and slightly improved social conditions had rapidly pushed the death rate down to 36.3 from 47.2 per thousand, the single largest advance in India's demographic history. Family planners, knowing what successes actually implied, were already ahead of the statistics. The first Indian birth control clinic was begun in Bombay in 1925 by a Dr. R. D. Karve. And in the 1930s, the birth control crusader Margaret Sanger's message was heard. But Mahatma Gandhi refused to lend his support to her, thinking birth control unnatural. He stressed abstinence, and the rhythm method, ignoring the fact that very few women in India in his day could count beyond ten or twenty. Between 1921 and 1941, 66 million people were added to the subcontinent. By 1951, another 44 million. By 1951 there were 361 million. The health ministers, meanwhile, all strove toward lowering the death rate and encouraging longevity. These were humane endeavors, after all, aided by the increasing sophistication of science and the outreach of pharmaceutical multinationals who saw a gigantic market for their products.[93]

By the early 1950s, the efforts of the nongovernmental Family Planning Association of India, established in 1949, were seen to be too few too late, for already the population growth rate had surmounted 2 percent, up from 1.5 percent during the previous decade. Independent India recognized that smaller families contributed to a healthier economy and to healthier women. The first five-year plan in India sought to stabilize population so as to foster the national economy. "Economics" was, and continues to be at the basis of family planning policies. Nehru recognized that the economic well-being of each individual would define the country. He was to say, there is not a population problem, there are four hundred million such problems.

In the early 1960s, when the National Family Planning Program was launched, its goal was to reduce the country's birth rate to twenty-five per thousand by 1975. 1975 came around and the country's population had swelled to 620 million. At that level of increase, it was projected that India would reach a population of 2.275 billion by the year 2025.[94]

When Indira Gandhi assumed power in 1966, she placed family planning under the Ministry of Health and by 1969 announced that family planning was "to be given the highest priority and to occupy a pivotal place in the economic development of the country." The government promoted IUDs, then passed in 1971 the Medical Termination of Pregnancy Act (legalizing it without a battle eighteen months before Roe v. Wade), as well as a law forbidding females from marrying before the age of eighteen (a provision difficult to enforce). By the mid-1970s, male contraceptive sterilization had become the vogue, following the success of several vasectomy camps in the states of Kerala and Maharashtra. For thirty days from late November to December in 1970, a mass vasectomy camp was held at Cochin in Kerala, called a Family Planning Festival. At the camp 62,913 vasectomies and 505 tubectomies were performed, exceeding by 400 percent all previous sterilizations. It was hailed as a breakthrough, the result of preparations in the press and a broad coalition of concerned writers, organizers, medical institutions, and government officials. Family planning cadres gathered together the data on eligible couples, publicity units went into the field throughout the Ernakulam district, one hundred medical officers with staff and equipment were assembled, the compound was made rain-proof and decorated festively with garlands. Free canteens, counters for issuing incentive money, an entertainment auditorium with twenty-four hour per day variety shows, and free condoms were all part of the appeal.[95]

A year later, more than one thousand vasectomy camps were held throughout Gujarat state and 221,933 vasectomies performed in a two month period. Circus-type clowns and jokers drumming tom-toms and walking on tall bamboo stilts advertised the camps from village to village. The success of these efforts has been hailed as an important landmark in family planning history.[96]

When the mass vasectomy camps were tried in Uttar Pradesh, however, four cases of tetanus deaths were enough to prompt abandonment of the camps. Subsequently, the governments of Haryana, Rajasthan, and Uttar Pradesh began enforcing sterilization practices through other means.

Financial assistance from the central government to the states was soon linked to sterilization performance. Legislative discussions regarding compulsory sterilization took place. (It should be pointed out, however, that compulsion is basic to most health programs. As social scientist Robert Gillespie, president of the Population Communication organization, has described, "There is no such thing as a voluntary program." The control of most diseases, whether yellow fever or small pox, has always made for required identification certificates, immunizations, even quarantine.) And then the pace of fertility control suddenly escalated. Indira Gandhi declared a state of emergency as a means of consolidating her authority when the Allahabad High Court tried to overturn her election in June 1975. She imposed censorship on the media and promulgated a

Twenty Point Program to improve the country. Her son, Sanjay Gandhi, was given the responsibility of focusing New Delhi's authority on three aspects of the initiative, namely, population control, adult education, and afforestation, a remarkably informed combination of counterdisaster coefficients. In October of that year, Union Health Minister Dr. Karan Singh sent a message to the prime minister which stated, "The problem is now so serious that there seems to be no alternative but to think in terms of introduction of some element of compulsion in the larger national interest."[97] The measures, deemed necessarily "drastic," drove sterilizations up from 2.6 million in 1975–76 to 8.1 million the following year. Sanjay Gandhi and his mother sincerely believed that there was no other choice. India was in a state of crisis, and Indira's emergency declaration was meant not only to preserve her own regime but to underscore the severity of the population bomb.

The findings of the 1978 Shah Commission inquiry revealed that Uttar Pradesh police and the Provincial Armed Constabulary had been given specific targets to achieve (the number of people brought in, not for questioning, but for sterilization). Homes, whole neighborhoods, were surrounded in the middle of the night by hundreds of police who would literally drag men and women out of their beds into the waiting clutches of surgeons. Those who resisted or protested were arrested.[98]

Fearing civil war, Indira Gandhi called for national elections in March of 1977. Not surprisingly, she and her party were disgraced. In Uttar Pradesh, the most populous state of India, the ruling party could not win even one seat in Parliament out of the eighty-five seats in that state. Such was the fury of India's illiterate masses. The incoming Janata Party did not want family planning even mentioned. Contraceptive prevalence throughout the country fell to below 6 percent, thus engendering the explosive growth being witnessed today.

By extraordinary powers of persuasion—a testimony to the Nehru dynasty's hold on the country—Mrs. Gandhi managed to return to power in 1980. This was also a measure of how badly managed the government was under the Janata Party. At first, Mrs. Gandhi down-pedalled family planning. But when the 1981 census showed that the population was rising at 2.2 percent per year, and that there were at least seventeen million more Indians than expected, she again pushed for population control, though noncoercively and with some tact. But the government was not keen to listen and, according to investigators V. Panandiker and P. Umashankar, family planning in India has been the "victim of electoral politics" ever since. For the next decade, family planning stayed in hiding. And it was during this uncertain time that female tubectomies replaced male vasectomies as the primary choice of contraception in the country. Today, rather than confront the lingering ill-feelings regarding family planning across the Bimaru states, many of India's parliamentarians are more eager to visit China, Indonesia, Singapore, and Thailand to learn about these issues. And this is one of the reasons that the runaway populations of Bimaru are going to be difficult to check, no matter how much money the government, with assistance from AID, UNFPA, and the World Bank, throw at the situation.[99]

In spite of India's rejection of compulsory family planning, the truth remains that the additional six million sterilizations under Sanjay Gandhi probably prevented two million births. Multiply that number times likely offspring, over several generations, and one is into a European-sized nation. In fact, if India's population growth had been checked at 1.5 percent a year since Independence (the original hope) versus today's 2.2 percent growth rate, there would have been some two hundred million fewer Indians, with all of the corresponding increases in the quality of life.

Only draconian measures seem capable now of altogether combating India's difficulties, yet these are the last sorts of measures any politician wanting to remain in office would advocate in India. The country has thus boxed itself into a democratic and economic corner.

One profound example of this is the dowry system. If the dowry could effectively be outlawed, punishable by the full force of the existing laws, population growth would decline. It might not change demographic fundamentalism, particularly in poor rural areas, but it would certainly impact urban parents. Knowing they had nothing to fear from the financial burden of a dowry, they would be less concerned about supplanting a daughter with an additional male child. However, the dowry system is more widespread than ever before, as are dowry deaths, or wife burnings. Few people have ever been convicted under the dowry law, even though the government knows the system is responsible for thousands of cases of infanticide every year, and the perpetuation of an encrippling economic and cultural bias favoring males.[100]

India's overall response to this complex bottleneck of fertility uncontrol has been characterized by some as a policy of resignation, of de facto destiny, of good intentions subsumed in mere rhetoric. Or as one former joint secretary in the Union Health Ministry has said, "The tragedy is that

prolific breeding is not a disease. Children are not an epidemic. An outbreak of population doesn't hurt anybody immediately. With the result
that no one really cares."[101]

Many people do care, of course. A barrage of control strategies have
been tried out, endless think tanks convened, more than a few careers
made and ruined on various micro and macro policy initiatives. A specialist was once called in, and he invented a bead necklace for women that
would help them remember the rhythm method. Green for dangerous
days, red for good days. But children got hold of the beads, mixed them
up and half of all the women in the program got pregnant.

Several years ago the application of government incentives emerged as
India's new hope for the future.[102] But the incentive schemes are vulnerable to corruption. Because the central and state governments were giving
out money to both doctors and clients, there was a built-in temptation for
both parties to lie. In 1988, at the First Conference of the Central Council
of Health and Family Welfare in New Delhi it was stated that the previous
year had been a milestone for family welfare, with an "all-time high
record" of 20.5 million fresh acceptors into the program. But as investiga-
tive journalist Raj Chengappa discovered, some 75 percent of all fresh
acceptors were over the age of thirty, and had already had more than four
children.[103] In addition, some of the new acceptors were said to have
obtained repeat vasectomies because, of course, they wanted the 180
rupees. prize money and the surgeons were willing accomplices (any doctor should be able to easily distinguish a client who has had a vasectomy,
and thus avoid a repeat performance).

To "solve" the population bomb, some have argued in favor of a national campaign to reintroduce breast-feeding. Others have focused on the
overall unemployment rate among females, which is 80 percent. The
Integrated Rural Development Programme budget has allotted 30 percent
of its financing to women, but little has actually happened. Many see the
hope for India with the rising middle class (a throwback to the classic
demographic transition theory). Others insist on no more targets, but simply maternal and child health care. Or getting more NGOs into the act, the
privatizing of birth control, and removal of the sterilization emphasis. All
of these components have been called upon in different states and union
territories, at various times, and to varying degrees. Many look toward that
magical moment when the sun pierces through the storm and the convergence of multiple factors come together to effect a transformation.

Despite certain dramatic successes—such as an estimated ninety million unintended births prevented in the last forty years[104] a fertility pall hovers over the country. The population rate has not gone down in twenty years. Nine out of ten babies in villages are still delivered by typically untrained dais. Refrigerators frequently breakdown, or do so temporarily as the electricity fluctuates. And when that happens, vaccines for polio or diphtheria–tetanus are ruined, though may still be blindly administered. Meanwhile, the auxiliary nurse–midwives or A&Ms are the least trained and most neglected and underpaid of the whole health system, yet they are the ones who are supposed to immunize children, conduct deliveries, and provide postnatal care. Medical training for pregnancy-related needs and problems (or for knowing how to detect repeat sterilization fraud) is inadequate. According to Bose, as much as 90 percent of all new alleged sterilizations in Uttar Pradesh may be falsely reported. If such levels of medical or bureaucratic incompetency seem unlikely, consider that in one recent study, according to Conly and Camp, "over half of government health staff failed to correctly identify when in the menstrual cycle a woman is most at risk of pregnancy."[105] I asked a leading official of the Indian Council of Medical Research about this rather astonishing allegation. The official's response was, "Why is it so important that doctors know such things about the cycle? After all, we are not advocating the rhythm method. It would be idiotic to offer a woman over the age of twenty-five anything other than sterilization, when she still has thirty years of childbearing ahead of her." Moving on, I asked the doctor about the cafeteria-style approach, referring to a multiple of contraceptive choices, the tried and true test of any successful family planning program worldwide. "Not in India," said the official. "Here, it needs to be 100 percent sterilization by the age of twenty-five. Only in the poor northern sector where the infant mortality rate is ninety or more should you insert the IUD after the second child. Once that child looks like it's going to live, then you counsel that woman to be sterilized as well."

This emphasis on sterilization, Sanjay Gandhi's own revelation about India's future, hinges upon the presumption that young couples will be in favor of it, which so far they have not been. Too many other psychological, religious, and cultural factors particularly acute during an average person's most fertile years (his or her twenties) have preempted this otherwise singularly effective approach. The burden of government-proposed contraceptive progress has thus shifted to other wider ranging methods, like two to three years spacing between the first and second pregnancy (best attained by a breast-feeding regime), and state of the art long-term contraceptives, such as Norplant, which was recently sanctioned by the Indian courts after being held up by feminists, ironically, on grounds that it would curtail a woman's freedom of choice. But the fact remains, however ingenious the new technologies, such as Norplant, India's huge population of sexual neophytes has thus far indicated little interest in any kind of birth control whatsoever.

How, then, is India to break through this numbing veil of conflict? The country is buffeted on the one side by seamless introversion, scientific self-assurance, and implacable custom; and on the other by political paralysis, and a rash of differing perceptions, superstitions, priorities, fears, and inflexibilities from village to village, from state to state.

One of the government's primary goals is to bring the IMF down to sixty by the end of the decade. However, that could pose other problems reminiscent of the 1930s. According to Dr. Prema Ramachandran, deputy director of the Indian Council of Medical Research, there is as yet no evidence linking a declining infant mortality rate to a hoped-for decline in the total fertility rate. What has been shown in many countries is a coincidental drop in TFR once maternal and child health care was improved. If an IMR of sixty should be achieved, without a corresponding increase in contraceptive prevalence, then India's net reproductive rate will soar even beyond the much-speculated two billion plus stabilization figure sometime in the next century.

Getting the IMR to sixty—part of the Child Survival and Safe Motherhood project—will require providing most of India's rural populations with safe drinking water. That poses nearly insurmountable ecological and economic problems the country has not yet managed to figure out. Other aspects of the government's program should be less difficult to achieve. For example, the country plans to escalate its war against anemia and typhoid and is currently strengthening its technology to anticipate more complicated deliveries and high-risk cases.

In addition, more than 135 thousand auxiliary nurse–midwives are being trained throughout the country. At the same time, the *dais,* or traditional birth attendants, are also being retrained, as money permits, and supplied with newly provisioned kits that basically supplant the Stone Age with twentieth-century appurtenances.[106] Such practical education programs coincide with the widespread recognition in India's medical circles that pre- and postnatal care are crucial to the whole ferility process, though with 80 percent of all births taking place outside of hospitals such screening and follow-up has been almost entirely absent from India's experience.[107] Further compounding the existing rural fertility dilemma is the fact that only about 25 percent of graduating physicians end up in rural areas, where the majority of Indians live, and where a few cents is the crucial determining factor in whether an infant's chance of survival is increased or not. It was calculated in the mid-1980s that the government of India was spending a mere twelve cents per person on basic health care. And yet, multiply that times nine hundred million and it surely adds up for a poor country.

But the money is there, if the sense of urgency is there. India numbers among its imperatives the developing of nuclear weapons, the cleaning up of the Ganga, subsidies for irrigation, and the building of hugely expensive hydroelectric plants to fuel more local industry. In a nation with thirty competing regional governments, ethnic turmoil, and a vanishing resource base, New Delhi's choice of national priorities has not been made any easier.

With so vast an impoverished population, it is understandable how the practice of monetary incentives as a means of stimulating popular interest in birth control has long played a part in the government of India's family welfare strategy, whether in cash disbursements, or a preferred loan for a water buffalo. Birth attendants are now receiving ten rupees for every delivery they conduct assuming they follow the prescribed checklist, which includes bringing in the pregnant women to an auxillary nurse–midwife for tetanus/toxoid immunization early enough and making sure that there are two to three prenatal checkups.

As an incentive, an acceptor currently receives nine rupees and the doctor six rupees for each IUD insertion. A vasectomy is worth a reward of 180 rupees, a tubal ligation 250 rupees. Government employees (1 percent of the total work force) are granted various benefits if either spouse volunteers for sterilization. The money for such enticements comes out of both state and central government budgets.

The nearly twelve thousand registered environmental groups and NGOs are deeply involved in India's ecological and fertility dilemmas, perhaps none more effectively than the National Family Planning Association of India, whose long time president, Mrs. Avabai Wadia is an eagle-eyed, girlish visionary who has seen it all. She believes, along with Einstein and Vermeer, that God is in the details. "If you try to take in the big picture," she said, "you get into paralysis by analysis. We know nearly everything. But it's the doing that counts." And she pointed out with justifiable pride that at Independence, the life expectancy in India was thirty-two. Today it is over sixty.

With eighty thousand members in some 3,164 local voluntary groups across the country, Mrs. Wadia has for many years been spreading literacy, installing water and sanitation facilities, and developing income generating schemes for women. In 1991, FPAI's endeavors were encouraging. In the district of Malur in Karnataka state, for example, 150 newlyweds from 138 villages agreed to delay their first pregnancy by two years, while five hundred boys and girls pledged to postpone their marriage by two years beyond the legal age. Over ten thousand men and women attained literacy and nearly thirty-five thousand boys and girls (near parity) were shepherded into schools and *Balwadis* (preschools). It also enabled 8,330 men and women to open savings accounts. Smokeless stoves were introduced into nineteen hundred households, while eighteen thousand people were provided with safe drinking water systems. Tens of thousands of tree saplings and fruit gardens were planted and nearly sixteen thousand new couples accepted family planning. Such efforts are inherent to the struggle that engulfs a country as rife with numbers as India. It breeds philosophy, a sense of perspective, a sense of hope that refuses to cave in to the equally galling premonition that whatever incremental gains may be won, the built-in population momentum and its ecological devastation are nearly irreversible. For people on the front lines, like Mrs. Wadia, irreversibilty is not what matters. Gains are what matters; gains and sensitive, sensible damage control.

As we spoke, Mrs. Wadia radiated optimism in her impassioned descriptions of small groups of illiterate hopefuls clustered together around a kerosene lamp in a hut during the monsoon rains learning from a teacher who was herself just in the process of becoming literate, one step ahead of her peers. To know that another 6,087 women were initiated into the world of reading and writing, into the dignity, equipoise, and freedom attached to those skills, was no small matter.

From a somewhat more satirical, but nonetheless affirmative perspective, Professor Ashish Bose also wrestled with demons in the night—the big picture—yet ultimately came back around to the details, and to the possibilities for unleashing an enormous reserve of energy and skill in the Indian people themselves.

Bose labels the entire family welfare program by one of his character-istic acronyms, namely, COMIC: Contraceptive technology that is unsuit-ed to the culture, Monetary incentives that are utterly fraudulent, and Information and Communication which are a disaster.

"If you can't bring drinking water to people, you have no right to ask them to enact birth control for two children," says Bose.

His solution to all these grievances is something akin to a literacy corps of engineers. Bose sees India's hope to lie in a people's movement, not in the dank corridors of Delhi's bureaucracy. He calls for a mobiliza-tion of every retired military man, government officer, teacher, and unem-ployed graduate. In just one district that he cited, there are one hundred thousand retired military men. And he pointed out that India is produc-ing thousands of graduates in English literature who are useless to the country. Mobilize all of them to impart reading and writing skills to the masses and there would be a true renaissance in English literature. Indian women who more and more want contraceptives but must keep their wishes hidden from their husbands, would all be able to read the instruc-tions on the boxes. It may not be Shakespeare or Tagore, but it's crucial reading nevertheless. He believes 100 percent literacy could be achieved within three years.

Bose is convinced that education is the only way. Not laws, not dire warnings. "We have doubled the population and are still surviving," he reminds me. "If you say to the Hindu that the situation is so bad, that there is no water, no food, no land, and so forth, then he will simply say, 'OK, only God can save us, Hari Krishna, Hari Rama.'"

Ultimately, avows Ashish Bose, India needs more of these village-based mobilizations. It's the only way. But, he confesses, India also needs a little luck. According to Hindu scriptures, without luck one is lost. "Unfortunately," Bose says with a grin, "Indians rely on that luck more than anything else."

THE LESSONS OF TAMIL NADU AND KERALA

FOR SEVERAL YEARS demographers and family planning experts throughout India have hailed the two southernmost states, Tamil Nadu and Kerala, as proof that India has what it takes to reverse its population crisis. Kerala, with a population equivalent to that of California, or just over thirty million, but one-third California's geographical size, is the only state in the country where women outnumber men, 1,032 for every 1,000; where the literacy rate is higher for women than their male counterparts, 93 percent versus 92 percent. Infant mortality in Kerala varies from seventeen to thirty-three per thousand, while the birth rate itself is between nineteen and twenty-three per thousand. These are the best figures in India, by far. In a 1988 survey of contraceptive use—including traditional "natural" methods—the State of Kerala showed the highest usage among couples, at 80 percent. More and more the thinking throughout India is that to firmly establish a two-child family norm in the country, nothing short of the "Kerala method," an 80 percent contraceptive prevalence rate (CPR), will do.

While the figures are also encouraging for Tamil Nadu—a 22.4 per thousand birthrate, and an average marriage age for women of 21—the state's literacy rate is at 55 percent (high by Indian standards, but not compared with its neighbor, Kerala), and its infant mortality is at 57 percent. This latter figure is extraordinary considering that it was at 93 percent in 1980. Tamil Nadu is a poor state, with little economic potential for women, at present. Kerala is also plagued by what many consider to be a depressed economy. Both states suffer from badly mired environments. Yet, in addition to Goa, a union territory negligible in size and population, and thus a bad model from which to extrapolate, these two southern regions offer abiding hope that India possesses the power of stabilization, under the right circumstances.

Some Indian demographers have viewed the achievements of Tamil Nadu as a more realistic example to strive toward in implementing similar, hoped-for curbs on the runaway Bimaru populations. According to T. V. Anthony, the former chief secretary and chairman for the state planning commission in Tamil Nadu for several years, Tamil Nadu offers the most realistic model of improvement for the rest of the country.

In the mid-1980s, Tamil Nadu under Chief Minister M. G. Ramchendran, initiated a remarkably logical, yet in all of India untried program, the Mid-Day Meal Scheme, to help defray protein deficiency among students who made it to kindergarten. Since then, every day a hot meal of rice and vegetable curry has been given to nearly a million children in sixty-seven thousand centers throughout the state. In addition, some one hundred thousand expectant mothers are given health food packets every afternoon. Two hundred thousand otherwise unemployed and poor women are recruited within their villages to pass out the food in the centers and schools and to reach the slum children. It is not an inexpensive program—at a cost approaching seventy-five million dollars, or approximately 25 percent of the entire family planning budget for the whole country, paid for not by Delhi but by Tamil Nadu. While there is no hard evidence linking the meal to a lower birthrate, the program does reflect unique political willpower on the part of the state government, a sense of urgency that has not yet caught on in most other Indian states. The impact of this one activity seems to have been extraordinary. Aside from improved health, female literacy has risen significantly, primarily because parents now want their children in school where they are likely to get their best meal of the day.

Every department in the local Tamil Nadu government has gotten involved in family welfare, from the Marriage Register and Revenue Department to the Social Welfare, Health, Education, Information, and Publicity Departments. Inspired by the chief minister's own passionate commitment to family planning, Tamil Nadu has seen a declining birth rate of about one per thousand every year after two to three years of preparation.

Antony believes that Tamil Nadu's success in the family planning arena is similarly replicable in the Bimaru states, given sufficient educational investments that are tailored to local customs and sensibilities, and realistic targets set for each well-studied factor (TFR, IMR, age of marriage, and literacy). Anthony believes that with but three years of preparation, the subsequent decline in birthrate of one point per thousand per year could be expected, with the success spreading throughout the country within three to four years.

What Antony calls for is nothing less than a whole new way of life, one that promotes the postponing of a first child until the woman is twenty-seven, and the pushing up the legal age of marriage for women to at least twenty-one. He advocates deemphasizing contraception and sterilization in favor of noninvasive planning and choice, ethical and cultural shifts in thinking, in other words. His prescriptions seem appropriate for Tamil Nadu, which has already begun the transition toward population stability. If those same stabilizing ingredients can be especially targeted toward towns adjoining ecologically sensitive parts of the state, then truly Tamil Nadu will be worth emulating.[108] In seeking to extend the lessons of Tamil Nadu to the rest of India, two relevant, if not key, components are finding the money for the midday meal and doing the same for expectant mothers' health packages. Given the central government's evident reticence to undertake such a project, it will thus be left up to all the individual states and territories throughout the country to recognize that healthy, educated children and parents will make a critical difference to the economy and the ecological well-being of the region. Whether environmental safeguards can somehow be incorporated into this scenario remains questionable, given India's experience thus far, and the fact that virtually no country in the world—whether heavily populated or not—has yet managed to increase its GNP without imposing considerable ecological damage.[109] Tamil Nadu's western neighbor, Kerala, is a case in point.

In spite of Kerala's demographic successes, serious ecological degradation persists. As of 1974, fish (from among the fifty-four or so exploited species) and prawn harvests began to fall in Kerala from both overfishing and industrial pollution. Economic overconsumption resulted from a simple idea, the mechanization of boats. As the profit motive expanded, fueled by a new international demand for processed prawns, the trawlers indiscriminately clear-cut whole shoals and sea-bottom species. Prawns, once perceived as the poor man's protein and priced at 240 rupees per ton in the early 1960s, were valued at more than fourteeen thousand rupees. per ton in 1985. As has been pointed out, "For capitalists, given their short-term perspective and under the given conditions of investment, the ratio of profits from indiscriminate harvesting of the commons to the profits from regulated and sustainable harvesting are large."[110]

While overfishing has wrought havoc in the coastal waters, declining profits and lack of available land has been at the heart of Kerala's agricultural stagnation and unemployment. The unemployed in Kerala exceed 18 percent, the highest level in the country. Much of the problem stems, paradoxically, from the fact that 55 percent of the population have various secondary school and college degrees. They're overqualified for most available menial tasks. Thus, in what must be judged a most perverse twist on Indian aspirations, that state which has best managed to educate and dignify its people finds that it can least support them, or do so without raping the environment. Education has also meant that Kerala's unions are pervasive and well-organized, and this has had a chilling effect on potential outside investors who realize that they will be unable to set up sweatshops in so literate a region. Adding a demographic twist to an existing paradox, some have observed that the reason women marry later in Kerala (thus ensuring fewer children) is the fact that they are not interested in marrying unemployed, and possibly unemployable males. It is a bizarre situation. Does it then imply that a depressed economy and high literacy are the real preconditions of a low fertility rate?[111]

The Portuguese had introduced fast-growing exotics into Kerala centuries ago, utterly transforming large tracts of natural forest into coconut, cashew, teak, pepper, and rubber estates. While natural vegetation covered 44 percent of the state at the turn of the century, today, there is less than seven percent left.[112] And while the forests are rapidly disappearing, agricultural expansion has nearly ceased in Kerala since 1960.

Kerala's unique backwaters have become inundated with dissolved synthetic fertilizers, giving rise to increasing eutrophication and exotic weeds.

Widespread ecological compromise in Kerala, a (relatively speaking) demographic panacea, poses very serious conceptual and ethical considerations. I say "relatively speaking" because thirty million human beings with short-term profit motives densely packed into a small state with a history of environmental malpractice are not likely to suddenly revert to ecological stewards, not unless they can figure out how to stabilize the economy for all of the people in a benign way, an unlikely occurrence given Kerala's extremely high density of population. Thus, the rest of India and the developing world might well try to emulate the basic fertility replacement patterns of Kerala. But unless a corresponding effort is made to redefine what's good in life, and to wean populations away from the crude reliance on GNP indicators toward ecologically sustainable, nonviolent business practices and ethics, then zero population growth by itself will not be the answer. India invented the term thousands of years ago—*ahimsa*, nonviolence. It is India's only hope. As Martin Luther King Jr. put it, this is not a question of violence or nonviolence, but of nonviolence or nonexistence.

Formulating specific economic policies that effectively induce population control while ensuring ecological sustainability has proven almost impossible at every level of bureaucratic, social, and consumer demand in India. The circumstances and needs vary from Kerala to Tamil Nadu, from Ladakh to Rajasthan, from Maharashtra to West Bengal, and often the energies and focus of population control and environmental restoration would seem to have nothing in common. The State of Haryana, for example, has the second highest per capita income in the country, and yet is very backward in some respects, the status of its women considered to be among the worst in the country, its forests almost completely denuded. A comprehensive financial package, targeted both toward women, as well as at afforestation and species protection, would be necessary to uplift Haryana. The money is there. The will, apparently, is not yet there, despite the state's proximity to New Delhi, and efforts by UNFPA and the World Bank to help Haryana. Contradictions abound throughout India. One cannot understand them, necessarily, through mere statistical analysis. Every village demands its own unique solutions and requires unusually creative thinking from any political administration.

It would surely be desirable to transpose Kerala's extreme fertility successes to other regions of the country, but not the state's devastating industrial and environmental shortcomings.

Tamil Nadu, her triumphs less pronounced thus far than Kerala's, having not enjoyed Kerala's nineteenth-century predisposition toward literacy and matriarchy, may nonetheless be the key to understanding how India might best focus on mass family planning and ecology mobilizations. The techniques for achieving these goals may be as uncomplicated and elegant a solution as providing free lunches to children at school (though by itself this is unlikely to solve the population problem). But such elegance will only mock Tamil Nadu if it is unable to control female infanticide within many of its villages, or check the state's massive animal abuse in the form of slaughterhouses, or curtail destruction of its beaches, turtles, and elephants.

THE JURY IS still out as to whether family welfare and environmentalism in India can, or will, pave the way for sexual caution, a widespread cafeteria approach to contraceptive methods, and the propagation of a true reverence for existing life, as enshrined in the legal codes, but sadly absent from any substantive monitoring or policing infrastructures. Two hundred fifty million females in India are currently of a childbearing age. Of the fifteen largest states in India, ten of them—the most populous ones—witnessed a disastrous and (at least officially) inexplicable drop in the rate of contraceptive prevalence and sterilization during the 1990s. The sharpest falls occurred in Assam, Bihar, Haryana, and—most discouragingly—in Tamil Nadu itself.[113] And most discouraging, in early December 1997, the government's National Population Policy, commissioned in 1991, was aborted as the United Front collapsed. The working policy document had stated, "It needs to be realized that if our population policy goes wrong, nothing else will have a chance to go right." Now the whole effort is in ashes, a victim of politic instability, and with it, a rational plan for India's leaders to halt what even conservatives in the country acknowledge to be a crisis. They project, at a minimum, 162 *crores* of Indians by the year 2050; that's 1.62 billion.[114]

The world's population is increasing at three children per second. In the decade of the 1990s over a billion people will be added to the planet. India will contribute about two hundred million to that figure, 20 percent, of whom will be below even India's generous definition of the poverty line.

Many Indian demographers look to China, but fear the political repercussions of coercion; they look to Thailand which has cut its growth rate from 3.2 percent in the mid-1970s to 1.6 percent today, through massive raising of consciousness and distribution of literature and condoms even at traffic jams (of which there are plenty in both countries). And they look to Indonesia, which has also seen a steady decline to under two percent annual growth from three percent two decades ago, though not without its own severe environmental problems, as will be discussed in the coming chapter.

In comparing India's situation with so-called RICs, or, rapidly industrializaing countries, such as Brazil, Mexico, or Sri Lanka, Indian scientists acknowledge that they are as much as thirty years behind these other nations in areas of income, education, and health. While India's TFR was 4.4 in 1985, South Korea and China had done much better than that twenty years before. Even neighboring Sri Lanka was doing better than India as of 1971. The consensus now is that India's family welfare program is trapped, and showing a state of diminishing returns even for its meager per capita investments.[115]

In the 1980s the Indian family welfare slogan was, "TWO OR THREE CHILDREN ARE ENOUGH." In the 1990s, it reads, "NEXT CHILD NOT NOW, AFTER TWO NEVER." Many argue that the future slogan of family planning should be, simply, "NO MORE"; that morality and population control need to be separated that voluntary sterilization programs must be urgently enhanced if India's internal war is ever to be peacefully resolved.

The greatest living source of paradox in India is the fact of decreasing mortality and persistent poverty, two demographic facts of life which translate into increasingly more numbers; men, women, and children who will be forced from the exigencies of sheer survival to rampage across every remaining hectare of India, like driver-ants. That situation, to date, has condemned the country to a most unfortunate syndrome of contradictions: that which is most loved—nature, women, and children—tends to be abused.

The World Bank projects population stabilization in India at 1.852 billion during the last quarter of the next century, though it will hit 1.35 billion in the year 2025. The government of India has cited other projections. It believes that the country's population could reach between 1.6 and 1.8 billion by the year 2035. Such discrepancies highlight the anguished labyrinths through which demographers must tunnel.[116] But as Ashish Bose reminded me, "Unless we go beyond the cold calculus of births and deaths and feel the heartbeat of the people, demography will remain a dismal science of population, dominated by doomsday predictions based on mechanical projections which can now be done in a matter of minutes on the computer. Statistical competence is not enough to understand the population problem. . . . We have produced a whole lot of technical demographers who cannot go beyond decimal points."[117]

What the numbers do tell us, however, is the cumulative weight of impact, whose science and detective work yields very real, very tangible problems, decimal points and all. At the turn of the century, educational costs for India's growing population will be roughly fifty billion dollars a year, a large share of the country's resources. Thirty percent of the country will still be illiterate.

The urban population of India will exceed 325 million by the year 2000. Even if allocations for sanitation and water should manage to be doubled, they will, at best maintain the status quo, which is desperately inadequate today, and at the basis of much disease, frustration, infant mortality, and population growth. Actual real dollar costs associated with disease in India have not been calculated.

By the year 2000, India will need to invest approximately twenty billion dollars every year starting now in the housing sector just to keep up with the increase in newborns. This, according to P. D. Malgavkar, is beyond the means of the nation.[118] And even if that money were allocated, there would still be hundreds of millions of untouchables living in substandard shelters, leaf huts, and urban slums of cardboard and dried buffalo dung. The so-called quality of life package for India's future, including environmental protection and restoration, access to safe drinking water for humans and other species, adequate nutrition, clothing, housing, education, and health care, all appear similarly to be beyond India's means, if one wishes to perceive it that way.

On the other hand, what else really matters to a nation, if not such basics of the social contract? What else is a government for? India's annual

GNP exceeds three hundred billion dollars. The country spends at present 17 percent of its annual budget on defense, but a mere 2 percent for health, and 3 percent for education.[119]

Considering India's overwhelming dilemmas, certain fiscal priorities are begging the kind of reappraisal that would leave ample economic elbow room to preserve what's left of the country, and ensure a dignified and creative future for its people. If only the voters and the politicians themselves are committed to doing so.

Otherwise, one of the oldest and most noble of human civilizations, along with the planet's most remarkable diversity of biological habitats and creatures great and small, will vanish painfully, like so many other human cultures and ecosystems during the past hundred thousand years of humanity's lineage.

PHOTO BY JANE MORRISON

~4~
Nature Held Hostage: Indonesia

THE INEVITABILITY OF THE MASSES

SOMETIME AROUND 4:00 each rain-sullen morning during winter in the stillness of sprawling Jakarta, the call to the faithful rasps and twines, as thunder rumbles gently across the distant hills. The muezzin's cries are no longer broadcast from atop minarets, but by city-wide megaphones. Sultry, grating, inflictive, and inescapable, these prayers tense and punctuate my sleep, filling me with apprehension, echoing beyond Java to all of Indonesia's nearly seventeen thousand islands. Overhead in the heavy darkness, the fan turns lazily, momentarily disorienting the mosquitoes.

Across three thousand miles Indonesia begins to rise. If you turn your ear toward the enormous industry of this rapidly developing world you hear the shuffling of the work day: of weavers taking up their bamboo baskets, of embroiderers and bricklayers, tilers and fishermen, garment makers and those engaged in the preparation of snacks, or the manufacture of brassieres, rattan wickerworks, or kerosene stoves. One detects the clatter of women walking to beauty parlour posts, rope makers bicycling to their shops, brush makers gathering their materials, sandal fabricators pulling their leather. By dim light, the workmen who decorate copper lamps can be seen huddling over an early morning breakfast of rice and tempeh. With poles and nets the caretakers of fish nurseries begin their myriad tasks, while processors of soy beans, pastry, and cakes take up their positions. Others can be heard scraping various husks for animal fodder, or harvesting, peeling, washing, cutting, cooking, and fermenting the cassava. Some are busy recycling rope, others pounding millet. Train stations are bustling. Taxi drivers are already at work. The middle class, those earning as much as $640 (U.S.) a year, are pouring coffee for themselves, reading the morning's *Jakarta Post*, while the storm-soaked streets steam in the unearthly cornelian glow of a clearing dawn.

The air is thick and mucilaginous, and through it softly strides a labor pool out into the paddies and fields, more than 20 million farmers, upon whom 185 million others depend. They toil, principally, for rice, maize, sweet potatoes, soy beans, ground nuts, coffee, tea, tobacco, sugar, clove, pepper, nutmeg, cassava, coconut, and corn, in a constant struggle with the loss of topsoil, and the corresponding deterioration of watersheds. The land is redolent with agricultural odor that dates back several thousands of years. But an estimated 10 percent nutritional deficiency now enshrouds all this effort.

Beyond the farms, small-scale industries proliferate in ten thousand directions. Rubber tappers, who collectively produce more natural rubber than any other country in the world; extractors of palm oil, manufacturers of various copra products, and the omnipresent animal jobbers who "produce" nearly six hundred million chickens, twenty-five million ducks, eleven million cows, three million buffaloes, eleven million goats, six million sheep, seven million pigs, and seven hundred thousand horses every year for commercial and dietary use (slaughter, by any other name). Well over two billion pounds of meat are now consumed annually by Indonesians.[1] In addition, Indonesia exports over eleven thousand primates, eighty-eight thousand live parrots, and over three million reptile skins in a given year. But the term *export* hardly conveys the truth of the activity, the hundreds of thousands of other animals killed in the process of obtaining live "specimens"; the fact that the young are frequently left to die without their parents. As with any other country whose economic indicators look positively at desecration and ecological disaster on the basis of subsequent contracts and jobs targeted at restitution, *export* suggests progress and prosperity. In the case of animals and animal by-products, it conceals the savage entrapment and horrid conditions of shipment, the animals subjected to torture and trauma, to wire cartons, asphyxiating cases, gunny sacks, and overstuffed crates that lack food, water, or enough space, even, for the animals to move, over a period that can last weeks, sometimes months, even years. Such export removes the resident creature from its rain forest paradise, in the case of Indonesia, to the dark basements of an animal research laboratory, some taxpayer-supported university where the doomed animals are needlessly and repeatedly tortured, then murdered; or to zoos where they are humiliated, frustrated, and condemned to unholy, forlorn lives; or to decrepit, diseased holding cells prior to distribution to pet stores and private owners, or other forms of hell. Or, finally, into department stores as leather belts, brief cases, shoes, and furs.

Such animal suffering infiltrates the country. While there are the odd vegetarian dishes, Indonesian food predominantly reeks of meat. Not surprisingly, the country boasts of more species threatened with extinction (approximately six hundred) than any other nation. Devastation has laid claim to at least 44 percent of all natural habitat in Indonesia.

I am inclined to single out such incidents not randomly, but in an effort to begin to grasp the broad swathe of devastation. The last mangrove preserve along the city of Jakarta's coast, a meagre 15.4 hectare area, was recently turned over to developers by the minister of forestry, in spite of the minister of environment's protest. This was home to long-tailed and Javanese black monkeys, as well as large numbers of migratory bird species. Now, it will be another strip of hotels and golf courses. Elsewhere in the city, a few blocks away from the World Wide Fund for Nature offices (the WWF, known in North America as the World Wildlife Fund), tens of thousands of rare, wild-caught birds, are kept in squalid cages, exposed to the heat of day, and sold to passers-by. Jakarta has become a magnet for poachers, a lawless epicenter for those wishing to profit upon the agony of other species. The WWF representatives know the poachers by name but are hesitant to interfere in domestic legal matters such as these when many greater priorities call for their fragile negotiations with the government, the saving of whole habitats, for example. Neither the WWF nor the government of Indonesia is financially able—all things considered—to police so vast a country, or rescue all the endless victims of human greed and ignorance, or relocate them to safe havens. Phrased in the popular jargon, Indonesia reflects a condition of necessary triage whereby the needy are too many, the means of amelioration too limited. The country, like the world, is simply too large and too cruel.

Even *identifying* safe havens is becoming problematic. As far as away as Indonesia's remote Aru Islands, southeast of Maluku, there are inexplicable mass deaths of pearl oysters occurring. People are hungry, oil-tankers are unmonitored, spills untreated.

One hears of Indonesian fishermen bombing coral reefs, even within park boundaries, to get at the fish; of military generals who have been given whole islands as perks and have then exhumed lagoons to build hotels.

Out amoung the mountains, miners are busy digging and dynamiting for sulphur, nickel, manganese, phosphate, gold, tin, silver, bauxite, and coal, their effluent streams percolating into the country's groundwater, and sending enormous loads of toxic waste downriver.

Beyond the paddies, amid primeval forests, smoke is rising. What used to be designated with admiring distaste as "the jungle" is now more formally described as "biodiversity." But there is nothing polite about what's happening in those woods. Iron sponge, electric machines, plywood, pulp, textiles, and a medley of other value-added forest-based products are now shipped around the world, while factories churn forth alkali benzene, polyethylene, methyl ethyl peroxide, and a host of other chemicals quite lethal if uncontrolled . . . a dizzying array of human activities in search of foreign exchange.

A multiplicity of priorities assails Indonesia, but there is no confusion: Indonesia represents enormous growth in terms of an energy-suppressed population. Over two hundred million consumers in the country demand an ever improved quality of life. At the same time, Indonesians are systematically attempting to reduce their birth-rate in order to increase per capita income. Everyone knows that fewer children at the dinner table mean more food to go around. But despite this conventional wisdom, and many years of serious family planning, the economics have not yet been reconciled: the country finds itself ecologically cornered. With a nearly 2 percent population increase per year, Indonesian human numbers are expected to double by the year 2030, assuming even existing levels of birth control and family planning do not diminish (and there is some cause for alarm in that regard). As it is, the country's population has more than doubled since the 1961 census, when the recorded figure was 97,018,928.

And yet, despite this doubling of size, it could have been much worse, for Indonesia has managed to increase contraceptive prevalance from 10 percent use in 1971 to over 50 percent today, thus preventing the births of over twelve million people. Life expectancy is sixty-one years.[2] Viewed even more broadly, if the number of users of some form of contraception continues to increase at least until 2005, as it has since 1971, fifty-seven million fewer Indonesians will exist than might have, the equivalent of the population of Thailand or France.[3]

To support this imminent quadrupling of inhabitants (from 1961 to 2030) projections for resources needed to sustain a future quality of life package, so-called, have already claimed more virgin tropical rain forest overall than in any other country, with the exception of Brazil. And this implies the calculated annihilation of perhaps millions of species, unless alternative technologies and economies can fashion a system of warranted utilization congruent with a wide range of local responses and rural poverty.

"Only if the poor can enjoy a better life will they be able to give their contribution to the solution of global environmental issues," said Indonesian President Suharto. Seven out of ten people in developing countries depend on forests for their heating and cooking; for houses, furniture, fences, tools, and household implements; for any foreign currency. In Indonesia, according to the Department of Forestry, those basic demands have resulted in the loss of more than five hundred thousand hectares of forest each year throughout the country, while only 40,500 hectares are annually reforested. To date, officially, eighteen million acres, or nine billion trees, have been felled to meet local needs, and this figure does not include the equally enormous attrition from private industry.[4] In addition, thirty million hectares of allegedly protected forests are, in fact, wide open to illegal logging and pioneer agriculture.[5]

Indonesia is the fourth largest country in the world. By comparison with China and India, its population is still "manageable," the country rather spacious, and its environmental and family planning leadership very much aware of its options. Yet, a converging tragedy has already been plotted on countless charts in Jakarta. But darkness and the demise of nature are on few Indonesian's lips. As elsewhere, the colossal debasement of the natural world has been rephrased in the lingo and currency of hope, feasibility, and furtherance. Because poverty has been identified as the source of all destruction, its alleviation has logically been deemed central to rain forest preservation, longer human life expectancy, a diminishing fertility rate, and a decrease in infant, child, and maternal mortality. Wealth, those enormous banks along Jakarta's swank, tree-lined avenues is viewed with the same hysteria as in the West, as the solution to everything. And yet, ironically, in the midst of this unabashed quest for dollars, Indonesia's leaders are quick to seize upon the vulnerability of the Western economic model. They point out that developed countries pollute, consume, and destroy far more than developing ones, and cite, for example, Austria, which exploits considerably more cubic meters per hectare of timber than Indonesia, or 3.3 versus 0.27. Moreover, Austria's total forest area is slightly less than 3.7 million hectares while that of Indonesia is somewhere around 100 million hectares, and these numeric differences separating the temperate and the tropical forest countries invite ethical and policy comparisons based upon population and country size, GNP, and—most importantly—the varying levels of biodiversity. Indonesian government officials, while not unaware of the fact that biodiversity is vastly more excelled in a rain forest than a temperate forest (possibly by a million-fold), are adamant about their right and their need to exploit their own forests. Indonesia is focused upon trees as a principal guarantee of international exchange. The economics, driven by Indonesia's population bomb, are fickle. No matter what policy of monetary gain the country pursues, regardless of the ethical and just positions it adopts to justify its financial aspirations, *nature* will suffer. Human nature itself recognizes that suffering, and well understands it has manufactured a social and political language of false certitudes so as to obfuscate and deny the truth, or to go on in spite of truth, or to satisfy itself with half-truths. Living in false consciousness, reconciled to compromise, Indonesians, like everyone else, have harbored a global lie and termed it "survival."

The lie comes from knowing better, even if "better"—the absolute safeguarding of even a small piece of wilderness—has proven nearly impossible to achieve. Within this context, a knowing Indonesia is attempting to fashion a compromise that is at least *a little better.*

India, China, and Indonesia together account for nearly 40 percent of the world's population. While India and China have already suffered untold ecological pillaging, their populations moving seemingly out of control, Indonesia still has time to implement life-saving measures in the two crucial antiwar sectors, family planning and conservation, in spite of its economic sweet tooth, a huge population of young people, and more biodiversity to lose than nearly any other country.

Among the Bata people of North Sumatra, following a three-day wedding shindig, the chief blesses the bride and enthusiastically implores her to bear sixteen baby girls and seventeen baby boys. But elsewhere across Indonesia, the pace of reproduction has been toned down considerably in the past twenty years, thanks to an aggressive national family planning program and a predisposition among countless rural, and some urban communities to honor the state's authority. The government is seeking to achieve a total fertility rate (TFR) of 2.1. At present, estimates of the TFR vary from 2.8 to 3.4, a difference between tens of millions of people over a single generation.[6]

But to put the country's indisputable fertility achievement in proper context, remember that Indonesia is 85 percent Muslim, making it the largest Islamic nation in the world.[7] And yet, except for Turkey (TFR of 3.31), most of the other forty Islamic countries show TFRs between 4 and 7.7 (this latter figure from the Republic of Yemen). Many countries, like Saudi Arabia, Pakistan, and Iran, exceed a TFR of 6. The more than one billion Muslims are the fastest reproducing religious group in the world. How then has Indonesia accomplished so much toward stabilizing its population already?

Some have argued that the achievement is the result of a "dramatic shift toward self-choice marriages," nuptials at much later ages, in addition to the increasing normal trend toward normalizing remarriage and divorce.[8]

But a more pervasive explanation pertains to how the Indonesian *ulamas* (religious leaders) have interpreted Muhammad's teachings. Many social scientists discount the influence of religion on contemporary family planning, whether in Catholic or Islamic countries.[9] But, without religious accommodation in Indonesia, much of the government's considerable efforts would have been in vain.[10]

Indonesian Islam favors birth control and was thus immediately receptive to the government's own family planning programs. Many Muslims insist that family planning is inherent to the Qur'an itself, once it is properly understood.

But that understanding is largely an Indonesian phenomenon, shared by few other Islamic countries. Consider that in Egypt a growing fundamentalist sector among its sixty million residents has denounced birth control as a Zionist plot, despite President Hosni Mubarak's constant reminders that the nation's resources are almost exhausted because of unchecked population growth. Mullahs in Iran have claimed that family planning is a Western plot, though that sentiment is slowly changing. In the Sudan, birth control is considered shameful by many, who believe that the best the poor can do for the world is to offer as many children as they can to Allah for his care.

Yet, the fact remains, if it is so interpreted, that Allah, the Prophet Mohammed, and the many collections of the hadith detailing statements by the Companions of the Prophet, all confirmed permission to use birth control, both pre- and postconception. "Go ahead," said Allah, with respect to contraception. "Nature will in any case take its course."[11]

According to most Islamic religious scholars, the four original *Imams* (Abu Hanifa, Shafe`i, Malik, and Ibn-e-Hanbal) accepted contraception. Long before Europeans were discussing openly the fine points of birth control, Islamic jurists were doing so, supporting the use of intravaginal suppositories and tampons.[12] Moreover, Islam prohibits intercourse during nursing, recommends suckling for two years, even accepts coitus interruptus (*azl*) as a form of contraception. Islam wants a large number of followers but unlike conventional Catholicism is not willing to propagate those minions at the expense of a quality existence. And thus, economics has always entered into Islamic feelings about family size.

Why, then, have most Islamic nations failed to achieve a low fertility rate? The answer appears to be the dogged devotion to two particularly simplistic statements in the Qur'an, namely, "Marry and beget children," and "Marry so that you multiply because I will make display of you in front of the other nations on the Day of Judgment even I will make a display of those prematurely born (*alsiqt*)."[13] Indonesian Muslims have managed to see beyond these provocations. They have not, however, granted the woman the free right to have an abortion.

There is no discussion of abortion in the Qur'an itself. Conservatives (fundamentalists) prefer, in absence of precise guidance, to err on the side of caution and thus prohibit it, except in cases of doctor certified mother's peril.[14] Among Muslim nations, only Tunisia, Turkey, and Bangladesh have legalized abortion. But many Indonesian Muslims would like to see legalization at least openly discussed in their country. Though the government denies it, Indonesians are aware that millions of "illegal" abortions are being carried out, often resulting in maternal deaths.[15]

One morning I sat with Abdurahman Wahid, head of one of the largest Islamic organizations in the world, based in Jakarta. At least 25 percent of all Indonesians follow this middle-aged gentleman. With the body of a former soccer star, and an acutely sensitive interpretation of human affairs, Wahid began by declaring his fervent support for birth control and environmental preservation. He argued that the government itself was faltering, having skirted the issue of permanent contraception "for fear it will be seen as too anti-Islamic. I know my people and how they react," he said. "If the scientists can give a level of confidence about recanalization, reversible sterilization is OK with the Muslims." The official government family planning agency, BKKBN (the Indonesia National Family Planning Coordinating Board, launched in 1970), has not advocated it because "they have no guts," said Wahid. And he went on, "let's open up the debate on abortion."

Islamic scholars, using relevant hadith, historical commentaries on the Qur'an, have stated that so-called "ensoulment" occurs 120 days after conception. Abortion prior to that time is not considered *wa'd*, or murder, though not all ulamas agree on this point. If the mother's health is imperiled, abortion is actually mandatory under Islamic religious codes, however. Interestingly, despite much that is made of the male's oppression of women in traditional Muslim societies, mutual consent for sterilization is also mandatory inasmuch as procreation is considered a "right" of both spouses. Man and wife must discuss the matter, in other words. The problem in Indonesia is that the most conservative elements of Islam have scared the government into relying upon shorter-term contraceptives and refusing to even open up the abortion issue for debate. Pronatalist Muslims have argued that "He who does not marry for fear of having a large family has no trust in God," as well as stating that "If they are poor, God of His bounty will enrich them."[16]

The government of Indonesia has been able to verify a 35 percent confidence level for reversible sterilization (the so-called *recanalization* technique) at seven official centers in the country. But most Muslim leaders want to see a 51 percent assurance rate before they will sanction it. Do the leaders speak for the people? Not in the rural areas, according to former UNFPA country representative Jay Parsons who explained to me that the authority of Islam in the countryside does not usually extend beyond the front doors of a Mosque, especially for women.

According to Wahid, Indonesians "cannot afford" too much traditional Islamic law. In other words, conservative inhibitions are no longer practical in a world where human population has exceeded environmental carrying capacity.

The problem Indonesia faces by refusing long-term methods of contraception is the high rate of short-term method discontinuance, a trend that does not bode well considering the government's recognized need to greatly accelerate the number of new contraceptive acceptors in the coming years. According to one recent study, "Even in the Asian nations where contraceptive acceptance is increasing, high rates of contraceptive discontinuation continue to plague program planners."[17] Demographers studying Indonesia have pointed out that—consistent with the psychology of contraceptive freedom elsewhere in the world—a woman's ability to chose her method is crucial to the likelihood of her maintaining contraceptive vigilance.[18]

One positive medium-term trend has to do with the fact that Norplant has been embraced more enthusiastically in Indonesia than in any other country. The reason for this cultural endorsement predates Islam's arrival there. Among the Balinese and West Javanese, it was considered beautiful for women to insert gold or silver needles under their skin or for a man to have stainless steel inserted under the palm of the hand. These insertions, known as *susuk,* were also believed to ward off illness, to maintain strength. Sometimes, the metal was inserted in the chin, the breast, or the face. Fortunately, the five-year life of Norplant has not been deemed "long-term" by the conservative Muslims.

Promoting two official slogans ("Two is enough, male or female, it's the same," and "Small, happy, and prosperous family"), the BKKBN government family planning agency employs eighty-one thousand workers, five hundred thousand village volunteers, operates seventy-six thousand contraceptive distribution centers (VCDC) across twenty-seven provinces, and, in addition, coordinates the activities of three hundred thousand family planning acceptor groups and tens of thousands of other volunteers. For twenty years the agency has distinguished itself through ingenious publicity, rigorous family planning administration, and impressive results.

With the exception of China, no other country has been so aggressive or successful at reaching the subvillage level, dispatching workers from door to door, a system compromised only by Indonesia's rugged terrain and endless island chains. Movement from village to village is frequently difficult, curtailing the predictable flow of monthly contraceptive supplies. This is one reason why long-term contraceptives are so crucial in Indonesia, and why the Islamic resistance to them (on grounds that any permanent check to children, or a mother's free right to have children, is morally wrong) has served to escalate Indonesia's population bomb, and corresponding ecological crisis. In fact, according to a confidential World Bank report in 1991, the shift to longer-lasting contraceptive forms seems to be the key to making family planning work in Indonesia. How does a government best manipulate the economy within an Islamic ethical system so as to foster long-term contraception? That is the issue, and it is not a simple one.

Most births in Indonesia occur unassisted by doctors in rural areas, where 83 percent of the population live, and where the rural literacy rate has actually fallen from 39.1 percent in 1971, to 28 percent in 1980, a level comparable with rural India.[19] The traditional village midwife is called *dukun* and she delivers more than 50 percent of all babies in the country, often under conditions of superstition and poor hygiene. As a result, Indonesia's maternal mortality rate is extremely high, 450 per one hundred thousand or seventy-five times that of other developed countries.

Just as infant mortality has always been linked to high fertility, one might assume that high maternal mortality would similarly be linked to low fertility; that the logic of death would intervene to check a mother's enthusiasm for more children. To a certain extent, this is true. What prevents the lower fertility is the lack of available contraceptive supplies, particularly in winter months when the rains and flooding are chronic. During these monsoon periods BKKBN workers are unable to reach many of the sixty-seven thousand villages throughout the country. And these are the same periods when millions of women get pregnant. The government is working to correct this situation by training and dispatching one auxiliary nurse–midwife, or *Bidan,* to each village.[20]

In spite of this well-organized and broadly defined mission to curb future births, Indonesia's population is growing rapidly because of the large existing number of young newlyweds and teenagers soon to be married. In wrestling with this paradox of numbers, the BKKBN has increasingly sought help from outside, nongovernmental consultants such as Dr. Firman Lubis, the executive director of the Yayasan Kusuma Buana NGO, which maintains six clinics in the poorer parts of Jakarta, oases of options for women.

There are visionaries throughout the world in family planning whose commitment and warmth is nothing short of heroic. Dr. Lubis is one of them. Born in Jakarta, the middle-aged doctor has given himself over to the poor. It is one thing to provide medical care as a doctor, to alleviate suffering among individuals; but to aspire to demonstrably change the world—to lower the birthrate and thus counteract the ecological fallout from a population boom—is an act of stubborn courage in the face of near futility. Refusing to be daunted by either the pervasiveness of poverty or the density of population, in 1981 Dr. Lubis introduced Norplant to Indonesia, the first person to do so on a large scale anywhere in the world. Over seven hundred thousand Indonesian women now use the implant.

The island of Java, on whose northwestern end Jakarta is located, constitutes 7 percent of the land of Indonesia, and contains the majority of the population, or 110 million. Its extreme density of 835 persons per square kilometer in a region the size of Wisconsin has resulted in the deterioration of every major watershed on the island. Java is losing 3 percent of its productive capacity, and nearly 737 million metric tons of soil each year, just in the highlands.[21]

Dr. Lubis does not hold with the BKKBN that Jakarta has achieved fertility replacement, or a TFR of 2.1 to 2.3, but rather (at least as of 1994) believed it to be between 3.4 and 3.5. His astonishingly higher estimate is consistent with the sheer number of children everywhere to be seen in a region like Pesangan Baru, where the density is sixty thousand people per square kilometer, the average number of children per couple between three and four, and average family income about eighty-five dollars per month. These are not the poor, who can be seen living along the canals and railroad tracks and have even more children, but the lower middle class. The government's position that Jakarta has achieved the two-child norm may, in fact, only apply to rich neighborhoods, an internalized demographic discrepancy similarly to be noted in the cities of Brazil, Iran, Thailand, even the United States.

Lubis started his clinics in 1981. Those who can afford to pay for his services are charged a minimum fee commensurate with their income.

Those who cannot afford anything are served for free. Dr. Lubis's teams are traditional pediatricians and family planners. They go into the homes. Moreover, the clinics themselves are like homes, spotlessly clean, among the most intimate and inviting I have seen anywhere in the world.

"We cannot depend on the government," says Dr. Lubis. "We are doing what the government is afraid to do. It is our task to help women. It is a matter of guts. We believe abortion is not a contraception, but a backstop. We educate people not to have it. But we do what we have to do," he says tactfully. And to that end, Dr. Lubis's six clinics in Jakarta are all medically licensed for various surgeries, like sterilization.

While wandering together through the Pesangan Baru, he explained that less than 5 percent of all teenagers and junior high-school students in Indonesia are getting real sex education, and probably only in a few major cities. Another 30 to 40 percent are getting basic reproductive health information through the religious organizations, but rarely any mention of sex.

Yet, teenage sexual intercourse by age sixteen is nearly 60 percent in Indonesian cities, as much as in most Western countries. Still, the government maintains an ostrich policy, all the more remarkable considering that there are an estimated three million unwed mothers in the country. When I asked officials at the BKKBN about teenage unwed mothers, they said there were none—the same response as in China.

At various private clinics throughout the city, a woman can get an abortion (menstrual regulation, they call it) under conditions of secrecy. It costs about one hundred dollars, or on average, nearly two months of a working woman's wages.

"Abortion, if legalized, would have a big impact in Indonesia," Dr. Lubis explained. He cited South Korea and Peru as two countries with similar TFRs to that of Indonesia, at least several years ago. Peru eventually reached a fertility impasse while South Korea's TFR continued to decline because of government supported abortion in that nation. (TFR in Peru today is a high 3.5, in South Korea, however, it is down to 1.7.)

Dr. Lubis definitely sees the day when abortion will be made legal in his country, and sterilization much more widely obtainable. "It might be fifteen or twenty years. But then again, it could also happen in a year if there were a political shift."[22] President Suharto is getting old. There is already talk of his successor. Perhaps that shift is on its way.

But whether Indonesia legalizes abortion anytime soon, will not by itself solve the country's population dilemma. In an ideal world, abortion should never be deemed a solution. What might more realistically inhibit the fourth largest country in the world from becoming the third largest, is a combination of concerted factors. By 2005, for example, the country hopes to reach a two-child family norm, or 2.1 TFR. That will require a 30 percent reduction in total fertility rate (based on the lowest AID estimate). To achieve it, the contraceptive prevalence rate (CPR) must rise from the current 55 percent (15.6 million female users) to at least 62.7 percent (25.4 million users). The 62.7 percent projected benchmark, if accurate, would be quite unusual considering that most countries have not been seen to reach replacement fertility until attaining a CPR of 70 percent for all child-bearing women between the ages fifteen and forty-nine. But for Indonesia, this means that over the coming eight years, roughly eighty-five million new contraceptive users—more new users than in all of sub-Saharan Africa—will have to be recruited, based upon the recognized allowance for large numbers of acceptors who discontinue usage every year. That figure represents a huge amount of work—consciousness raising, door-to-door lobbying, mass production of contraceptives, a policy of technical and cul-tural suasion. What makes this goal particularly ambitious (or just plain unrealistic) is the fact that there is great debate over actual CPR stats in Indonesia. As of 1994 the rate of new acceptor use appeared to be *down* by a whopping 75 percent since 1988. While an estimated 95 percent of all married Indonesian women know of at least one form of contraception, more than fourteen million of those women have unmet contraceptive needs. Yet, in mid-1997, the Population Reference Bureau reports that Indonesian CPR is up to 55 percent.

Malaysia and the Philippines both stalled on their fertility declines once the TFR fell below 3.5 children and the number of women of repro-ductive age using contraception of some kind reached 50 percent. Indonesia now faces that situation. The good news is that, in one donor-sponsored poll, some 65–70 percent of the women throughout the coun-try expressed a desire to stop having children, or at least delay them.[23]

However, according to the World Bank, even if all the targets were to be reached by family planners, an NRR (natural reproductive rate) of one will not set in for at least another century.

Thus, regardless of the BKKBN's best efforts, the intimation of near-ly four hundred million Indonesians grappling after a Western-style standard of living has cast an enormous pall over the land. All of the hard-won victories of official Indonesian family planning, and of committed individuals like Lubis and Wahid, will surely diminish, but cannot hold back the inevitability of many more people, and what those masses bode for one of the most spectacular biological regions in the world.

THE HOSTAGE SITUATION

THE SPEED OF human appropriation within a single generation will be slowed down by a combination of vigilant, enhanced contraceptive prevalence, the aggressive participation of private businesses, foreign capital assistance, ecologically sound technology transfers, and domestic enforcement of all conservation laws. But unless such relatively benign employment as ecotourism, computer biogenetic prospecting, nonpetroleum based sustainable agriculture, and noninvasive cottage industries, can be elevated to the economic equivalent of the present lumber trade, and quickly, Indonesia is likely to follow much the same disastrous path as India. The war against nature in Indonesia is being waged strictly for money.

Consider what's at stake here. Occupying 1.3 percent of the planet's surface, Indonesia's forty-seven distinct ecosystems encompass marine, rain forest, and alpine habitat. They host a fabulous plenitude of creatures, all vulnerable, that include panthers, bird-winged butterflies, black monkeys, Komodo dragons, green pythons, the largest flowers in the world, snake-eating eagles, a proliferation of orchids, leopards, and a few remaining rhinos. The country contains peat, freshwater swamp, heath, montane, and evergreen dipterocarp forests that harbor more than seven thousand tree species. In addition, the nation's lowland rain forests are the most expansive in all of tropical Asia. Indonesia also contains the third largest atoll in the world at Taka Bone Rata in the Flores Sea. Mangroves and beds of sea grass are to be found throughout the country's coastal regions. The Sulawesi and Maluku coral reefs are some of the most biologically productive on Earth.[24]

As with all other biomes on the planet, rain forests particularly so, the *known* number of species may be on average ten to seventy *fewer* than what is actually out there, not so much in the case of larger, more obvious mammals, but certainly with respect to smaller organisms. For example, in the rain forest of Sulawesi, two British taxonomists studying the hemipterans, or true bugs, recorded 1,690 species, of which 63 percent were unknown to science.[25] Only four countries in the world can be described as "megadiverse," namely, Indonesia, Brazil, Zaire, and Madagascar.[26] What is known about Indonesia's megadiversity is that the archipelago hosts 10 percent of all flowering plants (an estimated 25,000 species), 12 percent of all mammals (515 species, 36 percent of them endemic), 16 percent of all reptiles (600+ species) and amphibians (270 species), 17 percent of all birds (1,519 species, 28 percent of them endemic), and more than 25 percent of all marine and freshwater fish in the world.[27] The natural heritage is so "valuable," in fact, that it provides the direct, daily sustenance in one way or another for some 22 percent of the country's population, or forty million people, 30 percent of whom live in and around forests.

Three crucial facts about Indonesia's battleground need to be considered. First, in terms of percentage of its total political boundaries, Indonesia has 0.0 percent wilderness, according to the World Resources Institute definition of the term.[28] Second, this paucity of undefiled territory coincides with the fact that the country has more threatened species than any other nation, with the possible exception of Madagascar.[29] In the 1980s the Javan tiger went extinct. Eighteen known Indonesian bird species have vanished just recently. The Red Data Books of the IUCN (International Union for the Conservation of Nature, now called the World Conservation Union) list 126 birds, 63 mammals, 21 reptiles, and 65 other Indonesian species as threatened with extinction.[30] And third, the government is committed to protecting 10 percent of its land area, though, according to the World Wide Fund for Nature, the official agenda actually only covers 7 percent. But even 10 percent would mean that 90 percent will *not* be protected, and even that 10 percent will require extremely ambitious efforts yet to be undertaken, in most cases. Embracing the philosophy of compromise as a triumph, the Indonesian government has run the following advertisement in the nation's daily newspapers: "Indonesian Forests Forever—280 million acres PRESERVED forever—By designating 280 million acres as permanent forest, Indonesia is protecting and preserving its forests in their natural state. Over 43 percent of these forests will remain untouched, forever. The other 57 percent will be carefully managed for sustainable growth. . . ."[31] While some ecologists elsewhere in the world have been impressed by such official rhetoric, when carefully scrutinized the numbers actually reveal a sinister and slippery slope. After Brazil, Indonesia is the second largest exporter of hardwoods in the world. "Untouched forever" scarcely exists in a human-dominated world, certainly not in a region focused on converting tropical hardwoods into money. The effectiveness of "damage control," even of a holding pattern, hinges upon the quality of criteria applied not just to conservation, but to the very *idea of nature*. What are the rights of nature? Are they comparative or absolute? Are they more relevant among the rich than the poor? Supreme Court Justice William O. Douglas proposed a "wilderness bill of rights" in 1965 and a few years later argued that people in "intimate relation with the inanimate object about to be injured . . . are its legitimate spokesmen."[32] Back in 1933, conveners met in London to formulate a consensus on the Protection of African Fauna and Flora that endorsed the idea of "strict natural reserves," which—in contrast to mere parks—banned all human visitors, other than "qualified" scientists whose presence would be carefully regulated.[33] The arts and sciences have long acknowledged the concept of "pure wilderness" and its gradations, or as Paul Simon and Arthur Garfunkel sang in 1970, "I'd rather be a forest than a street." Conservationists have classified wild lands and marine habitats according to the extent of strictly defined levels of human encroachment and compromise. But for the general public, too often the notion of pure wilderness has been cloaked in nostalgia for what is lost, a phrase more given to longing, reduced to "mere" paradise in pastoral literature and mythopoetic pictorials. Or, by recasting the preexisting wilderness as some *future*, unreachable utopia, we have conveniently disavowed our responsibilities as powerful stewards, embracing the human condition as the only true reality, an excuse for everything we do. This has served us as a "rational" defense of destruction, an anthropocentric syndrome that is another form of the aforementioned "lie" which we repeat to ourselves under the brazen or apologetic rubrics of our survival needs.

If we are to rephrase our standards and practices, to become truthful denizens of an interdependent world, we must first insist upon the healing process, and that would mean safeguarding as much wild land as possible, to cease irritating an open wound. Given that some 50 percent of the planet's net primary production (the planet's natural green growth) has already been coopted by our species, at the very least, we must ensure, however monumental the task, that *Homo sapiens* are somehow inhibited from expanding their hegemony any farther. And once that restrained threshold has been stabilized, we must quickly act to take several steps back from our massive planetary swathe, curbing all future extraction, manipulation, and exploitation of living beings and inorganic deposits. We must recede, the way a destructive tidal wave recedes. But how? If we have not managed to accomplish even a remote semblance of this healing process in a rich nation like the United States, what is possible in a dollar-poor country such as Indonesia now on the brink of economic disaster?

At no other time in our history have philosophy and spirituality come to play such crucial roles in our politics and our relationship with the natural world. Until we forcefully assert new international laws that uphold the inherent rights of nature, we will blindly justify any action, and hail all compromise as manifest destiny. In India, the World Resources Institute definition of "wilderness" has been ideologically diminished in scope, scaled back from four thousand square kilometers to five hundred, with little or no social commentary. That country has felt it had no choice because of the sheer pervasiveness of its people. So that what is one man's suburbia is another's wilderness. Personal experience and economic circumstances, ethics, aesthetics, sensitivity, and political persuasion all cloud any realistic definition of what constitutes "wilderness" and "biological integrity." Governments are easily able to justify expedient ecological definitions; even when those marginal, haphazard, and largely false definitions backfire; when one learns, for example, that all the mammals have vanished from a region.

Such vagaries point to the fundamental truth of this war: the inevitability of compromise, however extreme, given the presence of too many human beings. Living with compromise, and with contradiction, is what the law of averages, and any human collective imposes. There is simply no known method whereby 5.8 billion large consumers can forge obvious or harmonious points of consensus. A democratic demographics is an oxymoron that does not suggest obvious compassionate antidotes to the governing mind. The role of science is to constantly remind us of our current compass reading in the vast sea of compromise; while the arts hold the promise of evoking and championing a more pure course. But it is the arena of policy making that should invoke balance. The difficulty with attaining or maintaining a viable path in a world politically, culturally, and linguistically fragmented, is the absence of a true processing, or *feeling* center. An individual's brain processes injury to its person almost immediately, sending out signals of alert and damage control. Though even before the brain responds, antibodies have already set to work. But in the case of the planet, the feeling centers are usually not connected to our person. An American cannot know to respond to injury in an Indonesian wetland. Time, distance, and political boundaries separate us from the causes of crisis, despite our superficial acquaintances through the media. And because destruction of the world occurs under much broader regimes than the course of an individual injury, we are largely disconnected from the Earth's needs and vulnerability, mired as we are in a hierarchy of denials. Emotionally, there are myriad other "priorities" which societies like Indonesia's have placed before some vague balance of nature. Indoctrinated with compromise, ethically imbued with a world biologically overrun by *Homo sapiens,* people have come to view money— blunt, cold, hard cash—as far more valuable than other life forms. Or, conversely, to hold with the sixteenth-century writer George Pettie, a man expressing the first Western frenzy of consumption, "What disease is so desperate which money may not medicine? What wound so deadly which coin cannot cure?" (*Petite Palace,* 1576) Can this illusory and disastrous mindset be reversed? There are few places on Earth where such a reversal is more critical to ecological stability than in Indonesia.

The country is looking for money to increase the power of its infrastructure and the lifestyle of its people, and much of that wealth is expected to come from the forests. That, of course, is the problem. Even if Indonesia were to quadruple its GNP, it would find itself in the unenviable position of a country like Russia, which is in an equally difficult situation. The economic threshold for ecological balance is simply unknown. For any given area, one trillion dollars might not redress what a no-cost policy of preventative restraint could have brought about.

Nobody knows for certain how much forest is left in Indonesia. Based upon dated surveys by the Dutch, officially (and in keeping with the government's newspaper advertisements), 66 percent of land area is still covered by trees. That means 143 million hectares. One hectare is equal to 2.4 acres. Thus, according to the government of Indonesia, that country still has 343 million acres, 10 percent of the planetary total, the third largest timber estate in the world. The Indonesian government is saying two things: that 280 million of the 343 million acres will be protected and preserved forever. That's 86 percent of existing forests! The government is also saying that only 43 percent of that, or 147 million acres, will be untouched forever. What is the general public to make of the difference between "protected and preserved forever" and "untouched forever"? The government spells it out. Bear with me here because the very uncertainty of the policy-dependent numbers and intentions are part of the problem, and hence the message. Of those 143 million hectares (or 343 million acres), under the four land use categories stipulated in the 1984 Indonesian Ministry of Forestry's Consensus Forest Land Use Plan currently in effect, 30.3 million hectares are designated for protection (that means approximately 72 million acres, not the advertised 280 million acres—a rather appalling discrepancy), 18.7 million hectares for conservation (hunting and other activities will be allowed), and 64.3 million hectares for out-and-out production. Another 30 million hectares are earmarked for agricultural conversion (total appropriation). What this dense cluster of apparent contradictions reveals is a dual usage of language, fortified by public relations, and misleading calculations.

Other data by WALHI, the country's leading environmentalist organization show Indonesia's forests as covering between 100 and 109 million hectares, not 143 million.[34] That is nearly a 33 percent difference. Because the estimated rate of loss was 1.2 million hectares per year in the early 1980s, prior to what has become an even more aggressive lumber industry, it means that there could easily be less than 100 million hectares today. If that is the case, rather than the high 143 million hectares government estimate, all total forest cover figures would correspondingly be reduced by nearly a third, which means that what the government had promised as 280 million protected acres (corrected to 72 million) is actually closer to a figure of 50 million, or nearly six times less than alleged!

Now the government has said it intends to protect 10 percent of the country, of which supposedly two thirds are forest, the other designated areas covering a broad range of ecosystems, of plant and animal life. With a 6:1 discrepancy in actual "untouched" protection status, that 10 percent is probably closer, in reality, to 2 percent. On an international scale, and forgetting the far greater need for safeguarding a megadiverse region, as opposed to, say, central Greenland's ice shelf, 2 percent is far below the already depressing world average of a mere 4.3 percent of national land area that is protected.[35]

Given the incidental loss of forests, the lack of certainty with respect to road-cutting damage (edge effects), watershed disturbance, the ratio of official selective cutting to official and unofficial clear-cutting, and the additional burden of shifting cultivation (nearly 40 million hectares of forest affected), nobody knows with any precision how compromised the official figures actually are. But the feeling is one of growing desperation among many ecologists in the country with whom I met. Selective cutting laws were introduced in the 1960s, at the beginning of the logging boom. But enforcing those laws—pertaining to stipulated minimum diameters of cutting and required regeneration times—has proven nearly impossible. Policing manpower is at the negligible level of one man per fifty thousand hectares of forest (about the same for India), so you can forget management of the selective cutting. Uncontrolled forest clearance is escalating. Wild fires are beginning to resemble the "controlled" fires of Brazil. In the fall of 1997, out of control fires across Indonesia created the worst smog conditions ever witnessed in the Indo–Malay Peninsula. I was in Singapore at the time, where visibility was approximately one thousand feet. One airliner went down over Sumatra, killing more than two hundred people, and at least four oil tankers collided due to lack of visibility.

But other problems escalate. For example, the haste to replant new land is double the country's population growth rate. For every new mouth to feed, two additional units of land are cleared for crops. Such clearance for agriculture has been deemed "the greatest threat facing Indonesia's biodiversity." Government sponsored habitat "conversion" for food production will consume at least 17.4 million hectares by the year 2000, in addition to the uncontrolled land-use, and the commercial "production" of forest. But these figures are all based upon current energy capacity, housing starts, the price of petroleum-based fertilizers, the proportion of national budget allocations to affordable housing, and any number of other indicators likely to change. With respect to demographics, if anything the numbers will be worse, and thus, all the other sectors dependent upon the number of mouths to feed, clothe, and house will also increase exponentially.[36] Already, fifteen hundred Indonesian rice species are known to have gone extinct in the race for fast-growing monocultural strains. Similar trends toward depletion can be inventoried for every facet of Indonesia's marine environment.

The existing legal framework for conservation in Indonesia is extraction oriented. While the 1990 Conservation of Natural Resources and Ecosystems Law recognizes biological integrity, it does so with an eye toward manifesting future exploitation. Agriculture, forestry, and fishing makes up 21.8 percent of Indonesia's gross domestic product (GDP).[37] Complying with the call for global free trade, Indonesia signed the GATT Code on Subsidies and Countervailing Duties, but tariff barriers in Japan and

Australia, quota restrictions in the U.S. and Europe, and new competition from throughout a financially strapped Asia have largely negated any benefits of the GATT Code on Subsidies, and forced Indonesia to aggressively focus on the the production and marketing of domestic timber by-products, hence adding to the country's pace of rapid forest encroachment.[38]

The Indonesian government provides a ridiculously small proportion of its budget for conservation. The largest national park in Indonesia (Gunung Leuser in Irian Jaya, a Biosphere Reserve, one of seven in the country, with 10,946 square kilometers), has an annual operating budget of $232,357. The PHPA—Directorate General of Forest Protection and Nature Conservation within the Ministry of Forestry—has few trained field staff, and virtually no marine biologists.

Indonesia is trying hard to implement strong global alliances for conservation, having joined the Global Biodiversity Conservation Strategy of UNEP, IUCN, and the World Resources Institute. It participates in the UNESCO Man and the Biosphere program, as well as working closely with the World Wide Fund for Nature (WWF). In all, 366 terrestrial conservation areas have been created. A total of 16.2 million hectares, or 8.2 percent of the country's land area, has been designated as preserved. Most endemic species and all known Indonesian birds appear to be represented in at least one or another of the preserves. Another 22.7 million hectares are being considered for preservation. Together, these existing and proposed preservation sites would add up to the official 10 percent figure. So far, however, many of the parks and reserves "exist on paper only." Many of the more remote parks and preserves have virtually no staff in place. There is no protection. Poaching and illegal trade are widespread. Backtrack further through the aforementioned numeric "discrepancies" and a kind of fuzzy illogic begins to surface, a house of cards that betrays any solidity or conservation comfort zone.[39]

As of early 1993, 575 concessionaires had legal claim to over 144 million acres of Indonesian rain forest. As of the mid-1990s, according to WALHI, there had been "little replanting" of demolished regions, while 106 primary dipterocarp tree species were threatened with extinction.[40] Says the forestry minister, the country is taking steps to convert two decades of reckless exploitation into sustainable management. And yet, the total *Reboisasi* (reforestation) and *Penghijauan* (afforestation) figures in the last few years have been lower than ever before in the history of the Indonesian forestry program.

As in India, the Indonesian government is attempting to convert its rapidly expanding burden of wasteland into commercial plantations for fast-growing wood fibers to support paper, pulp, and rayon products (HTIs, or hutan tanaman industries).

In principle, reclaiming wastelands is an admirable goal, a form of poetic redemption. However, most investors to date have shown little enthusiasm for redemption. Many of the fast-growing varieties like eucalyptus and acacia are subject to pest infestations. The *Acacia magnum,* for example, is attacked by as many as nineteen species of insects while still a seedling. In fact, no pest-resistant fast-growing varieties have yet been found.[41] The HTI fast-growing wood fiber programs, rather than deflecting destruction from natural hardwood forests, is encouraging it, because industries are clear-cutting existing forests, selling the lumber, the captured pigs, deer, monkeys, and other creatures they can easily get their hands on, and only then planting the fast-growing monocultural varieties which spell the total doom of the rain forest ecosystem. In other words, plantations are not precluding primary forest encroachment.

Indigenous rights are also being perverted. The government of Indonesia has avowed the right to regulate the legal relationships between people and the forests. Inasmuch as most indigenous groups have no maps of their community tribal lands, nor effective legal representation, their claims to traditional sovereignty are at the mercy of the government's own agenda. And that, in turn, is dominated by entrepreneurs and foreign investors. Millions of animals will go extinct so that we can all avail ourselves of Indonesian toilet paper, unless there are international boycotts, trade barriers, or other kinds of pressure exerted.[42]

In one Indonesian village, a paper company clear-cut and burned 3,379 hectares, destroying every last remnant of the local Sakai people's livelihood and legacy—its farms, even its burial grounds.

Foreign investors bankrolled an Indonesian conglomerate which went into Sumatra in order to produce pulp cheaper per ton than any other mill in the world ($226 [U.S.] per ton.) It did this by securing Swiss convertible bonds, Finnish thirteen-year interest-free loans, and Canadian consultants. The company avoided any environmental controls, according to WALHI, and manipulated Indonesia's relatively "innocent" bureaucratic system, in spite of the staunch objections of Indonesia's own minister of population and environment.

Throughout much of the country, economic imperatives have totally replaced sound ecological strategies. Indonesia is struggling for revenues.

Overpopulation has saturated many of the domestic markets, and the global trading blocs have disadvantaged the country's revenue stream from textiles, shoes, and electronics. As of November 1997, Indonesia was forced to liquidate sixteen insolvent banks as a condition of a thirty-three billion dollar loan from the International Monetary Fund, a desperate bailout for a country whose economic system—like that of Thailand and Malaysia—is rapidly deteriorating, and which views its forests as its most profitable commodity, its green gold. Tragically, Indonesians still see enough rain forest in place to imagine that the alleged crisis of deforestation will be taken care of by the implementation of a few parks, pious proclamations, and largely symbolic legislation.

According to Dr. J. Harger, an outspoken program specialist in the UNESCO Jakarta Office for Science and Technology for Southeast Asia, the saving of Indonesia is the most important ecological battle to be fought anywhere on the planet.

"The onus of arriving at a solution must cut just as deeply in developed, as developing countries," says Harger. "For years now the American policy has stated, 'Not open to negotiation.' 'OK,' says the South, 'we'll all go down together if that's how you want to play it.' Vice President Gore's statements are good," Harger avowed. "But it's easy to write this stuff. Has he paid his dues? It's a hell of a lot harder to take heat, harder than they ever thought. You take Mrs. Gro Harlem Bruntland. She's zipped out. She says catching whales is great. Any ecologist can tell you catching whales isn't great. If those guys can't find some other way to operate, how can the Indonesians? This is insane. Loosen up on some of the strategies that have brought you to dominance and give us some of the difference so that we can move forward and we can make some kind of a joint plan. North Americans have been brainwashed. They DO NOT understand the world rightly. Indonesians who have grown up with nature know what is the problem. The senior people in the developing countries understand—they live it, they see what's happening. They know that we are trapped in the ideological crisis of all times, a serious intellectual conflict of what should be done here in Indonesia."

One of those individuals very much immersed in the conflict is Dr. Emil Salim, the former minister of environment who met with me for an afternoon at his office in Jakarta. "In spite of active family planning we are going to see eighty million new babies," he said. "How do you accommodate these people? Either the developed nations open for migration, or for nonforest exports—like textiles, foods, and electronics. Our infant mortality rate is seventy. It will come down by half again but the population will go up. How do you raise income to cope with the increased population? Either you go outside Indonesia—but be realistic, that's not going to happen—or you open the door for industrialization outside the forests—shoes, electronics, textiles, manual labor. But what are the facts: we are now facing an embargo in the U.S., while the U.S. talks about a free market economy. It's hypocritical. Everyone protects their own economy so we cannot move fast in nonforest products. Our own economy is not enough to sustain the nonforest products market. So what happens now? President Clinton increases protection for his domestic economy. A tariff wall."

Because Indonesia had built up a number of small-scale industries around value added furniture, the tariffs have hurt the country badly, rewarding the mowing down of tropical hardwoods so that Western manufacturers could derive the economic benefits of raw lumber. There are two profound paradoxes in all of this. While the developed countries are crying for protection of tropical rain forests, they are as Salim says, also raising import duties for higher value added products, thus depriving the developing countries like Indonesia of their due revenues. This is a form of imperialistic schizophrenia. But there is an even deeper ecological malaise that can be read into it, and which even passage of the GATT in December 1993, with its associated 33 percent, on average, tariff reduction, is unlikely to mollify: whether America or Indonesia fashions the furniture, the trees still get chopped down. There are no guarantees that higher incomes in Indonesia derived from value added furniture products would actually favor less exploitation of the forests! Now that those import duties have actually come down, the likely incentive for manufacturing more and more furniture in a competitive arena is likely to result in increasingly aggressive conversion of primary forests to furniture for export.[43]

I reminded Salim that a rain forest possesses considerably more biodiversity than a temperate forest. And that just because the West has made colossal mistakes is no reason for Indonesia to repeat them.

His response was direct. "We are told, 'Look, Indonesia, you are a treasure for the world, maintain your forests . . .' If the tropical forest plays an important role, what do we get for not exploiting it? Everybody shouts, 'Save the forest.' But when you ask how do we meet the needs of the poor people, there is silence. 'I won't give you technology, I won't give you gene patents, you remain poor, you go to hell.' That is how your people (the Americans) look at us."

Salim himself has recognized the fallability of balance sheets when examining the natural world. Already, Indonesian economists have tried to pin him down for the benefit:cost ratio of certain species that have gotten in the way of development, whether bird, tree, or monkey. "Benefit:cost ratio nobody can say," Salim told me. He explained how the Ministry of Mining was looking for new opportunities and demanded to exploit a certain region. Salim said there were alternative regions for coal but no alternative regions for orangutans. Open pit mining was determined to be the most cost effective means of getting at the coal. No rehabilitation was planned. Said Salim, "The fact we don't know the value of a monkey should not mean that we can thus exploit it." And quoting the Qur'an, he reiterated, "God does not create something without a purpose. Man with limited knowledge does not know the purpose. God knows. There must be a reason God created a long-nosed monkey." He told me he wants Indonesia to be the "best in the world" when it comes to conservation. But he was not able to stop developers from eliminating Jakarta's last mangrove right in his own backyard.

Other forces at work are bound to increase this conflict, certainly in Indonesia. Salim believes that the country will run out of oil as early as 2010; that natural gas from the South China Sea is too expensive to pipe in; that solar energy may work for hot water, but not for commercial industries; that they have already utilized their full hydropower capacity. He argues for nuclear energy as the only possibility of supporting economic growth painlessly. But WALHI has argued that the government has grossly overestimated energy needs for the year 2000, even under the most ambitious GNP projections. "Indonesia's status as a developing country is often presented as an excuse for rapid energy growth," says WALHI. "But the fact that Indonesia is at an early stage of industrialization should instead be viewed as an opportunity to avoid the energy-inefficient history of the more industrialized nations." By applying more efficient technologies across the spectrum of Indonesia's nearly thirteen thousand large and mid-sized industrial ventures WALHI analyses suggest that 40 percent of total energy demand could be saved in Indonesia at a reasonable price. In the rural sector, small-scale, locally managed renewable energy sources have been identified throughout the country, including microhydro, solar, wave power, the use of agricultural wastes, wind power, and geothermal.

The debate rages on. Seventy-six percent of cooking fuels come from wood in Indonesia, not electricity. All the more reason, says Salim, in conjunction with limited nuclear, to promote fast growing trees species, particularly bamboo. He advocates a Chinese-style model of Green Walls in every province, and would like to see more Indonesians using kerosene for cooking oil. In deflecting demographic pressure away from the forests, Salim acknowledges that the urban population will swell from a current 17 percent to 30 percent by the year 2000. His goal, and that of the BKKBN, is to reduce pressure on the land by guiding urbanization into suburban buffer zones surrounding the major cities. But with increasing population those buffer zones multiply and spread out like an ink blot. The edge effects proliferate in the name of wise conservation policy.

Collaborators in the destruction of the rain forests are those who somehow encourage the market for tropical timber. But it is the governments who are most to blame, for they are the only concentrated force that can intervene to halt the cycle. So far, the cry of global recession and unemployment has stifled such mediation.

The problem can be summarized: even selective cutting that supports at least a partial biodiversity has long proven to be erratically implemented, at best. Corporate greed, laziness, deception, and ignorance, coupled with most developing countries' lack of enforcement capabilities, has perpetuated the clear cutting mentality. Energy consumption in Indonesia grew at 15.6 percent annually throughout much of the 1980s.[44] While the export of raw logs, as well as clear-cutting, have been banned, and a tax levied on sawn timber (except in Irian Jaya which happens to contain some of the largest tracts of forest in the whole country) settlers are nevertheless building roads and burning down large sections of forest for agriculture. "Wasteful logging" operations—in addition to the offical quasi-selective and clear-cutting figures—are resulting in some four hundred thousand hectares of lost forest each year in Indonesia. Illegal encroachment continues unabated for lack of policing staff, and it is also well understood that the remedial tree planting schemes, in which artificial ecosystems supplant real ones, are biological tragedies, in terms of biodiversity loss.[45]

An enforceable moratorium on all new exploitation of primary forest—the goal of India—would mean that Indonesia's entrepreneurial impulses and huge debt would have to be, (1) repaid via other nonforest means, (2) repaid through fast-growing timber estates created only on existing wasteland, with an eye toward regenerating the forest floor through a decisive diversity of planning, or (3) erased by the developed nations which might forgive the debt in perpetuity.

But consider that together, tropical countries are besieged by a nearly one trillion dollar debt, half of which is owed by those nations responsible for two-thirds of all deforestation.[46] Any sizable level of debt forgiveness is not likely to occur in today's economically depressed climate. Conversely, no nation has thus far indicated its willingness to compensate tropical countries for income voluntarily resisted, despite the fact that forest preservation benefits everyone.[47]

In a state of war, sustainability means the continuation of that war, a perpetual, profit-driven harvest of shame. Given what we now know is actually taking place in the forests—the immense losses, the permanent transmogrification—the goal must be to prohibit the cutting of any and all trees, whether temperate or tropical. Selective cutting will not do. World leaders would do well to impose a global ban on all extraction, export, and import of primary forests, while compensating concessionaires with alternative sustainably derived income generating land giveaways, interest-free loans, and grants. Anti–forest-poaching patrols must be trained, and dispatched in the same manner as anti–animal-poaching units. Up until now, such interventionism has been the province of radical fringe groups (i.e., Earth First!). But, I can well envision international antipoaching brigades, much like the U.N. Blue Helmets, financed by a cooperative world body. Skeptics will argue that there is not enough money to pay for the *existing* eighty thousand U.N. peacekeeping forces (despite Ted Turner's one billion dollar gift to the U.N. in 1997, and Clinton's determination to repay the U.S. debt). The counterargument rests upon the fact that the prevention of a few dozen multinational corporations from building roads into forests should be considerably easier to handle than, say, the resolution of hostilities in a region like the Sudan. The number of needed troops—in cooperation with the countries involved—would be relatively few.

A globally enforced ban would invite a more concentrated timber estate industry (such as exists in the American Southeast) in conjunction with the badly needed restoration of existing ruined lands. In addition, biogenetic engineering of hardwood surrogates would become more a bankable strategy.

In this age of ecological double-speak, the alleged practice of "sustainability" has shielded countries from criticism. Going much farther, by implementing a total ban, as I am proposing, would require tenacious diplomatic finesse and economic counterincentives by the world's lending organizations and the major banks (many of which are in Japan). The argument *against* such a ban rests upon several emphatic assumptions. Mohammad Bob Hasan, chairman of the Indonesian Forestry Community, points out that most northern countries have destroyed more than 95 percent of their forests, whereas some tropical countries have as much as 40 percent left. In addition, the north has safeguarded a total of less than sixty million hectares, versus eighty-seven million hectares in the south (discrepancies and vague sources of data—the fuzzy illogic syndrome—lend little confidence to these figures, however). Indonesian officials say that eco-labeling, punitive measures by the north against the south (such as trade boycotts, let alone a total ban), would further stress an already impoverished system, diminishing the perceived value of timber, and thus the incentives to protect it. "If we don't take care of the poor, they will take care of the forests in their own way," says Hasan. Unless the landless farmers, and increasingly unemployed poor can realize immediate financial gain from the forests, conservation is not going to happen. The government says that if the tropical rain forests are to be truly understood as a global commons (a notion India rejects), then the rest of the world needs to help finance their survival.[48]

Environmentalists insist that rain forest destruction is the result not of poverty, but of greed, corruption, and the lack of willpower to police logging by governments in tropical countries. As for the developed countries, those same environmentalists have argued that governments, pressured by corporate lobbies and the much bloated emphasis on unemployment, have willfully encouraged the destruction of old growth forests, while ignoring selective cutting abuses or higher market incentives for timber estates. The United States, for example, has been incapable of ensuring the livelihood of the old growth coniferous stands, with their thousands of precious species.

By now it should be obvious that such arguments hinge upon several glaring contradictions. For example, all the wealth in the world has not protected temperate rain forests. Alleviating poverty is thus no guarantee of anything. And while India has attempted to limit forest commercialization, those efforts have been overwhelmed by the personal foraging of nearly half a billion dependents upon wood. The argument strikes of lunacy: one side is asking to extract several liters of blood, the other just a few liters. Both sides are ignoring the fact that the patient is already hemorrhaging to death. In forty years, Indonesia's population will have doubled, at current fertility trends. That is the *large* picture, embroiled in grand conflict-resolution schemes. But, during a realistic day and night of an average village, in the private quarters of a real human life, where troubles are strictly personal, these statistical data and sophisticated *arguments* are somebody else's problem, a kind of morbid poetry.

INDONESIA'S PAST AND FUTURE

THE TRAIN TRIP past partially denuded hills and intensively farmed paddies to Bandung two hours southeast of Jakarta yields a composite picture of Indonesia's problems and possibilities, cloaked in haze and human high-density. Bandung used to be a mountain-cooled Dutch resort, tranquil and uncrowded, nestled beneath a still steaming caldera. The town maintains its village feel, though it is the second largest city in the country now, with some 2.7 million residents. In the last few years, tens of thousands of acres of volcanic rain forest have been mowed down to make way for migrants who put up bungalows and plant crops. Traffic is already gnarled, babies are everywhere, and the population increase is on a par with Los Angeles, namely, 4 percent annually. The pattern of forest encroachment is chaotic, imperceptible today, a gigantic bald spot tomorrow, as it is in India. But what distinguishes Indonesia's plight from that of the Indian subcontinent, is the amount of forest still remaining. Encroachment thus enjoys, for now, a luxury of proportion that masks its seriousness, and can only be fully diagnosed from a distant vantage point, or a satellite.

Descending toward Bandung one day, from twenty miles away along one of the surrounding volcanos, Tangkuban Perahu, I ventured off the road by foot into the jungle. I walked several hundred meters into the thickest tropic I could lay my hands on, kneeling, crawling, rubbing my face in it, taking in every penetrant odor, sight, and sound; sat down amid a teeming puzzle of life forms; took off my clothes in a faint drizzle and folded them neatly in a bundle beneath what appeared to be a rather rare Anggrek Bulan orchid; and waited.

Ants investigated my arms and neck, though none were aggressive. Butterflies of pale green and Antwerp blue dallied all around me. A dark

snake moved through the thicket, just in sight, while a medley of determined and unrecognizable birds went about their business overhead. I
dug through the grass and weeds and vines. Layers of dazzling life
egressed with each additional millimeter of exposure. In the rotting bark
of an immense softwood, beetles multiplied in a rousing chorus of
motion, shape, and color. Here, all around me, were universes within universes. I closed my eyes, grateful and spellbound.

It was in this very archipelago that Alfred Russel Wallace, sick with
fever, contemplating Malthus's *Essay on Population,* and noting a more
remarkable divergence of species than anywhere else on the known Earth,
first postulated his theory of "natural selection" in the mid-1850s. In his
writings, he recognized that the existence of any organism depends upon
"preexisting closely allied species" forming an interdependent web of life.
"Closely allied" pertained to a kind of coexistence or harmony. But what
harmoniously admixed species preceded man, let alone a few hundred
million of them? The mid-Pliocene *Pithecantropus erectus* (Java man) of
seven hundred thousand years ago? Dr. Eugene Dubois who made the discovery during the early 1890s, found hundreds of other skeletal remains
in the lapili bed along the now polluted Solo River in East Java—rhinos,
cats, hippos, crocodiles, hyenas, elephants, a gigantic pangolin, and countless smaller mammals that have all since gone extinct. Did Java man kill
them? Was he as ruthless a hunter then as now? *Homo soloensis,* or
Ngandong man, a later Javanese Neanderthal type, the possible precursor
of both Indonesian and Australian aborigines, slaughtered mammals,
fashioned hunting tools out of deer antler, and—based upon skull
remains—was probably a cannibal. Evidence from both of these paleontological layers suggests anything but prehuman harmony.[49]

Wallace, who was not yet aware of Java man, or the Ngandong can-
nibals, meditated for three years on the interspecies relationships
throughout these rain forests and hit upon the notion of the "survival of
the fittest." It was a concept that seemed appropriate to a balanced ecosystem. The population on Java by the time Wallace sojourned among the
islands was probably around nine million. What would he have said to an
Indonesian human population of more than sixty million, the estimate
following the country's first census in 1930? Would it have confirmed his
and Darwin's analysis of evolution? Or completely negated it? If sixty
million humans have a fitting place in a balanced ecosystem, what is it,
where is it? Is there some cosmic *purpose* to human folly and destruction

that we're not appreciating? What meaningful *raison d'être* for four hundred million Indonesians a few generations from now, in a country laid waste to?

More likely, the theory itself is inappropriate for describing or predicting the human maelstrom, which has drifted apart from evolution, like a continent coming unglued.

The forces of natural selection that had relished such spectacular biological largesse on the rain forests were already being grotesquely skewed by one species who stood out from all the others without precedent, even thousands, possibly hundreds of thousands of years ago. To sit alone in that sylvan cornucopia on Mount Tangkuban Perahu was to feel the brunt of this conclusion, to hear the distant sounds of human industry, and to know that it was only a matter of time before Bandung's quickly growing population would overwhelm the very garden spot of creation in which I sat, a paradise in which the Earth had invested several billion years of loving patience and creative impulses.

Now, all is impatience and harm. As in the Amazon, Indonesian transmigration and colonization have meant the massive construction of new highways through primeval rain forest, like the trans-Sumatra and trans-Sulawesi. Fifteen cities over half a million in size are rapidly absorbing Indonesians who harbor a dream of mercantilist security and gain. These are not hunters and gatherers content to wield tools of stone or antler. There are two important ways to view the growing city populations. Certainly, it can be held that urbanization lessens the immediate burden of the human presence on the forests and lowlands. In that respect, the more *metropolitan* a country, the better. But, from the standpoint of the concentration of power which is then employed in prospecting for wealth out beyond the urban peripheries, cities pose an inherent liability of monumental proportions.

Some policies have the weight of overnight reemphasis. Others are mere goals toward which the decade, or the generation is slowly turned. Wallace's rather pleasant "natural selection" is no longer an option, even under the most rigorous one-child policy, which nobody at the BKKBN has advocated.

Much of Alfred Wallace's splendid wilderness has been lost, yet much remains to be saved. Fourteen years ago there wasn't even a national park in this country. Not until 1990 were parks incorporated under any legal framework for protection.

For many years President Suharto has vigorously pushed family planning, motivating lower ranking officials, from provincial governors to village headmen.[50] At the same time, relative to other developing countries, Indonesia's national budget is weighted in favor of education, health, and social welfare which account for 10 percent of annual expenditures, versus 8 percent for defense. In the same spirit, this is the crucial decade for Indonesia to greatly enhance its national budget expenditures for conservation, tying those costs to the very preconditions propitious to population stabilization early in the next century. The country needs more medical clinics as it prepares to receive the next baby boom. But, according to Pathfinder's Does Sampoerno, the key is *education*. Better teachers are needed, and a government commitment to compulsory secondary school education.

UNFPA says that the majority of Indonesians are in fact already aware of the fertility problem. It's the *access* to medical services that is the issue. According to the BKKBN, the best way to meet the unmet demands for better education and access to medical services, in an effort to lower the country's total fertility rate, and thus its negative ecological impact, will be through that agency's program to dispatch trained midwives to all of Indonesia's sixty-seven thousand villages.

For their part, the World Bank and A.I.D. recognize that without a greater commitment to long-term contraceptives, Indonesia will not be able to further lower its birthrate. That commitment will necessarily involve political inroads to the conservative branches of Islam within the country.

All of these components of the fertility crisis are half the story, of course. An official recognition of the fact that under most Islamic tradition, "ensoulment" does not occur before the beginning of the fourth month of pregnancy, would pave the way for the legalization of abortion. That would significantly reduce the TFR as well, as it has in places like Italy, the Commonwealth of Independent States, South Korea, Germany, and Spain.

Yet, in spite of such gains, the country is going to witness a doubling of its numbers. Sooner or later there will be between 350 and 400 million Indonesians, or, a small village for every individual person that Alfred Wallace encountered. In the planetary sphere of things, such myriad human lives and wants challenge the status quo of tropical Asia's six-hundred-million-year-old wilderness, the Earth's heartland.

In my meetings with M. S. Zulkarnaen, the head of WALHI, he reiterated the urgent need for ten very compelling changes to existing ecological policies in the country. WALHI's published prescriptions are applicable, in fact, to every country with remaining forest. They are:

(1) Base all economic decisions on ecologically sustainable development, determined by local and regional environmental carrying capacity parameters.
(2) Reduce the demand for raw materials by recycling, and through the maximal use of viable fiber residues, normally left by loggers, as well as by increasing the quality and efficiency of the harvesting technology.
(3) Redirect a substantial proportion of all in-country paper production toward educational materials, particularly for those in the Outer Islands where school books, dictionaries, and writing pads are essentially nonexistent.
(4) Integrate local cultures and economies into plantation management.
(5) Substitute the country's excess of agricultural residues for wood fiber. Bagasse sugar cane residues, rice straw, and bamboo are all viable alternatives.
(6) Create community cooperatives owned by the local shareholders.
(7) Involve those communities in all aspects of the decision-making process, such as whether to establish a factory and plantation or not, with a thorough presentation of the ecological pros and cons.
(8) The national government should enforce its existing laws mandating environmental impact assessments.
(9) Phase out all toxins, such as those associated with chlorine bleaching, and implement a law of best-available-technologies for mitigating all pollution.
(10) And finally, establish a system whereby the investor, and the beneficiaries (i.e., consumers in the north) must pay for natural resource depreciation in the south, much in the "polluter pays" and "energy tax" manner. At the same time, northern countries must not be allowed to export any technology that is not at the standard of its own domestic environmental control levels.[51]

I lingered there, above Bandung, sprawled reflectively amidst the heartbreaking splendor of a fertile planet, trying to put myself in the place of those at the highest levels of government who must work with, and transcend, the shortcomings of human nature to effect curative policies. However one might visualize and practice the Zen of conservation and restraint, out beyond, down in the valleys, other human beings were making more noise, chopping down trees, chewing up the land, swarming far more furiously than those few ants which quietly meandered through the hair on my arms. If the fragmentary skulls of prehistoric Java man teach us anything, it is the lesson that while our personal spans are remarkably brief, our footprints, the damage we are capable of, may last forever. That message is, if anything, a challenge each of us must confront.

~5~

The Forgotten Ones: Africa

EVOLUTION AND ADVERSITY

BENEATH 19,340-FOOT Mount Kilimanjaro, the warm, dry dawns are accompanied by a chorus of life forms that have found their voice. Their gait and tempo are as well worked as a pearl, as fixed as amber, even if their population sizes are totally vulnerable to a host of vagaries, normal fluctuations that only recently have been skewed and subjected to shock. Tateva golden weavers busily flit about the dusty, sun drenched acacia thickets, their chattering as involved as any stock exchange. Elephants, who as adults have no natural enemies, sojourn among the yellow-barked fever trees along seasonal marshes and permanent swamps. The water, amid expanses of desert and salt flats, is fed by underground springs from the perpetual snowmelt atop Kili. The elephants sink neck-deep into the rush- and weed-steeped pools, satisfying their herbivorous diets, as do hippos, which rummage and snorkel blissfully. Above ground, churning up the volcanic soils, are thousands of brindled gnu (or blue wildebeest, as they are also called) heading out in massive phalanxes or in single file, toward their favored watering holes that day, along with Grant's and Thomson gazelles, impala, cape buffalo, zebra, and more discrete medleys of hogs, bushbucks, waterbucks, reedbucks, elands, gerenuks, dikdik, addax, oryx, and roan antelope. In all of Kenya there are known to be 314 species of mammals, 1067 species of birds, 191 of reptiles, 88 of amphibians, and 180 of freshwater fish. In Africa, only Zaire has a slightly greater variety of animals, but nowhere near Kenya's migratory density. Newborn Grant's zebras prance delicately, testing their still unpredictable legs and the endurance of their mothers' patience. Giraffes, in small groups, usually less than six, forage on tall *Leguminosae* trees, browsing for twigs and leaves twenty feet in the air.

In a matter of a few hours I witnessed well over forty exotic species—and probably twenty thousand individuals—at Kenya's Amboseli National Park, each of whom, upon even the most cursory observation, can be said confidently to be endowed with often memorable personalities. A family of spotted hyena conferred at dusk around their sandy burrow, father and pups playfully exploring the fringes of their family center. He was extraordinarily indulgent, his pups great charmers aware of their effect on their parents. To see the elephant young nursing, or the Kori bustards, Maribou storks, and cape buffalo commingling, is to recall—in its most basic configuration—the conscience and all that it is capable of dreaming. A similar crescendo of feeling is evoked by, and in, every species, which must share these precious oases and desert blooms, and which, together in seemingly ideal choreographies, meander at intermittent ease. An innate interdependency conjoins this glimmering ballet that suggests a widespread tolerance, even affability, as in the case of a white rhino that had joined a zebra herd, or the various teethcleaning birds that hang around the grinning crocodiles. There are scientific reasons, of course, for such relationships in the wild. But no precise rationale can altogether explain the obvious pleasure egrets exhibit whilst riding through the marshes at an even keel atop the hippos and elephants; or the seeming relish the wildebeest and gazelle, or ostrich and wart hog, take in one another's company. The biophilia, or natural affiliation among different species, may be commensal, biologically mutualistic—a shrewd, even necessary compliance with the fact of a broad, ecological community. Evolution has exploited the wisdom of biophilia. On the plains of East Africa, where the greatest terrestrial mammalian biomass on Earth is concentrated, it has come down to being poignant, emotional, and heartfelt.

Amboseli is the most frequented national park in Africa, with over 208 thousand human/day visits per year. A short flight, or few hours drive southwest of Nairobi, Amboseli elicits that part longing for, part horror of, Nature, and complicates the picture with the advance of *Homo sapiens*. In their wake, what was once pandemic to the African continent has become a mere island of ecological memory, increasingly beleaguered: a glorious, but dangling modifier of another time, lodged pathetically in the twentieth century.

Amboseli was reduced from 3,260 square kilometers to its present 392 square kilometers following protests to the Kenyan government by the dispossessed local Masai tribe. Africa's much-romanticized "warriors" had been forcibly relocated by the English and Germans in the late ninteenth century to the area of Amboseli, only to be relocated again by the newly independent Kenyan government. Outraged by what they deemed to be a gross injustice, their anger augmented by the government's construction of a faulty pipeline intended to compensate the Masai for lost water rights, the tribe slaughtered many endangered rhinos in frustration. The government caved in—the Masai now water their domestic livestock inside the park, which means added pressure on wildlife.

Humans and our ancestral hominids have been cohabiting with other wildlife in East Africa for at least three million years. Some *Homo* species were big meat eaters; others probably were not, such as *Homo habilis,* a contemporary of *Australopithecus boisei, Australopithecus africanus,* and *Homo erectus.*

Meat eating among early *Homo* species is revealed—whether in Africa, China, or Java—by the dietary remains, including at least ninety known species of mammals that they preyed upon. Abetted by the first manipulation and maintenance of fire (whose earliest African evidence, 1.5 million years ago, comes from an ashpit at Chesowanja, near Mount Kenya) this orgy of meat eating probably had a negligible impact on overall population stability among nonhuman life forms.

But in the last few hundred years, as populations in Africa have increased, this bloodletting has demonstrably altered a long preexisting homeostasis of numbers.[1] It is the accelerated, graceless rate of change that is particularly vexatious—that shift, driven by myriad local human population explosions, which exceeds any historical or biological precedent. On the sub-Saharan island of Madagascar, where humans have been settled since the eleventh century, 90 percent of all native vegetation has subsequently been destroyed, as well as sixteen known primates now extinct because of human aggression.

Nowhere is diagnosis of ecological agitation, human discontent, and strategies for coping with contradiction and subversion more urgently needed than in Africa, particularly East Africa, where the collision between rapidly expanding human populations and most other life forms is at a fever pitch. Human fertility in Africa is like a train screaming through the dark night, its headlights turned inward, to paraphrase Boris Pasternak. While the extent of population-induced devastation has been worse in West Africa than probably anywhere else in the world, there is an enormous amount of wildlife yet to lose—and thus, potentially, to save—in East Africa and much of the Central African rain forest countries. Forceful but empathetic African family planning, and a comprehensive nonviolence toward all remaining biodiversity on that continent, are, without doubt, among the most serious tasks confronting twenty-first-century humanity. It is a summons to the whole world. The plenitude of wildlife is not the only locus of pain and obliteration: human children are the other innocent victims. Children who are "led on" by all that being human means—to believe and trust in the aptitude and stewardship of their parents and the adult community, only to discover, too frequently, that such faith is premature.

Twelve percent of the world's population lives in Africa. That proportion will expand to beyond 16 percent of the world total by the year 2025.[2] Africa's mean total fertility rate (TFR) is over six, currently resulting in twenty-one million innocent newborns each year. That annual increment will continue to rise. Africa's population density of twenty-one per square kilometer equals that of Latin America, but compares favorably with the Middle East (twenty-nine per square kilometer) and Asia, and the Pacific Rim (each 113 per square kilometer). But that density masks the extreme competition for scarce resources around lush mountain areas, forests, lakes, water holes, and coastal regions, which serve as magnets not only for human consumers, but other wildlife as well. Eighty percent of Kenyans, and 50 percent of their livestock, dwell on some 20 percent of available agricultural lands, a ratio about equal to that existing on the whole planet. Outside these regions, other arid land is being "marginalized" as Kenya adds more than one million residents each year, and the fast-growing population seeks out new territory to plow, deforest, and graze upon. The real problem is that some 95 percent of all Kenya Wildlife Service–protected reserves, such as Amboseli, lie in those very outer areas (keeping in mind that the animals have already been repeatedly evicted from one location after another for well over a century), thus posing inevitable daily pressures on the already declining genetic stocks of wildlife. There are well over one million pastoralists in Kenya, each household, on average, possessing about one hundred sheep, goats, camels, and cattle. The pastoralist tribes, like those of the Rendille, the Samburu, Gabbra, Boran, and Turkana, are competing for space with a tidal wave of more sedentary farmers. As arable land vanishes, the competition gets worse, and wildlife—and its habitat—is the ultimate loser.[3] The patchwork nature of human survival almost guarantees that whatever remaining crucial migration corridors for animals exist will be rapidly infiltrated and destroyed, leaving the official reserves as isolated islands cut off from the rest of Africa, from migratory genes that might otherwise revivify dwindling populations.[4]

Average densities also fail to account for the rapid urbanization of Africa—24 percent to 31 percent in just fifteen years—with countless expanding slum populations, and the increased spread of diseases. By 2025, 56 percent, or 763 million people, of Africa is projected to be urban.[5] In sub-Saharan Africa, six women are becoming infected with AIDS for every five men. The Kenyan minister of health has predicted that every hospital bed in Kenya will be needed for the many AIDS victims in the year 2000. And yet, in spite of AIDS, malaria, TB, hunger, and wars, the population will triple across Africa by the year 2025. Everything about such calamities will have a *negative* impact on family planning, and on twenty-five years of efforts by the governments and NGOs to bring down child, infant, and maternal mortality.

At present, life expectancy on the continent has been elevated to an average of 51.4 years for males, 54.6 for females (much less in many African countries), but that figure will fall as AIDS takes its toll. And as it drops, more and more women will have more and more children to compensate. As it is, Africa's contraceptive prevalence rate (CPR) as of mid-1994 was a mere 4 percent, the lowest by far in the world.[6]

It has been estimated that for every 10 percent increase in the CPR, the fertility rate declines by 0.62, meaning that fertility replacement—or approximately 2.3 children per couple—requires about a 75 percent

CPR. That means seventy-one additional percentile points yet to be achieved across Africa.[7] Unfortunately, as Thomas Goliber has pointed out, a slightly increased CPR in a few African countries, like Zaire, has not pushed down the TFR (total fertility rate) but merely heightened "the decline in postpartum abstinence," thus increasing "the time a woman is at risk of pregnancy and inevitably the fertility rate as well." In essence, then, the traditional tribal and Islamic two-year abstinence between births has been diminished with the slight advent of contraceptives, but not the number of children or desired family size. And thus, concludes Goliber, "at the outset of Africa's transition from high to lower fertility, there is no direct connection between contraceptive prevalence and fertility. As family planning programs expand in Africa, they are not necessarily going to result in immediate fertility decline; indeed, fertility may actually rise in the short term."[8] There is no other situation quite like that anywhere in the world.

The paradox is a gripping one: if the African TFR remains at six for just two more years (until 2000), it is almost guaranteed that by the year 2045 there will be 2.1 billion sub-Saharan Africans and an additional 250 million North Africans, many undernourished. The stress and civil unrest of population-induced problems is already being felt across North Africa, from the Sudan to Algeria. If by some miracle, a TFR of 5.2 were achieved by the year 2000, there would be several hundred million fewer people throughout Africa by the year 2045. A TFR of four—the short-term goal of Kenya—would mean nine hundred million less persons in 2045.[9]

In all Africa, only Zimbabwe, Botswana, Mauritius, and Kenya have achieved high CPRs, though the figures are taken from married women, not those unmarried, with the exception of Kenya—43 percent in Zimbabwe, 33 percent in Botswana and Kenya. Only the remote island of Mauritius has managed to achieve a high CPR (by international standards) of 75 percent. But Mauritius is anomalous, statistically minute. And even its population of just over a million has exceeded the carrying capacity of the island, in a manner less discussed, less dramatic, but no less unfortunate than the crisis in Madagascar to the west.[10]

As for Zimbabwe, Botswana, and Kenya, many of those who study these trends have already perceived that a plateau may have been reached, beyond which CPR is unlikely to increase, or TFR to decrease. Modern methods of birth control are frowned upon throughout Africa, and many are unaffordable. Condoms are used to fight AIDS in some cities, but not for birth control; social marketing is new and, as yet, unproven. And while more and more women are indicating their uneasiness with large families, in most African nations, with the exception of Kenya, the global recession and increased poverty is enhancing the perceived economic value of more young ones. Indeed, 7 percent of African governments have declared their growth to be "too low," and at least half of all African nations oppose any family planning intervention.[11] This policy inertia is economic in nature, motivated by the male-dominated laws of inheritance, the lack of social welfare, and the self-perpetuating tyrannies of poverty, whose primary victims are women, their many children, and all of Africa's unique biodiversity.

THE EAST AFRICAN CONUNDRUM: KENYA

UNITED NATIONS PROJECTIONS for the fourteen-nation region of East Africa—with its 6.5 TFR—range from a low variant of 476 million, to a constant fertility rate of 674 million in the year 2025.[12] More than 80 percent of all those people are rural, usually in direct competition with wildlife for fast dwindling resources, a situation that is most pronounced in Kenya, where 85 percent of rural households fall below the poverty line (below fifty dollars per year). The total income generated domestically by 450 million sub-Saharan Africans is less than that of Belgium, with its 11 million residents. At least twenty sub-Saharan countries now face food emergencies, yet the annual food deficit is predicted to spiral downward fifteen times below even its current debacle. It used to cost a Kenyan one shilling for salt each month. Now the cost is fourteen shillings. The government used to pay all school costs, but now it can afford very little.

The high literacy rate for which Kenya was famed all over Africa is now slipping steadily just at the time when the country needs it most. The importance of such deterioration to family planners is clear: in Kenya married women with at least some secondary education are three times more likely to use a modern method of birth control than those with no formal education.[13] Life expectancy in Kenya has attained virtually the highest level in all of Africa, fifty-nine—up from a mere thirty-five in 1948—and the infant mortality rate (IMR) is less than seventy per thousand, as compared with 262 in 1962. But these figures are also bound to slip downward as the economic crisis continues to worsen. Already, the IMR appears to be going up in the slums and the poorest provinces.

When I asked one still young-looking Masai father at Ekongu Narok Manyatta village how he expected to feed and care for his two wives and eight children, he smiled and dismissed my alarm by referring to a much-lauded government minister from his tribe who has eighty-four children by four wives. There is no limit to the number of wives a man can have. Male TFRs are never discussed in family planning literature. Like most of Africa, Kenya is polygynous. I walked with one Masai herder and two of his children one day beneath Mount Kili and we discussed family planning. He said, "Maybe when the Masai add another million or so, then we'll start talking about family planning." His primary concern was that a man must have children because, as he stated emphatically, "When you're dead you're dead."

Meanwhile, the growth rate in Kenya overall had risen slightly from 3.6 percent in the 1980s to 3.7 percent in 1990, one of the fastest growth rates in the world.

The same graceful and prolific Masai father of eight complained to me that his wives and many children were not the problem, but rather the prohibitive costs for their health and education. How then, given such decomposing economics (and local interpretations of bad times), do family planners reasonably expect to meet targets in Kenya that include reducing population growth rate to 2.5 percent per year and increasing the CPR to 40 percent by the year 2000? To increase the number of Norplant users from fifty-four hundred to twenty-four thousand, and birth control pill acceptors from 217 thousand to 320 thousand. Where will the money come from?[14]

Eight children by two wives is actually a restrained family size for Kenya, where the average TFR is closer to 5.4 children per wife, 10.8 for two, down from 6.7 (or 13.4 per two wives) just eight years ago, if one accepts the most recent 1993 Kenya Demographic and Health Survey (KDHS).[15] That survey declared the new 5.4 TFR to be the continuing result of "one of the most precipitous declines in fertility ever recorded."

In addition to the 20 percent decline in fertility (5 percent per year since 1989), several other encouraging facts emerged in the Kenya Demographic and Health Survey with regard to CPR, male and female awareness of family planning, preferred family norms, prenatal care, and President Moi's personal commitment to family planning.

There are some within family planning circles who believe that these new trends in Kenya are actually the result not of a particular slogan or outreach effort, but of diminishing per capita income.[16] Once the economy begins to flourish again, nobody knows whether the TFR will also rise, as it has in China, Costa Rica, Singapore, and elsewhere. Does international largesse toward Kenya, and the rest of Africa, engender long-term stability or simply induce a dependency that perpetuates the fertility crisis? Are there scenarios according to which poverty is best suited toward accomplishing population control, or is economic prosperity essential? Third World governments have argued for decades that the best form of birth control was wealth. But in Kenya, poverty is pushing down the TFR. At the same time, NGOs and multilateral organizations are trying desperately to conceive of ways to help wean governments like Kenya off donor assistance. Unfortunately these efforts are occurring at the very moment that the country is economically on its knees. To move Kenya from mere awareness to action, and to discover ways in which to link population programs to environmental restoration in recessionary times, is indeed a challenge.

But from the family planning perspective, Kenya has enormous promise for holding back total tragedy. The signs are extremely positive. It is important to realize that family planning began in Kenya when there were five million people, not three hundred million as in India. While still characterized by a high TFR and percentage of growth, the country seems to be making unprecedented strides to curb a runaway population boom. That's the positive side.

But there is discouraging news as well: in spite of the fact that there are currently some 154 separate projects in Kenya addressing population concerns, the population is expected to double (again) in eighteen years or less.[17] Part of the problem is Kenya's enormous population momentum, with 60 percent of the country under the age of fifteen. By the year 2025, there will be nearly 61 million Kenyans; by 2050, 86.5 million. And, according to the World Bank assessment of recent trends, Kenya's population in the year 2150 could be over 112 million, or more than four times its current size.[18] Moreover, if the KDHS is overly optimistic (as some officials have suggested) and the TFR is actually higher than stated, or it should begin to rise, the U.N. "constant fertility variant" for the year 2025 shows 94,409,000 Kenyans.[19] The country's *official* doubling time is twenty-seven years.

Now add to these ill-boding premonitions the debilitating influence of Catholicism, which dominates some 25 percent of the nation and has attempted to demolish most family planning efforts in the country. While

Kenyan NGOs attempt to circumvent Catholic-dominated policies regarding sex, the country lacks any official policy concerning high-risk adolescents, despite the fact it is understood that the secondary school ratio of 144 boys to 100 girls is, in part, directly atttributable to the high dropout rate for girls due to early pregnancies.[20]

Family planning has failed the youth in Kenya. While the legal age of marriage is sixteen for girls—eighteen for boys—in places like Kilifi on the coast, girls are getting married at the age of nine. The country meanwhile is expanding at a rate of a million a year. Abortion is encoded in the legal system as a criminal offence in Kenya; a woman and her doctor go to prison if they are caught. Still, there are at least twelve abortions performed every day of the year just at one hospital in downtown Nairobi. Those women who don't make it to a hospital (most do not) endure the high probability of death during a botched procedure.

Already, with some twenty-nine million people in the country, 30 percent of the population is undernourished. Agricultural production is dropping, desertification on the rise, the demand for fuelwood and charcoal, 73 percent of all energy supplies in Kenya, is now three times that which is available. Accelerated poverty is already beginning to nullify the very triumphs recorded in the 1993 KDHS. Out beyond the city of Nairobi, in the Dagoretti Constituency, the TFR is eight in a population base of two hundred thousand. Whatever inroads had been accomplished to help control maternal and infant mortality in an effort to bring down the fertility are fast disappearing.

"We don't know what is going to happen," says Mrs. Leonola, who trains volunteers out of the Chandaria Health Center in Dagoretti. "We regard porridge for lunch as the single meal every twenty-four hours. It's at least enough to get the children through the night," she says. "So they can sleep a little. There is simply no food, no money, no jobs. We're defeated." Money in Africa is everything: fertility control, sustainable development, and the ability to sleep at night. Neither cultural norms nor indigenous wisdom seems capable of surmounting the daunting obstacle of persistent poverty here.

But perhaps the most disturbing report of the impact of recent economic hard times on family planning services comes from the region of Mount Kenya, a lush tropical highland fed by glacial streams. On the mountain's eastern slopes, 120 miles north of Nairobi in the Tharaka-Nithi District, Chogoria hospital is still considered the busiest and best family planning clinic in all of Africa, serving a population base of four hundred thousand people.[21] As of 1985, the CPR in the region was 42.5 percent, the TFR 5.2, and IMR about 50—at least a decade ahead of the rest of the country. Moreover 34 percent of those in the Chogoria catchment area were using modern contraceptive methods. (At that time there was only a 1 percent usage throughout the rest of Kenya.)[22] Since 1985 statistics at Chogoria have gotten even better. The key explanation seems to hinge upon four critical strategies: community involvement, including community leaders who themselves pass out supplies; dependable service and provisions; integration of primary health care and family planning; and a thorough system of monitoring.[23] Today, CPR in and around Chogoria are the highest for all of rural sub-Saharan Africa, over 54 percent. But there are terrible changes in the wind.

The collapse of tea and coffee prices has shocked the system. The government gives Chogoria hospital no subsidies. Clients pay for services, though at a minimal rate. But worsening inflation, the escalating cost of education, the loss of government jobs, and the continued marginalization of lands, have had a chilling effect on the Chogoria hospital program, and on demographics in general. Landless women are particularly hard hit. Many have wandered into cities like Embu and Nairobi, which has driven up the HIV seropositivity among such migrants.[24] Five to ten percent of all adults in Kenya are now estimated to be HIV positive.

"We are broke," was the constant refrain I heard from hospital staffers. Locals simply cannot continue to afford to pay for services, and the hospital is finding it difficult to pay for its staff.

Thirty minutes away from the hospital, in the village of Gaatia, one of Chogoria's sublocations, I sat with thirty-three traditional birth attendants who described their current difficulties. They have no kits, neither sterile gauze nor razors, neither scissors nor medicine, no pain killers, nothing. They have virtually no money.[25] They cut umbilical cords with sharp stones or the edges of banana leaves. And without money, or any kind of communal self-help, or government assistance, Chogoria hospital can do less and less to support the very midwives it has trained; neither can it protect mothers or children. Money well spent toward inhibiting more children in a place like Gaatia would mean the difference between contraception and desperation. That difference would directly connect to the fact that Gaatians, and others like them throughout Africa, throughout the world, are compelled to kill off other life forms in search of food, shelter, and economic breathing space.

The superficial Eden that is Gaatia haunts the nation precisely because there are already too many people, and insufficient white maize, wheat, millet, sorghum, rice, pulses, starchy roots, tubers, and milk (the main diet in Kenya, along with a heavy preponderance of meat) to feed them. Micro- and macroeconomic analysis of the nutritional carrying capacity, energy intensity, and future productivities, however interpreted, fails to reconcile nearly thirty million Kenyans.[26] While nature in East Africa has not changed in millions of years—evolution, adhering to its biological code of ethics—suddenly, in the course of one century, the populations of heavily consumptive *Homo sapiens* in East Africa have exploded.

The dynamics of boom and bust, as described earlier, whether among lemmings or deer, hares or locusts, dinosaurs or butterflies, always leave— as in the ecology of fire—an aftermath of splendid resurrection and realignment. Only one species, *Homo sapiens,* has flatly disrupted this biology of reincarnation, the ratios of predator to prey, the recycling of nutrients, the balancing of populations. Humankind's own personal will- fulness has violated the karma of whole ecosystems. If some greater law, or destiny, has ordained such wholesale carnage, then more than likely, what I call the small claims courts of human ethics—our feeble laws and meritorious treaties—are unlikely to alter cosmic necessity. But if, as many today believe, there are solid grounds for an alternative future, then what is occurring in Africa must be viewed as but one more horrendous battle- ground in this criminal and useless global war. The combatants are des- perate, the stakes as high as anywhere on the planet.

One way to gauge the dimensions of this war and of our species' popu- lation overshoot in Africa is by considering the needs of other carnivores (which, with the exception of leopards, lions, and crocodiles, are smaller than those of man). Five hundred cheetahs (the suggested absolute mini- mum number needed to sustain the genetic population of any local group of carnivores, and a tenuous number at best) require thirty thousand square kilometers of unencumbered habitat; five hundred lions, 6250 square kilo- meters; five hundred leopards, 12,500 square kilometers; five hundred spot- ted hyaenas, 3333 square kilometers and five hundred wild dogs, 100 thou- sand square kilometers.[27] Now, consider that the total amount of preserved land in all of Kenya is a little more than thirty-one thousand square kilo- meters. Tanzania has about one hundred thousand square kilometers, Uganda a mere thirteen thousand square kilometers. Tanzania's Serengeti, which is connected to Kenya's Masai Mara (for a total of thirty thousand square kilometers) is the only area left in all of Africa that can be said to contain a sizable constituency of mammals—an estimated one and a half million wildebeest, 250 thousand zebra, 500 thousand gazelles, and several thousand predators, for a total population on a par with human Nairobi.[28] Those proportions in the wild are indicative of the carrying (and caring) capacity of the natural world. Only a very small number (relatively speaking) of predators can be accommodated. Forgetting, for a moment, the technology of human carnage, which has completely eclipsed the evolutionary rules of behavior on the killing fields of Africa, there is simply no way to incorporate the nearly seventy million human carnivores of Kenya, Uganda, and Tanzania in just those three biodiverse, politically defined regions. Mass starvation, habitat destruction, and extinctions of other life forms are inevitable. Now add the fires of deforestation, the greatly shortened fallow periods, the poacher's machine gun, and the full scope of the ecological holocaust emerges.

The end result is a dark tunnel of human appropriation, a meteorite shower of consumption, unchoreographed, propelled by short-term exigencies. Caught up haplessly in this peppering of many conflicts is all of nonhuman Africa.

Poaching is escalating throughout Africa. In 1970 the continent's black rhino population stood at sixty-five thousand. In some countries, inventories of carcass-to-live-elephant ratios define the very terms of coming extinction for the pachyderms.[29] As of 1997 the moratorium on the sale of elephant tusks in three countries was lifted under a new CITES compromise ruling, a hotly debated decision to hinge compassion and ethics upon economics—a heavy blow to conservation in Africa. According to Dr. Michael Fox, a vice president of the Humane Society of the United States, behind "a facade of concern for wildlife" that has "lured funds from non-African nations, for supposed conservation programs," there is abundant "documented evidence of the mass slaughter of wildlife—including animals belonging to threatened and endangered species—by wealthy safari hunters and even local government officials."[30] Dehorning of rhinos, culling of elephant herds for meat, and other methods of so-called biodiversity control have transformed parks like those of South Africa's Kruger into government abbatoirs.[31] Only the Kenya Wildlife Service (KWS) remains determined to stop poaching, and has built up an antipoaching air force of eleven planes. Rejecting killing-as-management, the KWS sees controlled ecotourism as the only ethical and ecological way to finance conservation, a methodology that is at best imperfect but far more ethical than its alternatives. But the KWS also recognizes that "the future prospects for wildlife are undoubtedly partly dependent on the success the government may have in bringing population growth under control."[32]

Kenyan parks constitute approximately 6 percent of the total land area of the country (where, as stated, an estimated 50 percent of all remaining wildlife reside). Of course, the percentages are inexact, considering the nature of animal movement and migration. What is more precise is the fact that Kenyan population growth, with all that it implies, is rapidly shrinking the available territory for all species. While most "official" poaching has ceased for the time being, the increasingly severe economic times will force more and more of those Kenyans in rural areas to hunt for their dinner. The regions surrounding Nairobi, the Rift Valley, the lakes of Naivasha, Victoria, and Nakuru are all under siege. Southwest of Nairobi, along the coast, the last forests are threatened by developers determined to clear the "bush" and put up high-rise hotels.[33]

Most subdivision occurs without environmental impactment or appropriate land use consideration, purely haphazardly, for profit, or for the perceived survival needs of locals. As farming belts are divided into thousands of small plots (a predictable fragmentation equation based upon high TFR's and inheritance patterns), landholding sizes diminish, fallow periods cease, the soil is depleted, water tables vanish, and hunger for humans and all other life forms increases.[34] With such stress comes competition, particularly between farmers and elephants.[35] The KWS and Ministry of Tourism and Wildlife are struggling with blueprints for survival that encompass both species.[36] And it is worth remembering that while humans have massacred over 146 thousand elephants in Kenya in the last twenty years, elephants have only killed between sixty and eighty humans, in nearly all cases by accident, or having first been provoked.

Pressured by rising conflicts, officials are considering methods of elephant "family planning" so as to prevent any harsher "solutions" being proposed in the future, along lines taken in countries like Zimbabwe. Such fertility regulation has already been undertaken elsewhere in the world with many other species, such as white-tailed deer, elephant seals, and, of course, cats and dogs. In the case of the elephant, the KWS is examining the use of RU-486 embedded in fruit, of exogenous progestin, steroidal hormones, and immunocontraception. Delivery of the last three would be by darts shot into the elephants' muscle tissue. Techniques that induce abortion, or sterility, in a percentage of females, are also being considered.[37]

The suggestion that family planning be implemented among the pachyderms (albeit, mercifully), a species that has already been devastated by *Homo sapiens,* points out the degree to which the human war against nature in East Africa has escalated. It would be like saying, give one group of combatants birth control pills so that their enemies will have fewer of them to kill. But this is precisely the ethical conundrum confronting every human being, burning activist and bewildered armchair conservationist alike.

VICIOUS SPIRALS

HOWEVER PROBLEMATIC THE conflicts between overpopulation and the environment in Kenya, elsewhere in Africa they are even worse. Africa replaced Europe as the second most populated region in the world as of 1992, with over 680 million residents. But in the year 2025, the continent's projected population ranges from a low variant of 1 billion, to the unlikely possibility of a constant fertility variant of 2.1 billion. The median projection by the U.N. is 1.58 billion for the year 2025.

Throughout Africa populations are growing at about 3 percent per year, despite the highest death rates in the world—fifteen to eighteen per thousand. Life expectancy in nearly half of all African nations is under fifty, a benchmark, according to demographers, for projecting any kind of positive inroads that might be effected by family planning. Keep in mind that death rate data does not include infant mortality rates. An IMR below seventy has been discerned to be key to resolving the fear of family extinction. However, throughout most of sub-Saharan Africa, the IMR is 120 per thousand (versus ten in the U.S. and six in Sweden). In most countries of the world, the IMR (which pertains to the first twelve months of life) is deemed the critical hurdle: if the child can survive its first year, his or her chances of making it past five are excellent. This is not true in Africa, where a child has the same likelihood of dying within four years as during those first twelve months. Even in cases where infant or child mortality rates have declined (as in Kenya), the persistence of low life expectancy will inevitably supersede any "awareness" of contraception. The innate compulsion to perpetuate a family will not obey slogans handed out by bureaucrats recommending small families. In several sub-Saharan countries, the preferred family norm (PFN) is nearly nine children, more than the existing total fertility rates. The percentage of use of modern methods of birth control in

Mauritania is 0.0. In addition, while the number of students enrolled in both primary and secondary school has increased markedly in many African countries over the past twenty-five years, in some nations—the Central African Republic, Malawi, Lesotho, Tanzania, Somalia, Kenya, and Mali—it has actually declined.

At least 75 percent of all chronic and acute hunger on the planet (more severe conditions than mere malnutrition or iron-deficient anemia) is to be found in sub-Saharan Africa and South Asia. But only in Africa are tens of millions of people faced with actual imminent death. Those in the "hunger business" claim that 36 percent of the developing world was deemed chronically undernourished in 1970, compared with what is alleged to be 20 percent today. However, computing approximate population growth since 1970, the numbers of afflicted turn out to be about the same, and the majority are Africans.

Africa comprises 20 percent of the land surface of the planet. Most of the continent is plagued with drought and desertification. The U.N. Food and Agriculture Organization in 1982 stated that there was sufficient cultivable land across the continent to feed 940 million people, without any fertilizers or conservation effort. Yet, by 1975 half of all sub-Saharan populations, inhabiting a third of the land area, were losing the battle to maintain food self-sufficiency, and today they lack the cash liquidity or even credit to import food to stave off chronic malnourishment. "There were some exceptions," says the World Bank, "but sub-Saharan Africa has now witnessed a decade of falling per capita incomes, increasing hunger, and accelerating ecological degradation. The earlier progress in social development is now being eroded. Overall, Africans are almost as poor today as they were thirty years ago." According to the World Bank, if Africa is to avert total starvation its economies need to grow by at least 4 to 5 percent a year as a minimum target; and the target growth for industry should actually go to 7 to 8 percent a year. Nothing like that is taking place; in fact, the economic growth is declining, not increasing.[38]

In Nigeria, an early oil bonanza utterly undermined population control programs in the country by providing a false sense of economic security. When oil prices fell away, however, the government panicked and vowed to achieve a TFR of 4.0 by the year 2000, as in Kenya. In actual fact, Nigeria is likely to become the third largest country in the world by the middle of the twenty-first century, with a population greater than in all of Africa in 1984. There are 3.6 million Nigerians born every year. Currently, the population exceeds 109 million people, with a TFR of more than 6.2.[39]

With the exception of Zimbabwe, Botswana, Kenya, and a small region of southern Nigeria—consisting of thirty million people[40]—as well as in a few local areas of Togo, Cameroon, and Senegal, such blatant conflicts appear inherent to sub-Saharan Africa, where the contraceptive prevalence rate is below 5 percent, and where a woman has 1 in 21 chance of dying from pregnancy, versus a 1 in 6,366 chance in the U.S. If fertility is such a roulette game for the African mother, why does she persist? The answer has as much to do with the psychology of poverty as it does with male oppression. Ancestor worship, the economics of fertility descent, polygyny—which affects nearly half of all African marriages—separation in the male's mind of "reproductive decisions and the cost of child raising," weak political initiatives in the family planning arena, the absence of sex education in schools, the inaccessibility of contraceptives for young people, the woman's inability, or fear, to take the lead in contraceptive use, and the African bias against modern contraceptives, have all contributed to this low CPR.[41] Such human demographics, translated into population pressure on natural resources, have devastated the ecology of Africa. In countries like Brazil and Indonesia, approximately ten tropical trees are burned or cut down for each one replanted, a disastrous ratio. But in Africa the ratio is twenty-nine to one! In every African nation where forests remain, the conflict is readily observed.

Half of Tanzania is expected to be desert by the year 2000. All its natural forests will vanish by 2015.[42] Across the seven tropical forest countries of Central and West Africa (the second largest contiguous moist tropical forest region in the world), inappropriate macroeconomic policies, and rapid population growth, economic downturns, total forest-based economies, weak and corrupt management, and administration incapacity are causing deforestation rates to increase violently.[43] In Zaire, one million square kilometers of closed forest are often cited as the current remaining amount; however, as in Indonesia, there are vast discrepancies in data. The IUCN suggests that half that much remains. But since the demise of the dictator Mbuto in 1997 (who, for all his other faults, inhibited most development in the forests), even those remaining forests have been targeted for exploitation. From Equatorial Guinea to Gabon, the numbers are ghastly. In the Cote d'Ivoire, with a population growth rate of an astronomical 4.6 percent between 1965 and 1985, 95 percent of all tropical rain forest (140 thousand square kilometers) has been burned or cleared, the result of shifting cultivators. Less than ten thousand square kilometers of forest are still standing.

Beyond the rain forests to the west, Africa's woes multiply even faster. In Nigeria the last black rhinos were exterminated at least fifty years ago, and countless other large mammals are also gone. Even nonhuman scavengers, such as jackals, are now threatened with extinction. In the local dialect of Hausa, *nama* means both animal and meat, a perceptual bias ingrained in the nomenclature of biodiversity loss. In March of 1978, when author Peter Matthiessen traveled through Senegal and Cote d'lvoire, he reported that there were an estimated four million muzzle loader rifles used for hunting meat in the back country of those regions.[44] Increasingly, rural Africans are killing whatever they can. The situation is grimmest in the seventeen countries of West Africa, which currently host some 275 million human residents. And that number is expected to reach 925 million by the year 2050, and 1.36 billion in the year 2150.

Sub-Saharan Africa presents a biological enclave of desperate proportions. "If no measures are taken," the minister of environment for Mali told me in a calm voice, "it will be a catastrophe."

The Case of Mali

In a survey of three Malian villages in 1991, a traditional plant classification system was discovered. Malian healers have detailed knowledge of sixty-seven pharmaceutical species, but none would share contraceptive recipes for fear of competition (much like the great chefs of Tokyo).[45] This is not a climate conducive to birth-control policies. Life expectancy has improved from a mere thirty-five in 1960 to forty-seven in 1998. But this has meant, of course, a surge in population.[46] Current TFR is 6.7. The country's population of just over ten million will double in a little more than twenty years.

In Mali, 50 percent of all women who die do so during or just after childbirth. Abortion is illegal. Teenage pregnancy is at epidemic proportions. Only 11 percent of all adult women, and 27 percent of the men, are literate, yet school enrollment of any kind remains sadly stagnant: 19 percent for girls, 38 percent for boys. Girls are, routinely, forcibly circumcised so as to prevent their enjoyment of sex, prior to being married off—often into polygynous unions—by the time they are fifteen, if not younger. Gender equality, favored by the Companions of the Prophet, and by Muhammad himself, has been reinterpreted in Mali and surrounding countries, such that women must obtain their husbands' consent to use contraception, and are discriminated against by inheritance laws.[47] Estimates for mean per capita income vary from $210 to $270, placing it among the nine poorest countries in Africa, along with Burkina Faso, Tanzania, Mozambique, Malawi, Guinea–Bissau, Zaire, Chad, and Ethiopia.

Incredibly, a French colonial law prohibiting family planning is still in effect in the country. However, the government of Mali insists that it intends to increase the CPR from a current 7 percent to an astonishingly hopeful 60 percent in the year 2020, though UNFPA finds such optimism less than plausible. In fact, the UNFPA in Mali acknowledges six different sets of conflicting demographic data. As in the case of donor decisions pertaining to the refurbishing of Mali's beleaguered Boucle de Baoule National Park, so too, human health and human ecology are the victims of international triage in a country like Mali. There is only so much donor money to go around. Many find it easier to simply "write off" sub-Saharan Africa. Even traditional "planned giving" now views charity as the perpetuation of dependency; a perspective which holds, in addition, that dependents—trusting to the outside world for their allowance—will feel comfortable maintaining a high fertility rate.[48]

But for those donors who are actually targeting their money, their labors, and their professional idealism, in countries like Mali there is no ambivalence, no confusion: these are not donations, but lifesaving transfusions. As one foreign official told me, "We're doing this for individuals, not for principles."

One of the most exciting of these initiatives—a true reason for hope in West Africa—is the Katibougou Family Health Project, funded by the Centre for Development and Population Activities. Since 1986 this program has provided community-based distribution of contraceptives in rural areas of Mali. The contraceptive prevalence rate in those regions covered (nineteen villages, fourteen thousand people) went from 0 to 57 percent! This suggests a remarkable unmet need that one presumes could easily span the whole sub-Sahara, if there were sensitive financial targeting by agencies.

UNFPA maintains the largest platter of population projects in the country. Its overall goal is to bring down the TFR to about 3.5 by the year 2020, which would mean a million less people in the country at that time. Of course, since most government ministers themselves have three or four wives, and five children by each, UNFPA—hoping the government will set an example—is going to have its work cut out for it.[49]

SOLUTIONS

WHETHER IN EAST or West Africa, antidotes to the population crisis have been set forth by many experts. There is little mystery about the methods, only frustration enshrouding their execution.

In Kenya, for example, the thrust of UNFPA's program hinges upon "achieving future increases in the contraceptive prevalence rate," which it says "will depend upon creating specific messages to fill identified information gaps, in addition to improving upon the quality and coverage of family planning services."[50] In achieving these messages, UNFPA would conduct research into the "wide gap between knowledge and use of family planning," the awareness threshold that is proving so difficult to define, worldwide. In Kenya, 96 percent of all women (married and unmarried, from age fifteen to forty-nine) have evidently "heard of" at least some method of contraception, be it traditional or modern. And while 89.8 percent of all women know where to get pills, only 9.6 percent of them actually do so. Awareness is slowly closing the gap, at the rate of about 2.25 percent per year of increased usage, but UNFPA obviously wants to speed it up. Among men, the awareness gap concerning condoms is smaller (99 percent awareness, 54.8 percent current practice), yet it is unknown to what extent these same men were actually using condoms with women other than their wives, to avoid contacting an STD, rather than to prevent pregnancies. Furthermore, only 38 percent of all married men indicated they wanted no more children, compared with 46 percent of the women, further suggesting a large discrepancy in the awareness factor among men.[51] Closing the discrepancies between awareness and action presents the greatest challenge facing family planners.

In the Kariobangi slum of Nairobi, I walked with Alice Githaes, a nurse who has started her own family planning clinic for the poor. She had borrowed twenty-seven thousand Kenyan shillings (about one thousand dollars at the time) from her former cooperative, leased a small office, installed four beds, worked nights, and raised funds for drugs. Nearly eighty patients can now be accommodated. Equipped with a surgical theater, her clinic has literally provided a medical mecca in Kariobangi. Over twenty thousand people visit Alice every year. She offers free sterilizations (though it is not unusual in any one year for nearly all sterilizations to be among women—the men have said "No," a typical dilemma across Africa). Birth control pills cost thirty cents each, a Norplant insertion, roughly $4.25, if the patients can afford it. If not, she provides the service anyway. When Alice came to this slum in 1969, everyone was having eight to ten children. You still find up to seven, but not ten. Outside her door hangs a condom dispenser. They are free for the taking. Her annual budget is thirty thousand. Alice has a big heart, and a generous hug for everyone. She is precisely the sort of person to break the crisis of confidence throughout Africa, that pessimism which so easily breeds self-fulfilling defeat.[52]

Family planners all know many such "Alices," women who are, in fact, closing that awareness/action gap. They lighten an otherwise overwhelming horizon, in Africa and elsewhere, and remind family planners and the whole community of demographers and health workers what it is their profession is all about.

Indeed, to repeat, family planners know what needs to be done. They have urged host governments to maintain vigilance regarding the type and quality of contraceptives; to increase sensitive counseling, examinations, follow-ups, and the implementation of national programs for community-based distribution of the contraceptives; they have emphasized working with NGOs and establishing clinics like Alice's that are solely devoted to fertility control; and they have experimented with countless methods of popularizing family planning. But all of these essential components evaporate, ultimately, if women themselves—who consistently bear the brunt of responsibility for population control—are not free: free to be educated beyond primary school, free to work at the job they choose, free to find happiness, dignity, and love. That freedom is not solely dependent upon money, of course. But money helps. It surely does. Alice could not, and would not, have started her clinic in Nairobi's slums, I suspect, without her initial one thousand dollar loan. And, in Zimbabwe, the government could not have increased the distribution of condoms from half a million in 1986 to sixty-five million in 1992—which in turn tripled CPR from 14 to 43 percent—without foreign assistance.

And yet, by itself—as I have been arguing throughout this book—family planning is not enough. The rise of contraceptive prevalence in Zimbabwe has not deterred poaching and culling of wildlife in that country, and there is no reason to believe that it would have done so in Kenya without Richard Leakey's inspired efforts initially at the helm of the Kenya Wildlife Service. Nor has the partial CITES ban on ivory trade deflected the Asian obsession with ivory amulets and other animal-derived aphrodisiacs.

In southwestern Madagascar, it was a group of biologists concerned with the fate of three rare primate species which resulted in Ramomafana, one of the very few "sustainable parks" in all of Africa. But again, money was needed from the outside world. Inaugurated in 1991, Madagascar's fourth national park now supports a village-based economy ensuring dignified employment and nonimpactful labor beekeeping, local gardens, rice paddies, the cultivation of endemic trees and fruit-bearing trees rather than eucalyptus and pine, the offering of park-related careers to the locals, the building of kilns and making of locally stamped ceramics, and the founding of women's cooperatives. In addition, the park consortium is providing training to a new generation of local biodiversity systematists. And finally, strong health and family planning elements have been woven into the overall delivery system.[53]

In Mali there is an enormous potential for such parks. For example, the last remaining northern chimpanzees and elephants of that country—if they can be rescued soon enough—would be of enormous interest to tourists.[54] In addition, the birds and butterflies of Mali even right outside Bamako at the Montes Mandingues Foret Classee have much to offer visitors, as do the shores of Lake Selingue, the islets of Gao, and the region of Lake Faguibine.[55]

But in truth, most of Africa's wildlife have been forgotten by the rest of the world, regardless of the jubilant tour packages and glossy nature documentaries on television. Unless biodiversity concerns become the focus of all long-term economic strategies (whether the funding comes from other missions or multilateral banks such as the African Development Bank, the IMF, or the World Bank), a country like Mali's future is grim. Again, money and vision are the keys. Local conflicts over natural resources require enlightened resolution that will ensure social justice for both the transhuman grazers and the permanently based communities with whom they are increasingly at odds. Finally, the government of the Republic of Mali continues to spurn the CITES III international treaty, allowing influential locals to hunt elephants and all other species. Even the forest agents are involved in the killing. "There is need to make a decision quickly," says Peter Warshall, or "there will be no large mammal reserves in Mali."[56]

Which brings me back to endangered Amboseli, beneath eternal Mt. Kilimanjaro, and that ancient sunrise. The record of human biology, both in its origins and current plight, can be interpreted in support of an evolution favoring violence or nonviolence. However accurate the former notion—steeped in predation, meat eating, and self-aggrandizement —it has ecologically speaking, become an untenable anachronism, to be replaced by a new species of individuals driven not by destruction but by creation myths; souls that must, in turn, embrace a new credo of diversity and compassion.

Accepting the premise that human evolution is now about sustainable ideas, not physical force or digital thumbs, implies that we can alter our mindsets, choosing love over hate, sharing over greed. Evolution neither condemns nor liberates us: only our choices can do that. All people harbor an ideal of tranquility toward which we have been moving—in fits and starts—for millennia. That ideal today marks the fragile birth of a new human nature, of a noble creature of aspiring grace, who is fraught with ecological anxiety but with little time left for conceptual, let alone practical, reconciliation. But we can, and we must, effect this grand reconciling gesture. The clear high snows of Kilimanjaro, and the blessed animal plains below, challenge the human heart to get it right.

~6~

The Price of Development

> Know ye that on the right hand of the Indies there is an island
> called California, very near the Terrestrial Paradise . . .
> —Garci Rodriguez Ordonez de Montalvo, 1510[1]

THE GLOBAL CRASH

DURING THE EDO Period (1721–1846), Japan maintained a steady-state population of thirty million. By contrast, China's population doubled during that same period. Edo (Tokyo), numbering about one million people, was the largest city in the world, but the Japanese leadership was persistent in its efforts to counteract such crowding. For 125 years, the country deliberately worked at stabilizing its numbers. This effort resulted from a determined Tokugawa shogunate (that also banned all armaments from Japan) and a peasant class that evidently recognized the wisdom in inhibiting large family size. Writes William LaFleur, "It becomes clear that many people in Edo, Japan were limiting their children in order to enhance the quality of their lives."[2] Part of the strategy of limitation—indeed, two key elements, according to LaFleur—which saved the country from outstripping its scant resources, were infanticide and abortion, or *mabiki*—literally the culling of seedlings. Most Japanese, and most Buddhists, saw population control as a means toward achieving nirvana. This is not to say that abortion was treated casually among the Japanese. Even today, the so-called *mizuko* rituals honor the dead fetus publicly. Families gather together at special temples and graveyards where the fetuses are buried. They recite prayers and engrave the recitations on stones. *Jizo,* or protector spirits, are invoked to watch over the aborted fetuses during their journey into the realm of departed souls.

There are approximately 126 million Japanese, roughly twenty-one million of whom are boys and girls under the age of fifteen. While there was a baby boom after World War II, there was also a dramatic increase in *mabiki*. In 1948, the "health of the mother" was advanced as the legal justification for abortion.[3] With a current total fertility rate of 1.55, Japan is projected to begin experiencing a declining population growth after the year 2015. Indeed, toward the end of the twenty-first century, the country is expected to number twelve million fewer than at present. Furthermore, Japan shows the lowest infant mortality rate of any country, at five per one thousand. A Japanese baby is thirty times more likely to live than his counterpart in the West African country of Guinea–Bissau. If the least harm and greatest good to the largest number of people were one criterion for assessing the worth of an ethical system, Japanese abortions would have to be considered a form of long-term empathy—much like long-term thinking and long-term economics—the eschewal of short-term gains and gratifications (i.e., the pleasures of a baby) for a higher, more lasting purpose (the pleasures of an entire society). Until this century at any rate, Japan's artistic soul had extended the logic of this expediency to the natural world. One need only glance through the country's vast pictorial and poetic archives to appreciate the depth of Japanese nature religion, an astonishing harmony that once infiltrated most details of everyday life. (This generalization is still born out, in microcosm, by a casual stroll around Kyoto's peripheral greenbelt.) Corresponding to this aesthetic relish was the concerted, even penitent, recognition that over-population is harmful to the quality of the experienced world.

Until the "opening" of Japan by the West in the 1850s, the country in many respects was swayed by such potent affiliations. But much has changed now. Tokyo, still the largest city in the world, boasts nearly thirty million residents. It virtually connects with Osaka, three hundred miles away, their respective city limits separated by an inorganic expanse that cannot possibly suggest anything like the paradise in which earlier Japanese so sincerely believed.

Indeed, Japan now exhibits all the customary ills of human concentrations: near total human appropriation, heavy metal wastes from mining operations leaching into cultivated fields, toxic bioaccumulation in rivers, an enormous increase in oil spills and oil imports, a doubling of nuclear power generators, a global pattern of energy scavenging—be it plutonium from France or tropical hardwoods from Malaysia—and the decimation of wildlife. Tokyo Bay, not surprisingly, is gravely ill.

In 1990, a seasonal armada comprising 10 percent of Japan's squid fishermen combed the choppy waters of the North Pacific, as they have year after year, stringing enormous driftnets over many square kilometers of ocean surface. This tactic of the hunter, in sunlight and in storm, through calm and burdened seas, managed to kill vast quantities (metric tons) of living beings. To be precise—in addition to countless squid, the fishermen caught 1758 whales and dolphins, 30,464 seabirds, 81,956 blue sharks, 253,288 tuna, and over three million pomfret. This tangle of death, an infinitesimal fraction of far greater demolitions, was but one clue, virtually unnoticed, to Japan's and the industrialized world's so-called economic success.[4]

Japan consumes twice the amount of fish of either the U.S. or China, and six times that of India and Indonesia. In addition, its countrymen consume some two thousand tons of whale meat, and well over three million metric tons of chicken, pork, and beef each year, paying as much as $360 per pound for champion beef (called *wagyu*). Not surprisingly, the biodiversity of the open seas and more heavily populated coastal waters around Japan has been drastically reduced. Only the six-hundred-mile chain of Nambo Islands, (due south of Tokyo Bay and actually part of the greater Tokyo Municipality), retains any sense of natural integrity, in part because some of the islands have been elevated to national park status.

Most rivers in Japan have been heavily polluted, diverted, and built over. Sewage treatment in the country lags behind that of nearly all other industrialized nations, while the heavy air pollution is as acrid and enervating to the human organism as in places like Mexico City, Athens, and New Delhi.

Even Japan's financial citadel—the envy of the world's money managers throughout the 1980s—seems all but moribund, recessionary and scandal-ridden in 1997. There is unemployment, the country's stock market has laid dormant for two years (1996–97), and a crisis of layoffs has infiltrated the once impermeable system of long-term hiring. Confidence in Japan is waning among investors.

In short, Japan's modern experience—fortified no less by a unique tradition of responsible family planning, a sophisticated and artistic consciousness, and great wealth—has been to repudiate most of the ecological dreams of its history. This appears to be the contradiction, or the price, inherent to all development. But there are other contradictions, as well. Despite economic hard times, Japan during the 1990s contributed more money to the Third World than any country, much of it environmentally targeted. There is no rule that money ill-conceived need taint money well-intended. Prosperity has frequently invoked disparities, neighbors coveting neighbors, nations harboring designs against other nations, but it has also elicited great philanthropy, gentleness, and altruism.

America's economic rebuilding of Europe following World War II marked the zenith of forgiveness and idealism. And while poverty has never proved necessarily pacific, it has universally been shown to enshrine a level of generosity far beyond its means. The response of human beings to hardship can be graceful, even miraculous. Add up these many sides of the human personality and one is confronted by the middle class, a social phenomenon whose birth, following the Renaissance, has signaled an insistence on increasingly higher forms of well-being and security, the presumed precursors of homeostasis. Such economic equipoise has created a population explosion whilst isolating the consumer from the ecological violence inherent to consumerism. Whether forgiving or inflictive, the middle class—fearful of poverty, aspiring after the example of the rich—has proved to be an engine of adversity, the very definition of development. Is there any way out of the syndrome, with its billions of pounds of dead animal flesh, millions of abortions, sprawling megacities of concrete and unbreathable haze, thousands of years of protective and expansionary warfare? Is there a way to survive en masse, and to remain truly human?

The question presumes that we still know what "truly human" even means. Four of the leading "mass man" philosophers of the twentieth century—George Orwell, Jean-Paul Sartre, Elias Cannetti, and filmmaker Godfrey Reggio—doubt that we do. Nonetheless, we are quick to seize upon an answer, namely, the so-called "developed world," routinely touted as the exemplar, the grand resolution to all such dialectical agitations.

In 1950 the United States had a population of about 150 million. By the end of the millennium, just a few years hence, it will number 272,793,000 persons, plus or minus 3 percent.[5] By the world's standards, most of those people will be middle class. At that time all of the industrial nations together will account for roughly 20 percent of the world's population, about 1.5 billion people, who will be responsible for some 80 percent of all global consumption, not necessarily individual consumption, but mass consumption. The difference between the individual and the mass applies, for example, to a day in the life of a rural African, whose energy intake is essentially one on one: a plucked branch or two for cooking fuel, a scooped-up jug of drinking water, hand tillage of a garden patch, or small-scale cattle grazing. Versus a North American, like myself. I'm not quite sure how I manage it, but in the space of about twenty-four hours I figure that I have conspicuously contributed to global greenhouse gases, to the rape of both temperate and tropical forests, to the death of countless animals (in spite of my being a vegan), to long-term ocean pollution, acid precipitation, ozone depletion, scandalously inefficient mobilization of energy, the purchase of a stealth bomber or two, yet another unneeded freeway, the government-subsidized butchering of cattle kept on public lands, and any number of other ecologically insane expenditures. By simply being an American, I have conspired with the tax collector, and the textile, computer solvents, plastics, and weapons manufacturers. My clothes, electricity, gasoline, phone calls, mail, travel, and packaged foods all contradict my deepest convictions. I seem to have lost touch with the most basic cause and effect, with the web of life's delicate connections. I have driven seventy miles an hour over nuances at sunset. And I am told that in my own virtual backyard, five endemic California plant species are going extinct, because of people like myself.

Whether in a rich or a poor country, the U.S., Japan, or Mali, the net effect of such development and concurrent consumption, when driven by demographic pressures such as we are now confronted with, will invariably spell painful doom for much, or most biodiversity. This is, in my estimation, the central fact of the twentieth century and the crucial factor in considering the whole planet's destiny. This predicament is what I term the *end-loser syndrome*. But it is even more complicated than consumption and guilt, for this ecological no-win pattern has less to do with developed worlds, or developing worlds, per se, than with *development* itself. Rich, middle class, and poor—each are trapped by, and forced to contribute to, the patterns of global destruction.

Individuals are programmed by nature against grasping the large devastation caused by themselves, against internally processing too much shock and bad news. At the same time we are constantly habituating to smaller annoyances and increments of harm. These are possibly neurological adaptations that help us to anticipate and sort out our greatest defensive imperatives from amongst countless lesser dangers and anxieties. These subtle survival stratagems do not necessarily curtail our ability to hear the cries, to investigate, to empathize with victims who are actually far removed from our own immediate orbit of vulnerability. Children with whom I've spoken at schools throughout the world know that the ozone layer, penguins, topsoil, and black rhinos are in jeopardy; that their own air and water are polluted; that pesticides can cause cancer. They are familiar with the oft quoted "football field per second" worth of rain forest being destroyed. While such sayings convey an imperfect analogy that can scarcely account for the actual tragedy of rain forest destruction, given the global scope of that calamity, one "saying" is probably no more off the mark than a whole book, or a library of books, or some bureaucratic conference in Geneva, or Rio, or Cairo. Even "Chico (Mendes) and his *companheiros* were unaware that the devastation they were fighting against, the local deforestation in the municipality of Xapuri, was part of a much larger mosaic of destruction," writes Alex Shoumatoff.[6]

After all, how could the individual make sense of the fact that by the mid-1990s earth's rain forests were down to much less than their prehistoric amount? Never before in geological history have different floristic species in vast quantities been driven to extinction all at once.[7]

Because so much of the destruction is occurring in small, local outbreaks (what E. O. Wilson terms "a world peppered by miniature holocausts"), adding up in one's mind the cumulative and irreparable damage to species and habitats is a desperately imprecise task, bound to underestimate the true picture of horror that is emerging. An overall estimate, conversely, cannot begin to intimate all those countless small-scale disasters.

Of the eighty-seven major tropical regions in the world, with a combined total forest area of 1,884,100,000 hectares in 1980, the yearly destruction, by region, is causing the forests to shrink at a speed that most nonspecialists probably would not recognize, or not day by day. Our ability to clearly discriminate among large numbers, additions or subtractions, is severely limited, both perceptually and psychologically. In the decade of the 1980s, Africa's forests shrank from 650,300,000 to 600,100,000 hectares; Asia's from 310,800,000 to 274,900,000; and Latin America's from 923,000,000 to 839,000,000.[8] Every year the rain forests are being lost at a rate of 1 to 2 percent, or some seventeen million hectares. In fifty years or less, they will be gone. What does that effectively mean to the average American?

Fishermen in Finland or the Caribbean, are probably unaware that half of all ocean fisheries are being exploited beyond the estimated sustainable yield. A trout fisherman in Colorado is probably not conscious of the fact that 20 percent of all freshwater fish are extinct or nearly so. A chemist in Louisiana is doubtless aware of, but not overly worked up by, the more than two hundred major (and countless lesser) chemical accidents take place each year in industrialized nations.[9] A shoe salesman in Moscow and his clients are probably not remotely concerned that billions of animals will be slaughtered in this decade to meet consumer demand for an estimated twelve billion pairs of new leather footwear. A supplier of birds for pet stores in Buenos Aires is likely to feel all the more justified in his or her profession when informed that over 80 percent of all living birds are threatened with extinction, or are declining rapidly. A judge in Los Angeles takes it upon himself, in a real estate litigation in late 1997, to singlehandedly decide to cast the rarest songbird in North America to extinction. Such tidbits of attrition are fused in a blurred image of destruction that causes us to turn inward, but probably not to cease activities that directly or indirectly hasten the demise of such creatures.[10]

The World Conservation Union publishes its Red Data Books noting which species have gone extinct, are endangered, vulnerable, and rare. Throughout Europe more than one third of all insects and invertebrate species are threatened or endangered. Largely on account of collectors, the fungi are witnessing an even more devastating loss, potentially a biological nightmare. From the killing of freshwater fish in Africa's Lake Victoria, to the extirpation of profuse plant taxa in Turkey, to the eradication of tree snails in Tahiti—the mindless vandalism wreaked by humans is on the scale of a planetary cancer.[11]

To live on a finite island like Madagascar is to encounter first-hand the sound and the fury as eleven thousand acres of uniquely prolific rain forest are cleared, on average, every year, as the population expands. To inhabit either the state of Sao Paulo or of Parana, two of Brazil's Atlantic coastal regions where only six out of one hundred trees are now left standing, must invite certain unavoidable observations. As will soon be discussed, a recent poll in Los Angeles indicated that as many 70 percent of residents questioned said they would like to emigrate if they could afford to. That was after the riots of 1992 and the fires of 1993, but before the earthquake of January 1994. The number of malcontents may be higher now.

An observant resident of Burkina Faso related how "the region used to be full of wild and ferocious animals . . . graced with every species of bird on the planet . . . Now these times have become something of a legend, and the animals have disappeared as if under a spell."[12]

Twenty-one countries have no protected wildlife areas whatsoever, not for any known lack of interest, but from the sheer exigencies of national survival.[13] Seventy-six countries now possess no region biologically described as wilderness; of undefiled habitat of a size necessary to ensure the largest average of plants and animals with healthy genetic populations. Ironically, the largest two countries with the least human population density and the largest percentage of wilderness (relative to those countries' sizes) are Lesotho and Mauritania. In fact, of the top ten wilderness nations in the world, by percentage of overall national size, seven of them are in impoverished Africa, reaffirming that disproportionate environmental damage is wielded by the wealthy nations.[14]

What these sometimes contradictory assessments suggest is that the world is hemorrhaging and must be surgically viewed by region, inasmuch as most species are regionally oriented in their evolutionary adapatation. And because ecological boundaries, not cultural or political ones, are the crucial frontiers, only a transnational analysis of, and commitment to, data and subsequent remediation can effectively soften the burden of global abuse.

Ninety percent of all species exist on land, it is believed, which is where the human population dynamic has enacted its colossal appropriations. As the human population doubles in the coming decades, most analysts concur that the global economy will expand by 500–1000 percent.

Probably more than any other sign, the dramatically accelerated rate of species extinction over the natural background level argues for humanity's extreme economic dysfunctionalism. Add to that the *momentum* of human population growth, which systematically fuels that extinction rate, and one begins to recognize a malignancy unique to the annals of evolution. The less human beings suffer, the more the rest of nature tends to be adversely affected.

Human power leaves its traces in the form of billions of corpses, dead zones, burned out and bulldozed terrain, encroaching deserts, algal blooms, in the alteration of biological cycles, the proliferation of toxins, and the skewing of genes by technology and hybridization. As one scientist in Los Angeles put it, "The Lord made chromium to be eaten, not breathed. . . . It is an environmental sin to put chlorine atoms on a carbon atom. Nature does it only at the bottom of the ocean. Do it on land and it creates freons, dioxins, and hydrocarbons, all of our worst ills."[15]

Economic hubris seems to have redefined our nature. This situation is particularly distressing in the developing world where the largest concentrations of biodiversity and human population size are pitted against each another. While the damage incurred by the developed countries is still far more interregional and extreme than in the developing countries, that relationship may be reversed a few decades from now. Just at the time when the Earth's immune system may well have been totally exhausted, we can look forward to a new wave of exploitation unleashed not by the rich (who may well have fashioned remedial schemes by then, such as have been outlined in Japan's ambitious New World Agenda blueprint for the next century), but by the countless billions of poor, hungry, and angry people, most not yet even born, who are clinging to the development ideal as their last hope.

The inherent peril of human population momentum, in concert with this penchant to corrupt all preexisting biological homeostasis, places in doubt our ability to project anything about life in the future, or to actually gauge the full extent of our impact in the present. All that can be said with certainty is that human power is rarely benign, more often destructive and, given current trends and behavioral averages, inevitable. The portrait of that power, and those averages, in country after country, is a study in physical, mental, and moral degradation. The sum of destruction transcends its parts, just as human actions and awareness fail to connect with the larger picture. Accountability and the motivation to rectify injury are obscured. In Bosnia, wrote the poet Joseph Brodsky, "one always pulls the trigger out of self-interest and quotes history to avoid responsibility or pangs of conscience . . . the Balkan bloodshed is essentially a short-term project. . . . For want of any binding issue (economic or ideological), it is prosecuted under the banner of a retroactive utopia called nationalism."[16] The warfare of our past was endless, as are the many ongoing regional skirmishes around the world—human beings locked in conflict to the point of murder. But all of these battlefields combined do not begin to match the level of destruction, the megatonnage of harm meted out by the more silent, gun-free wars of "progress" and "development." These two words sail through our consciousness, breezy, proactive, full of promise and supposed comfort. They are the watchwords of every government policy, town meeting, corporate incentive, and social justification. Some would even argue that they are human destiny in an otherwise merciless, unfeeling universe; that without progress, there is . . . nothing! We speak of "underdeveloped" fetuses, capacities, ideas, intellects, and nations, with a mixture of cold detachment, disdain, and caution, whereas we rarely begrudge, or even acknowledge, that which is overdeveloped, except in certain medical cases pertaining to the thyroid or hydrocephaly.

Yet, it is precisely overdevelopment that has distorted everything good and potentially humane about our species. Because the number of people is so huge, and the instruments of its progress so potent, every new condominium complex, golf course, or air conditioner conceals even a far more devastating pain upon the world than a trigger finger in Bosnia, though they all stem from the same confusion—somewhere between nothingness and infinity. And truly, as Norwegian philosopher Arne Naess describes it, "it is painful to think" about this self-indicting situation, the ramifications of our presence, our biology, our very name.[17]

There was a time when being did not mean development—when certain of our ancestors lived truly harmoniously. The notion is bizarre, a hopeless sentiment, because to actually envision this harmony in all its guises, day after day, is to repudiate virtually everything we know to be the truth about our contemporary selves. More to the point, even if we should manage to imagine a plausible sequence of events, of our new life in ancient Arcadia, we nonetheless persist in the way we are, not the way we were. Even if individuals know better—and quite a few of them do—as a species we do not know how to reconcile the imagined better past with the imperfect present. We cannot stop ourselves. And because we are so many, and multiplying so rapidly, *Homo sapiens* have fled into the future, frantically squandering the visible resources around them, stealing from their children. The argument of survival has been inverted. Rather than searching for solutions in our anthropological and spiritual beginning, an ontologically sensible course, we are fixated on upward mobility, more money, more security, immediate returns, and a host of synonyms connoting gratification. *Development* is the implacable school of thought that enshrines these many activities. Now that there are nearly six billion of us in a state of feverish development, it is impossible to avoid the realization that development is tantamount to war. This is ironic, for it will invariably drive people away from acknowledgment.

This war is all in the cumulative weight of numbers. According to calculations worked out by Paul and Anne Ehrlich, a child in the United States will yield a destructive force 280 times that of its counterpart in Nepal, Haiti, or much of Africa; 140 times that of a Bangladeshi; 35 times that of an Indian child; 13 times that of a Brazilian.[18] What can such data mean to an American child, let alone an immigrant to Los Angeles (where, ironically, 22 percent of all children under five are poverty-stricken)? In South Central Los Angeles, 44.1 percent of all children under eighteen are in poverty.[19]

Indeed, one need not journey from South Central L.A. to Calcutta to sense the truth of biological damage, and the escalating blur of psychological and perceptual habituation our very presence incurs. Beneath the textual discussions, policy debates, and economic warfare, exists this vast human intransigence, the result of countless genetic eons, the brevity of our life spans, and the essential selfishness of individual organisms. The underlying question is whether income generation, the substitution of wealth for poverty, has anything to do with a nation's ability to prevent ecological damage. "The fact is that nations with lots of resources (capital, scientists, engineers, technology, a per capita GNP of over four thousand dollars) are better able to deal with environmental threats than those without monies, tools, and personnel," writes Paul Kennedy.[20] He goes on to allege that there is a "feedback loop," which presupposes that those who are educated will have an "enhanced ecological consciousness, and a willingness to prevent environmental damage."[21]

Reinforcing Kennedy's claim is the attitude of Jaime Serra Puche, who was head of the Mexican negotiating team for NAFTA (the North American Free Trade Agreement), that a four thousand dollars annual per capita income indeed would be the miracle cure-all, the supposedly predictable threshold for environmental protection.[22] With a per capita income exceeding the four thousand dollars threshold by five times, the U.S. must be environmentally pristine, which it assuredly is not. The presumption also suffers from at least two other chilling reality checks. First, out of nearly two hundred countries and territories in the world, only thirteen of them have actually reached that threshold. Most nations are far from it, and, in many countries—poor and wealthy alike—per capita income and the dollar value of the so-called quality of life package are dropping, not rising. Second, many of those countries exceeding the four thousand dollars per capita level are running colossal deficits, most disturbingly the United States, which faces a six-trillion-dollar national debt.

However triumphant a nation's economic progress, there will always be human victims. But the real end loser will be biodiversity, whether the country is rich or poor. This appears to be the brutal and bewildering blind spot of our age.

THE GOSPEL OF PROGRESS

CONSIDER WHAT THAT blind spot, that "American dream" has meant, ecologically speaking, in other countries that are either among the elite club of wealthy nations, or struggling to get there. I've chosen to describe, briefly, a handful of such nations that I consider representative of nearly all such countries.

In the Netherlands, a nation that supports 1031 people per square mile only by importing vast amounts of food and resources from elsewhere—millions of tons of cereals, oils, pulses, and minerals, even fresh water—the very earthworms are dying throughout the southern part of the country because of the intense build-ups of chemical runoff and sludge pollution from poultry farms. Ecologists have devised a term, the Netherlands Fallacy, to indicate a densely populated region that appears to be prosperous, but in fact has utterly exceeded its environmental carrying capacity. In the case of the Netherlands, that has meant that the country is dependent upon external inputs.

In Saudi Arabia the rapidly expanding population has been exhausting its nonrenewable groundwater reserves as fast as Brazil destroys its rain forests, or 2 percent per year, in order to irrigate twenty times more farm land today than existed in that country as recently as 1975.[23] The Saudi population is growing faster than almost any other in the world. With a current total fertility rate (TFR) of 6.4, the country's more than twenty million could surpass eighty million late in the twenty-first century.

Italy should be an exquisite example of the best that money and progress have achieved. The nation's (ironic) fertility discipline has resulted in a declining population, and a TFR of 1.2 as of late 1997. With 57.7 million people, and a per capita income of over sixteen thousand dollars, it boasts the fifth largest GNP, and one of the loveliest legacies of art and cultural sensibility the world has ever known. Yet, by many estimates Italy is the most polluted country in Western Europe. Pursuing industrial stardom, the nation has brazenly eschewed most environmental regulation or enforcement.[24] Northern Italy's perpetual smog only intimates other, unseen horrors, such as the countless chemical spills, and the largest garbage dumps in the world, their uncontained toxins percolating into aquifers and the drinking water of Italy's urban populations. The country's topsoil degradation has been likened to that of Somalia; so severe that any kind of restoration is impossible.[25] And, as of 1975, Italy had already lost 95 percent of its wetlands and Mediterranean littorals.[26]

Throughout Europe, at least fifty million acres have been directly despoiled by industrialization. The near total absence of the ancient temperate rain forests previously found in England, Ireland, Scandinavia, and even Iceland, is one clue to this pall of development. (In addition, since World War II, England has lost 98 percent of its old pasture.) It has been estimated that at least thirty billion dollars per year would be required to even begin to redress the damage to European forests from pollution.[27] But biodiversity loss is beyond compensation. In Germany, of the 933 plant species at one time identified, fourteen went extinct between 1870 and 1950. But since 1950, following the U.S. Marshall Plan to rebuild the country, 130 more plants have gone extinct, 50 others are threatened, 74 seriously endangered, and 108 in decline. These are astonishing statistics that reflect a continent-wide despoliation in the face of vast dollar wealth.[28] The largest number of endangered species—proportionate to the number of species within a region—are to be found throughout Europe. This fact alone should immediately call into question the assumption that more money will necessarily translate into environmental restraint. The long, unflinching history of Western human persecution of other plant and animal species is almost implausible but for the recognizable consistency of its cruelties, which so resemble our own killing of one another, most notably in two world wars, both fostered on European topsoil.

But if Western Europe's environmental track record is deplorable, today's Central European battlefields are even worse. These are the RICs, or rapidly industrializing countries, which have their hearts set on achieving that four thousand dollar magic number. The ghastly environmental legacy of places like the Katowice–Krakow areas of Poland, and the Bohemia region of the Czech Republic make a mockery of World Health Organization pollution standards. Poland's Bay of Gdansk is considered the most polluted body of water in the world. Lead and cadmium pollution in the Upper Silesian soils around the towns of Oikusz and Slawkow are the highest levels of contamination ever recorded anywhere.[29]

Government officials throughout the Commonwealth of Independent States have revealed a veritable Armageddon of ecological statistics, such as that more than a third of all food (two-thirds of all fish) and nearly three-quarters of all water in many of the states are seriously contaminated.[30] Throughout immense Siberia, the wasteful burn-off of natural gas flares are said to pollute the atmosphere as severely as the fires of the Persian Gulf War. In addition, millions of tons of uncurtailed Russian spills and leaks have damaged the soil and plant ecology of much of Western Siberia, where poaching has become a way of life.[31]

Each of the RICs throughout the world has shown the same economically driven devastation. By definition, no city today is anything but a brute, negative energy flow. Outside the urban environment, the RICs have spread their ruinous traits. Forest losses have quadrupled in these countries during the last twenty-three years. In Thailand, with a per capita income double that of Indonesia, forests are less than 28 percent of the country total, down from 55 percent in the early 1960s.

In rapidly developing Malaysia, whose per capita income is nearly four times that of Indonesia and double that of Thailand, the National Forestry Policy of 1978 is touted as being the closest to so-called sustainable logging in any tropical rain forest in the world. But only along the Malay Peninsula. In fact, throughout most of Sabah and Sarawak, where at least 50 percent of all hardwoods in the world originate, the destruction, and the profits, are scandalously out of control. The International Tropical Timber Organization has stated that the old primary forests of Sarawak will be gone by the end of the decade. With population pressures doubling, the country is predicting a doubling of its electrical capacity during this decade, which some predict will "tax Malaysia's reserves of fossil fuels and its fragile ecosystem of rivers and rain forests as never before." The president of Malaysia has expressed his desire for a Malaysian-produced motor vehicle, prompting a pronatalist stance based on the presumption that you need a more sizable consumer base than merely twenty million people to effectively sell a new line of automobile.

When the United States suggested targets for controlling population at the 1974 Bucharest Conference on Population, many Third World nations responded by calling for a "new international economic order" that would assure them access to world markets. "Development is the best contraceptive!" was the motto at work in both the developed and developing worlds. Development, it was universally felt, would ultimately provide the human race a way out of overpopulation. But, in Mexico it didn't happen. Development, and the country's Green Revolution successes, have been negated by the rapid growth in human numbers. Throughout Latin America, a 10 percent decline in per capita food production has coincided with increasing wealth for the few, poverty for the many, and rapid population growth of 2 percent per year. While Mexico's GNP grew by over 9 percent annually throughout the 1970s, boosted by oil development, the hidden costs included the loss of some 2.4 million acres of forest each year. Considering that Mexico hosts one of the largest diversities of mammalian species in the world (larger even than Brazil), such forest attrition is utterly heartbreaking.

The standard demographic equation that holds that rapid development should eventually result in population decrease, has not proved to be the case in either Mexico or Brazil, thus far, where 1.8 and over 3 million newborns, respectively, need to be fed and housed each year. Mexico's TFR is over 3.0 while Brazil's hovers near 2.5 Mexico's population will exceed 118 million by the year 2010. As for Brazil, she will harbor 187 million people at that time, the population of Indonesia in the early 1990s. Industrialization in both countries has merely widened the gap between the rich and the poor, exacerbating preexisting environmental ills. More than half of all Mexicans and 58 percent of all Brazilians are below the poverty line.[32]

Brazil has come to typify absolutely everything that is wrong with economic development. Nearly three hundred thousand square miles of rain forest have been destroyed in that country. In fact, the burning rate increased 28 percent between 1996 and 1997, ten thousand square miles at current rates, according to late 1997 data compiled by the World Wildlife Fund, the Environmental Defense Fund, and the Woods Hole research Institute. Despite such horrific revelations, the Brazilian government continues to arrogantly downplay the tragedy, attributing the fires to small farmers who are hungry, and excusing itself on the grounds that the U.S. is the real villain, for its high fossil fuel emissions. Brazil continues to build roads into the Amazon and has pumped $1.2 billion into new surveillance techniques for finding minerals beneath the rain forest. The country's population is 75 percent urban, as in the United States—the precise metaphor for the concentration of wealth and power (an annual per capita Brazilian income of $2550) that will not differ substantially in its destructive manifestations from an essentially rural population, such as India, Indonesia, and China.

Despite Brazil's higher income levels (relative to most of Latin America), at least half of the nation's couples are having more than two children during their fertile years. In Brazil's interior, many women have already given birth eighteen times by the age of forty-two. According to Julia Preston, that is "not an unusual number. . . . Burying children is a routine function of motherhood. Maternal affection is an acquired luxury that mothers rarely experienced when they were young and cannot consistently give to their families."[33]

Between 50 and 90 percent of the rapidly industrializing countries' exports are primary products—like forests, fuels, and minerals. This means that the adoption of American-style consumerism is not increasing service industries (whether consultants, plumbers, lawyers, or educators), but rather, directly brutalizing all life forms for primary resource extraction at giveaway prices. At the same time, much of the revenue from that encroachment is earmarked, not for recompensating nature, but for additionally inflictive public works projects. In Southeast Asia, for example, six hundred billion has been collectively budgeted for new roads, telephone lines, bridges, and viaducts. In the developing countries the game of catch-up has engendered military spending at a pace three times that of the industrialized world. The quest for what human beings imagine to be economic security is simply bankrupting our capacity to restore ecological and moral balance to the world.

It can certainly be argued that human economics has replaced the forces of human evolution. Economic impulses are destroying faster than nature can replenish. The law of averages knows no biological analogy, and thus offers no theoretical resolution. While our life and death spans are fixed, more or less, it seems plausible that we might be capable of destroying everything around us, sustained by nothing more substantial than that conceptual big bang, an explosion of ideas during the past fifteen thousand years. Physically, we have scarcely changed. Mentally, we are a new species, unrecognizable to our late-Paleolithic forebears who lavished such splendid images on the cavern walls at Lascaux. Mental speciation, without a corresponding physical accommodation, implies a disease, a form of chaos. So deeply embedded is this developmental paradigm, this world view of economic construction and destruction, that today's human organism seems lost (though not unimaginable) without it. A species sustained by mentation, and increasingly global, technological homogenization, prefigures a true monoculture, correspondingly vulnerable to its own biological downfall. When does the biological bottom line engulf us, like a mythical sky falling on our heads? We speak of an ecological price to pay, but is any price relevant to a civilization that has already been bankrupt for many years? Whether the debt is six trillion or one hundred trillion dollars, we would outpopulate and outproduce our attrition. A billion babies may starve to death, but does that matter, in biological terms, if four billion newborns replace them?

The World Resources Institute has stated that if the engineering and global proliferation of sustainable technology does not precede the anticipated fifty-trillion-dollar world economy in the next century, then "the environmental impact could be devastating."[34] And in his book *Qne World, Ready Or Not: The Mani Logic of Global Capitalism,* journalist William Greider points out that as such capitalism expands, it will depend upon the guarantees of a free society. But in a world that is ecologically caving in, amphetamized by more and more people, democracy will be threatened like never before, and hence, the mechanisms and instruments for controlling the environmental fallout will be terribly undermined.

The devastation is already upon us, obviously. It encompasses not only the RICs (rapidly industrializing countries), but also the NICS, or newly industrialized countries, including Singapore, South Korea, and Taiwan—countries whose spectacular growth has become the envy of 150 other nation states. Hence, the terrible, ethical predicament that few are willing to discuss openly: in our proudest moments of city life, we actually stand on the brink of complete obliteration of nature.

Taiwan, one of the world's most densely populated countries, along with South Korea, uses more pesticides per hectare than any other country in the world, while treating less than 1 percent of its human waste. Estimates for ecological clean-up have exceeded three hundred billion dollars. In South Korea, which recently topped the four-thousand-dollar per capita magic threshold, 75 percent of its sewage remains untreated and much of the tap water is deemed undrinkable.

It is estimated that current trends in global energy use, if unabated, will result in a quadrupling of the annual global energy demand by the middle of the twenty-first century as a result of population and economic growth.[35] For places like Siberia, that can only mean a point of no biological return. Siberia's degradation will eventually alter an enormous biological heritage of swamps, temperate forests, and tundra, fragile systems the size of Europe that will never be the same. Ironically, given the widely understood alternative solutions to nonrenewable energy exploitation, such damage is avoidable, technically speaking. The solar/hydrogen/fuel cell economy represents the best option for solving human energy needs in a virtually benign manner. Sadly, the U.S. Department of Energy spends the vast majority of its budget on conventional fossil fuel and nuclear projects, not alternative energy research and development.[36] Yet, even energy conservation and restitution, by themselves, are not enough to curtail population-induced ecological warfare.

In California, the technical acumen, enlightened public utilities, sophisticated city and county management, and the general public, are as energy conscious as nearly any in the world. But California, particularly Southern California, is an environmental paradox of grim proportions, despite its good looks. Imperceptibly, over the course of a mere century, California has succumbed to the same irreversibility as Western Siberia's ecodisaster, the dramatic human trespass witnessed in the state of Kerala in southernmost India, and the transmigrational tragedies afflicting a city like Bandung, Indonesia or Shanghai, China. Remarkably—and it says much about the American personality—people in California are talking about three things: taxes, crime, and health care. But few are referring to the overtaxed biology, the crimes against nature, and the awesome breakdown in the health of California's total ecosystem—all symptoms of an unsustainable population boom which rivals that of any developing country. Like the word applied to the Netherlands, one might similarly call this the California Fallacy.

The California Fallacy

California has always been understood in the light of beauty and freedom, of behavioral unrestraint and psychological deliverance. And without belaboring its rich gratifications and braggadocio, the dream of California has exercised the same persuasiveness over much of the human species as the New World itself once held for Europeans. England pursued an industrial revolution; America searched for California. The gold rush has never ceased. Consider that in the two most teeming nations, China and India, the birthrate is approximately twenty-one per thousand and thirty-one per thousand, respectively. But in California, particularly Southern California, the birthrate in 1990 was an astronomical 84.6 per thousand, a 2.1 percent per annum growth rate overall. California's population is growing at a rate of 646 thousand a year, not including illegal immigration. That fertility penchant is three-and-a-half-times greater than the average population growth rate for the world's more developed countries; it is even higher than the world average of lesser developed nations. One demographic research analyst I interviewed in the Planning Department for the city of Los Angeles told me with a heavy sigh that "fertility numbers have tripled." And he went on to say, "I can't even publish them (the data) they're so outrageous." Data was published, however, on the front page of *The Los Angeles Times* August 25, 1997—"Population Surge of 18 Million Seen for State by 2025" wrote Faye Fiore, citing research from the U.S. Census Bureau projecting 49.3 million people in the state at that time. A chief economist at the Economic Development Corporation of Los Angeles County labeled the news "a call to action—a fire alarm."

While at least a few people questioned the ecological implications of the data, evidence suggests that the news came and went with scarcely a blink. Why aren't people more concerned? For two obvious reasons. First, the more people, the more sales. That same economist cited above qualified his projection of "alarm" by pointing out that a California of nearly 50 million people "will be a promised land for retailers." And second, in rich, spacious America, few people care or understand what these numbers bode. The U.S. has no official population policy.

The Reagan/Bush years were utterly pronatalist. Clinton tried to change that by sanctioning abortion counseling at four thousand federally funded clinics, ending the ban on fetal tissue research, opening the way for the importation of the abortifacient RU486, allowing for abortions at U.S.

military hospitals abroad, and renewing funding for international organizations that performed or promoted abortion, but Congress later rejected some of the initiatives, thus continuing the fertility enslavement of economically disadvantaged women, and escalating the number of maternal deaths. As of mid-1998, the number of pregnancies and maternal deaths throughout the world were at an all-time high according to the Population Reference Bureau in Washington and the World Health Organization.

America's TFR is 2.0, its annual percental of growth, 0.6. In Southern California, however, the annual population increase is over 4 percent. California is the eighth largest economy—after the G-7 nations—in the world. It produces 50 percent of all fruit and vegetables for the United States. Its energy needs and global impact are intense. By perpetrating the American dream around the planet, California's population growth adds an enormous amount of kindling to World War III.

Combating not only the population crunch in California, but a global TFR hovering around 3.0, at least some in Congress are trying to wrest an annual commitment from the United States of $1.4 billion (in 1990 dollars) by the year 2000, or seven times America's commitment a decade before. That increased budget share would help provide fuller access to contraception for every person on the planet by the end of the millennium, and that includes high-school students in Los Angeles, who are reproducing faster than teens anywhere in the world other than India. More than half of all those on welfare in Los Angeles are teen mothers. Forty-four percent of the high-school dropouts in the city are girls, 80 percent of whom are pregnant.

For nearly seventy years, the American public has recognized the inherent economic and social problems associated with overpopulation. Even when their lawmakers vacillated on the subject Americans have consistently upheld the concept of population control. The condom (first introduced in Gabriele Fallopio's *De Morbe Gallico*, a treatise on venereal disease published in 1564) was popularized in this country around 1914, when Margaret Sanger, a New York nurse, began publishing a monthly magazine, *The Woman Rebel*. She was arrested and indicted under the odious Comstock Law of 1873, which made it illegal to disseminate by mail information pertaining to contraceptives, declaring such material "obscene." Sanger fled to Europe, where the public was considerably more sophisticated and practical about these matters, but she insisted on returning to Brooklyn in 1916 where she opened the first birth control clinic in the

United States. Police promptly closed its doors. But eventually, Americans sided with birth control; in 1925, in 1931, and finally in 1937, the religious and medical communities came to accept family planning as fundamental to medical practice.[37] (At the same time, many U.S. scientists were promoting the concept of eugenics, which the emergent German Nazi party employed to initiate compulsory sterilizations. In fact, as early as 1917, sixteen states in the U.S. had formulated compulsory sterilization laws for the mentally disabled, and for criminals.) In 1965, President Johnson advocated U.S. aid for birth control projects abroad. In 1968, however, Pope Paul VI's encyclical, *Humanae Vitae*, banned artificial contraception. That same year, Paul Ehrlich countered the Pope with his astonishing book, *The Population Bomb*. A year later the state of Virginia and the country of Singapore both passed the first set of nonrestrictive sterilization laws, and President Nixon allocated funds for birth control and family planning within the U.S. In 1973 the U.S. Supreme Court upheld Roe v. Wade, which was intended to safeguard a woman's right to an abortion. In November 1970 Pope Paul VI again rejected birth control programs, stating at a United Nations conference on food and agriculture, "There is a great temptation to use one's authority to diminish the number of guests rather than to multiply the bread that is to be shared."[38] In 1984 in Mexico City, the U.S. under Reagan favored the Vatican's position by declaring that population growth was a "neutral phenomenon." A year later, the U.S. Congress dropped its support for the United Nations Fund for Population Activities, as well as the International Planned Parenthood Federation, and suspended all participation in those programs that in any way supported abortion.[39]

The dogma propagated by those politically and spiritually to the far right has never obscured the truth that there is no greater ecological tool nor more powerful technology, no more egalitarian ethic, and no better investment, than contraception. According to the Alan Guttmacher Institute, for every one dollar spent on family planning, California taxpayers save nearly twelve dollars in welfare costs. In fact, each unintended pregnancy costs California $3317, multiplied by nearly one hundred thousand unintended pregnancies a year since 1990. Across America, 60 percent of all pregnancies are unintended, a figure that has not changed since birth control was first legalized in 1965. Teen births noticeably started rising across the U.S., particularly in Southern California, in 1987. According to the former surgeon general, Dr. Jocelyn Elders, America does "the sorriest job of any country in the world providing family planning.

We're always running around hollering and screaming about abortion—and abortion is not the issue. The issue is providing family planning services for all women who need them. Right now, the rich have them, but we don't care about the poor," she said.[40]

Under twelve years of the Republican White House, over one thousand health clinics specializing in birth control were closed, creating a social time bomb of unwed teen mothers in neighborhoods of soaring illiteracy and unemployment—"greenhouse conditions" for a baby boom. The conservative politics of fear responsible for keeping so many women away from family planning clinics have no doubt traumatized many of their lives, particularly those teen mothers unprepared to raise children. Along with the Philippines, Saudi Arabia, Malawi, and Haiti, the U.S. was recognized in 1991 by Population Action International as among the least progressive countries in the world in terms of expanding access to family planning services.

Net immigration now comprises about a quarter of all population growth in the U.S.—Third World consumers suddenly stepping into the consumptive cornucopia of the First World. Among them, Latinos have the highest birthrate in L.A. County—in the whole United States for that matter. Latino women are having four or five children each, on average. The Latino population of Los Angeles is expected to reach four million by the year 2000, the size of Mexico City in the early 1950s.

According to Melinda Cordero, the coordinator for the Promotoras Communitarias, a Mexican-originated family planning outreach program that now operates in Los Angeles, Latin women tend to believe that it makes them "more of a woman to have more children," or at least that's what they've been told. In fact, their birthrate is higher in Los Angeles than in Mexico City.

Cordero and I drove out past the housing projects, through the smog-bound southeast portions of the city—Maywood, Southgate, Boyle Heights—all heavily Latino areas. At a community center in Montebello, she spent an hour with fifteen mothers and two fathers and countless children, describing contraceptive options. She sat casually on a table before the crowd, speaking in Spanish, using a pointer, anatomical chart, and video animation to expertly illustrate aspects of a woman's monthly cycle, talking about the female body and self-esteem, and offering cartons of free condoms and foam for the women. After the talk, most of those in the audience swept up the supplies into their handbags.

Some of those women had eight children. I asked one twenty-six-year old, somewhat frazzled-looking mother of four whether her childbearing days were over. "If God wants me to have another child what can I do?"

Women in California have the largest number of abortions in the United States, by far. Yet, California has no legislative mandate to teach sex education in the schools. In fact, the state has ordered that "no student may be required to attend sex education classes" and "parents must be notified that sex education material is going to be taught and given the opportunity to review it, and to refuse permission for a child to participate."

Whether they are Latino, Hmong, Filipino, Mexican, Korean, Chinese, Polynesian, East Indian, Pakistani, Irish, or Guatemalan, more than half of all immigrants to the U.S. find their way to California, most to the L.A. area.[41] Every week six thousand legals enter California, in addition to thousands of illegals. The amnesty program and the Immigration Act of 1990 have increased this flow. In the next decade, as many as ten million legal and illegal immigrants will enter, with at least half of them coming to California for permanent residence. Some demographers believe this immigration pressure will push California's population over more than sixty-three million by the year 2040, and Southern California will account for thirty-seven million of that total.[42]

In planning for so many people, the Southern California Association of Governments has cited a number of critical shortfalls and anticipated ecological deadlocks. For example, there will be five times more traffic congestion, diminishing average commuter speed from forty to ten miles per hour. Millions of new homes—eight hundred every day—and offices, and at least one school a day for 640 new students, will be built upon 650 thousand acres of already scarce open space. Many new roads will be built, adding to the existing 21,086.5 paved miles in the city of Los Angeles.[43] Every major pollutant type—from reactive organic gases, carbon monoxide, nitrogen, sulfur oxides, and surface ozone, to particulate matter—will increase, as much as 500 percent.[44] But perhaps the greatest shortfall of all was already expressed by late November, 1997, when *The Los Angeles Times* discovered that the L.A. Department of Water and Power, the principal supplier of electricity to Southern Californians, was showing a deficit of over seven billion dollars, tied to a long-term contract with an inefficient, uncompetitive coal-burning power plant in Utah, that threatened to bankrupt the City of Angels.

Population density throughout the state of California is about 184 per square mile. But in most of Southern California it rises to over two thousand and in Orange County is nearly three thousand per square mile. With a doubling or tripling of density, what is the impact on the environment likely to be?

California ranks with the ten industrial countries of the world for its contribution to global warming and ozone depletion. A resident of Los Angeles literally warms the planet nearly nine times more than a Chinese and 14.3 times more than an Indian.[45]

Los Angeles county produces fifty thousand tons of garbage every day, more than twice that of Tokyo. Of the hundred million pounds per day of waste, at least one hundred thousand pounds are toxic and hazardous.[46] DDT concentrations off the Palos Verdes Peninsula just south of Los Angeles, are the highest in the U.S. Correspondingly, Southern California marine life have the highest bioaccumulations of toxic chemicals of any fish in North America.

Add to this the so-called "sleeper" issue, namely, nonpoint (difficult to analyze) pollution sources in the state. The EPA lists 295 California waterways as polluted. L.A. basin ozone emissions damage millions of ponderosa and Jeffery pines, and even the seedlings of the giant sequoias hundreds of miles away. There are still no environmental impact records kept on countless numbers of unrestricted pesticides. As for the restricted ones, over eighty-five million pounds are annually applied throughout the state.[47]

In addition to the ground-based wastes, runoff, air pollution, pesticides, and marine contamination, countless other fallouts from Southern California urban life add to this perplexing picture, from vast sources of electromagnetic pollution, to sick-building syndromes.

In the mental health realm, it is known that there are more psychiatrists per square mile in Los Angeles (some two thousand) than anywhere in the United States.

Crime in the U.S. is twenty-one times higher than in all other industrial countries. There are two hundred million firearms in the U.S., a country where men rape women seven times more frequently than anywhere else in the world. And within that country, Los Angeles shows the highest number of such crimes.

Hundreds of sirens can be heard throughout the city every twenty-four hours. And every day 4,696 airplanes take off or land somewhere in the Los Angeles basin—17 percent of the nation's total and the largest combined source of aerial noise and pollution in the world.

Yet, the colossal combination of all these physical, chemical, and psychological ills and assaults has not dampened the enthusiasm of millions of pilgrims who make their way to Southern California each year. Between its grateful immigrants, starry-eyed tourists, fourteen million heterogenous locals, and 130 thousand gang members, its rich and famous, its millions of poor, and forty thousand homeless, L.A. utterly challenges the doctrine of progress.

The real victims of this two-hundred-year old spasm of development are not merely the millions of people who do not particularly relish the urban experience but have no easy way to alleviate their situation: the true end losers are California's plants and animals. And this is where Los Angeles, and much of the state, has set a melancholy example of irresponsibility that the rest of the world appears bent upon following.

THE END LOSER SYNDROME

WHILE THE HUMAN fiasco in Southern California is veiled beneath the illusion of success, its impact upon other life forms is less concealable.

I set out one day to calculate the amount of "green territory" left in the metropolitan region of Los Angeles. The city *proper* contains 470 square miles, or 300,800 acres. The county officially lists 4,025 square miles, or 2,576,000 acres, within its boundaries. But according to Paul and Anne Ehrlich, a million people in a city need four hundred square miles of surrounding land in crops for even a vegetarian diet under theoretically maximally efficient utilization.[48] That means that Southern Californians need tens of thousands of additional square miles to sustain their appetites. This is the essence of what was previously described as the California Fallacy: To look at Los Angeles is to peer through a haze of deftly concealed ecological costs, a dense conurbation of bills and unpaid-for destruction.

Today only sixty acres of actual cultivated area are left in all of L.A. Farming in the city environment is virtually cost prohibitive, and actual zoning regulations specifically forbid "farming." It is ironic that where the most people live, the production of food is virtually illegal.[49]

The twenty-eight thousand existing public acres contain many buildings, whether police stations, public utilities, city halls, community centers, or fire stations. Even the parks can hardly be described as "green." Most have been retrofitted with public bathrooms, parking lots, tennis courts, basketball courts, artificial lakes, park benches, and gardens shorn of most biodiversity. The last stretches of marshland in Los Angeles have been all but covered over. There are a few hundred acres remaining of the

Ballona Wetlands on the ocean, and they have been the subject of the largest ecological battle in recent times: over seventy-two environmental organizations versus a would-be Hollywood studio that wants the marsh, despite several endangered species inhabiting that fragile, final oasis.

Add to this litany of human appropriations the concretized industrial sections of the city south and southeast of downtown, in addition to all the highways, and Los Angeles exhibits an astonishing ratio of inorganic material-to-organic material, of nearly 90 percent. Despite the Santa Monica mountains comprising America's only urban mountain range, Los Angeles city proper has less open space per thousand people than New York City.

California hosts a known 7,850 plant species, a third of them found nowhere else on the planet. In addition, there are 742 species of vertebrates, 540 bird species, 214 terrestrial and aquatic mammalian species, an estimated 28,000 species of insects, 47 amphibian species, 82 species of reptile, 110 different species of fish, 1,200 species of lichens, nearly 5,000 different types of gilled fungi, 300 to 400 slime mold types, and 660 species of mosses and liverworts.[50] This profusion places the state among the most biologically diverse regions in the world, and renders it exceedingly vulnerable to all of the above-mentioned human activity. Biologists consider Southern California one of the eighteen "biodiversity hotspots" on Earth.

At least seventy-three major plant and animal species have gone extinct in California in the last one hundred fifty years, including the grizzly bear, the state's official mascot. The last one was killed in the mountains of Tulare County in 1922. In the findings of the 1987 report requested by the California Senate Committee on Natural Resources and Wildlife, an astonishing 33 percent of all California mammals, 25 percent of all birds, 33 percent of all reptiles and amphibians, 40 percent of freshwater fish, and 12 percent of native tree, shrub, and wildflower species, were deemed threatened with extinction, based upon current trends. Is it any wonder? Over seventeen million acres of wilderness have been completely destroyed in California.[51] Many have predicted that at current population and agricultural growth rates, with the associated impact on water levels, a startling proportion of California could become desert during the twent-first century. This is all the more devastating when one considers that California contains 25 percent of all plant species in the United States and Canada combined, with 2,140 of those species unique to the state.[52]

And the trends are getting worse. Concluding from their many case studies, the authors of *In Our Own Hands* project that "between one and two million acres will be urbanized in the next decade to accommodate population growth."[53]

All of this carnage—most of it largely unseen by Californians themselves, the unwitting agents of destruction—translates into an estimated 663 plants and 220 vertebrates that are on the brink of extinction as of early 1998. In metropolitan Los Angeles, there are (officially) 174 endangered species.[54]

Despite the foregoing, only 6 percent of land in California is biologically protected. And that would include a place like the center of Yosemite Valley, with its hotdog stands and summer haze from congested camping—ten thousand people a day during the late spring and early summer. Poaching in California (most of it within that 6 percent region, where any wildlife remains) is at epidemic proportions. Poachers clandestinely lay miles of drift lines studded with thousands of hooks just offshore, by dark. And, as journalist Paul Dean writes, they "mow down elk, including their calves, with AK-47 assault rifles. Or run over wounded deer when bullets run out. They harvest organs and paws from bears and leave the carcasses to rot. They bring to this war forged permits, spotlights, diving gear to take lobster and abalone from protected areas, off-road vehicles, police radio scanners, infrared spotting scopes, military weapons, illegal lines that fish a mile of ocean. . . . And, an understaffed and outgunned state Department of Fish and Game can't slow the slaughter."[55]

While its exercise of policing power, protective custody, and formal scientific definitions may be hamstrung to a certain extent, the Department of Fish and Game does not mince words when it comes to listing the human causes of extermination, the very verbs of warfare. The following activities are deemed responsible for the demise of plants, in order of magnitude: development, livestock grazing, off-road vehicles, roads, agriculture, other exotic plants, water projects, human and equestrian trampling, fire management, feral animals, mining, landfills and garbage dumping, collecting, logging, flood control activities, energy development (pipeline and power lines), water quality degradation, hybridization, vandalism, disease, and finally, climate. For animals, the course of degradations is as follows: development, water projects, newly introduced predators, agriculture, livestock grazing, off-road vehicles, other human disturbance, pesticides and other poisons, flood control, exotic plant imports, climate, energy and mineral development, roads, logging, disease, habitat fragmentation, extinction of habitat, hybridization, water pollution, and collecting. If one were to catalogue the behavior of *Homo sapiens* throughout history, many of these activities, in one form or another, would be recognizable as of twelve thousand years ago, a period noted for the beginnings of agriculture in what are Iraq, Thailand, and Israel. But what distinguishes today's peril, of course, is the sheer *number* of people engaged in such enterprises.

In trying to protect what's left of Southern California's biological integrity, the Department of Interior in Washington has suggested a compromise model, beginning with the rare gnat catcher. Interior has agreed to "minimal development" in the area of the bird's nesting grounds, one of the only times in the twenty-year history of the Endangered Species Act that the Interior Department has compromised with respect to allowing any development whatsoever. There could be no clearer sign of the escalating war against nature than a compromise from the one public trust mandated to protect America's wildlife from greed, when all else fails. But this incident of compromise is much larger than the Southern California gnat catcher; it is a codified pattern. Under the provisions of the Endangered Species Act it is legal and allowable to "take" a species, even though it is listed as endangered or threatened. Hence, the true ground rules of compromise. And what does "take" really mean? It means that one can "harass, harm, pursue, hunt, shoot, wound, kill, trap, capture, or collect, or attempt to engage" if the activity is "incidental to a legal activity"—that is, if it is not the primary activity—but is somehow the byproduct of a legal activity. In addition, such killing and so forth must meet the criteria of a "habitat conservation plan" such that the activity does not jeopardize the overall survival or recovery of the species."[56] Such grammar fosters destruction under the guise of good intentions. From 40 to as many as 59 percent of all species protected under the Endangered Species Act in the U.S. are declining in number. Only five species out of more than six hundred have made recoveries. Less than seven hundred thousand acres nationwide have been set aside for endangered species. Habitat destruction is the key to their demise and virtually nothing is being done to curb America's trespass. Yet the U.S. inspector general's office estimated in 1990 that it would cost no more than $4.6 billion to save the six hundred or so most endangered domestic species. The figure is difficult to assess considering a pattern that seems to authorize as much or more budget allocation to lawyers and additional studies as to actual restoration of habitat. The U.S. Fish and Wildlife Service did not have the political muscle between 1987 and 1991 to stop 1,966 federal construction projects that directly and knowingly accelerated the demise of existing endangered species, all in the spirit of so-called "compromise."[57] Humanity appears almost incapable of marshalling the necessary reserves of intelligence and compassion to forge an end to the war, even in a place as blessed, as wealthy, and seemingly aware, as California.

AMERICA'S CHALLENGE

WHILE EVERY CITY in the U.S. can be viewed in terms of the aforementioned war zones, rural America is more difficult to biologically analyze, at least at first glance. But the derterioration is everywhere, in the form of barbed wire fencing, overgrazed pasture, desertified agricultural lands, rural sprawl, decentralization, military proving grounds (a landsize equivalent to a fourteen-mile strip spanning the entire U.S.), strip mining, and vast clear-cutting lumber operations, and the sheer preponderance of tarmac—a burden of highway spanning sixty thousand square miles, the size of Georgia, paved over so that not even a blade of grass can ever grow. In addition, over 131 million acres have been given over to railroad tracks in the U.S.

Such incursions into the natural heritage are amplified by America's production of over six hundred thousand tons of pesticides, nearly a million tons of plasticizers, fifty-seven million tons of petroleum, and thirty-three million tons of plastic and resin in a given year. Paper, tobacco, printing, primary and fabricated metals, leather, and electrical processes release more than 1.5 million additional tons of toxins into the environment annually.

Add to this systemic refuse the realities of over seven thousand major oil spills in and around U.S. waters, as well as the tens of thousands of inland spills and the perpetual problem of leaking pipelines. The beneficiaries of that oil—most Americans—travel over 1.5 trillion automobile miles each year and consume approximately seventy billion gallons of gasoline doing so. That auto traffic kills over three hundred million animals every year in the U.S., the second largest source of American slaughter after meat eating, which numbers in the tens of billions of animals massacred—America's cruelest reality.

Rural population density in the United State is around twenty per square mile, relatively low on a perceptual scale, though sufficient to interrupt the normal ecology of many wild populations. But again, that is not a readily discernible fact. We do not knowingly miss the New Mexico jaguar, the last of which was hunted down in the early 1800s (though two lone felines were spotted, like ghosts, in Arizona and New Mexico in 1996); nor do most Americans know or care that several thousand species of apple and pear trees had gone extinct in this country by the year 1900.[58]

Hunting takes a more immediate toll on the biodiversity around us—some 250 million animals are killed every year in the United States. Only upon dedicated inspection, often with the eyes of a biologist, the stealth of an informed environmentalist, or simply the sheer stamina of someone with a diligent conscience, are the signs of this professionally hidden warfare revealed, however.

But the facts cannot be obscured. The U.S. is the largest producer of forest products in the world, and the second largest exporter of raw timber.[59] Most primary forests in this country, and the vast majority of biodiversity dependent upon them, are gone forever.

In 1700 less than 10 percent of the world's population lived in cities. By 1950 the world figure was 30 percent, but in the United States and Europe, urban populations had swelled to 64 percent and 56 percent respectively. In theory, this presumes less and less impact on more and more open space, a trend that would logically lead to the most efficient concentration of human populations and the ultimate liberation of a maximum "quantity" of nature. Unfortunately, the data is not supporting that hope in the U.S., any more than it is in Brazil, India, or Indonesia. In the United States, metropolitan populations have doubled since 1950, from 85 to 180 million residents. But all that concentration of energy capacity and jobs has only served to build up a far-reaching infrastructure of exploitation: the defoliation of tens of thousands of square miles; the accelerated proliferation of toxins around the world; the exacerbation of the gap between the rich and the poor. Thirty million people are hungry in the United States. Ten percent of all Americans are dependent on food stamps. The U.S. places last among industrialized nations in child mortality and life expectancy, and approximately as high as Indonesia in terms of the numbers of endangered species.

The more people there are, the more possibilities for injury, pollution, and aggression.

Where there is poverty, illiteracy, and crime, there is less money or sensibility that can be mobilized in defense of the environment. Ironically, where there is wealth and a relatively high level of universal secondary school education, there is an epidemic of hedonism that has clearly turned its back on Mother Nature.

The numbers, the death tolls, the production figures, miles of paved road, tons of toxins, decibels of noise, percentages of growth, all conspire to transcend our ability to exert ethical controls, or even to think clearly. Do the larger numbers and disasters actually dissociate truth and meaning from the human capacity to comprehend, to be moved by feelings, to act upon life-threatening information?

Can we even distinguish one inconceivable number from another, let alone attach a hierarchy of ethical determinations to the varying quantitative levels and degrees of disaster? Are we any more distressed by the knowledge of a billion hungry people in the world than we would be by, say, nine hundred million? Or is the prospect of saving one hundred million children from starvation even enough to elicit a twenty dollar donation, a call-in to an 800-number on television, or an incentive for a congressional resolution? If it is not, then how can there ever be a serious understanding and application of family planning in any country? How can we fathom the thousands of superfund sites, or billions of slaughtered animals, or hundreds of thousands of homeless people, or billions of curies of radiation in the soil?

We are good at rallying around the plight of a single individual, or certain slogans—"family values" or the "war on poverty." All of America clung to the radio for a week once, when a little girl named Kathy Fiscus fell into a pipe in Texas. The country put all of its resources into extricating her. But in 1994, six dead Bosnian children, shelled while innocently sledding, elicited no more than a few moments of news. The fact is, the more people, the more quantities of problems, the less likely we are to deal effectively with them. Specifically, how can we formulate and execute any policy involving mass numbers of people, when Darwinian behavior, the ethics of personal survival at any cost, appear to be enshrined in our genes? We seem incapable of collective altruism, preferring personal escapism in the hope that we will somehow muddle through.

Economic development, the outgrowth of overpopulation, is the policy by which this biological contradiction is furthered. We have for so long insisted on the acquisition of wealth, there seems now little hope of turning back.

How does the impatient individual, increasingly aware of the seriousness of the human predicament and the many frustrations belonging to compromise, go on living a productive life? How is any progress or sustainable development possible, given the dark tenor of the definitions and semantics, as I have here employed the terms?

For purposes of developing an internal compass reading, I start with the principle of absolute zero impact: what would it require? What logical number of people might be sustained, and by what means? Aristotle believed that the ideal city must never exceed a population of fifty thousand. Plato reckoned on a mere five thousand inhabitants in his utopian Republic.

Such ideals have long been surpassed by human demographics. But the root questions remain: To what extent is human decency, kindness, joy, dignity, love, and, for that matter, art dependent upon the advances of civilization, technology, and heavily-crowded cities? The debate is academic, but the causes and consequences of America's deteriorating environment are not: our population explosion at home. Of the developed nations, only France and the Netherlands have official population policies, and only the Dutch have advocated negative growth. The U.S. still has no such policy.

WE LIVE IN A world more fraught with disaffirmation and the antithetical than ever before. Yet every disparity declares a priority, invokes a conviction. Our convictions are being tested today by new amplitudes and proportions, a crisis of harm that must force us to requestion all the fundamentals of our existence: who we are, and what we're here for? And while these conjectures have always been current, forever relevant, the massive, unchecked multiplication of our presence now challenges the core of our humanity and ingenuity.

Consider what, if anything, humanity has accomplished, judging not by its own standards, which are necessarily self-serving, but according to those of the Earth? By simply shifting this crucial point of view—the goal of all ecology—we cannot fail to register a certain regret about the industrialized nations; to recognize everywhere the calamity of our presence. The inventory of damage has left traces in our consciousness, to be sure, and in our lungs, mammary glands, and children. Moment by moment the list of atrocities, of incoming data, escalates, and we are increasingly unsure of ourselves. We are less capable of justifying our very presence, which in turn, incites a host of ontological difficulties. For example, some may question the notion of a divinity because it does not seem reasonable that any God would condone the ecological blasphemies of one species out of so many hundreds of millions of others that have gone about their business without leaving so much as a footprint. Why *Homo sapiens*? Friedrich Nietzsche remarked that we, alone, are the "sick species." We are assailed not just by terrible choices, but by circumstances whose magnitude offers no earlier analogies. The full force of this "logic jam" is perhaps best appreciated in terms of human demographic paradox, the subject of the succeeding chapter. I call it paradoxical, because in assessing the coming decades demographically, I am struck by a remorseless conundrum that nearly has a mind of its own, an already desperately overpopulated species furiously breeding, poised to double, triple, even quadruple its numbers; an organism that claims to desire peace and tranquility, but whose collective violence is fast escalating in all ways; a genetic population whose territorial imperative has utterly condemned that thin veil of other life forms gently covering the planet. In this condition of knowing abuse, chaos, and pain, we still proudly hail ourselves as "the civilized world."

The crude mathematics of our situation have persistently knocked at the door of all biological laws. Should we actually open that door, as we appear to have done in cities like Los Angeles, Shanghai, Mumbai, Tokyo, Mexico City, Sao Paulo, and elsewhere, there is simply no telling what might happen next. Some theorists believe that nothing will happen. That life will continue to drag along in depressing fits, some positive, some negative, a severely asthmatic life, wan and sapped of vitality. Others argue our fertility momentum has already unleashed every expression of misery. Whether one is a firm believer in the power of the human spirit or not, does not alter one irrevocable fact: that unless governments, and those billions of human beings they supposedly represent, act now, in a globally concerted fashion, to reduce our numbers and refine our economic impulses, all other "solutions" are likely to be useless.

Whatever we hope, or say, or do, our species—and all others—are caught out in the fire storm of human development—in the uncontrolled flood of human newborns at the heart of the population explosion. To ponder this virtual double bind is to taste a form of insanity. "When elephants make war," says an African proverb, "the grass gets trampled. When elephants make love, the grass also gets trampled."[60]

~7~

Demographic Madness

CHOMOLUNGMA

IT IS ESTIMATED that every second more than twenty-eight people are born and ten die; that every hour nearly eleven thousand newborns cry out. Each day more than one million human conceptions are believed to come about, accompanied by some 150 thousand abortions. Among those newborns, every day thirty-five thousand will die by starvation, twenty-six thousand of them children. Meanwhile, every twenty-four hours the pace of war against the planet increases, sometimes in major affronts, other times imperceptibly, at least by our limited perceptual standards. That war includes the loss of fifty-seven million tons of topsoil and eighty square miles of tropical forest and the creation of seventy square miles of virtually lifeless desert every day. At current birth and death rates, the world is adding a Los Angeles every three weeks. If average human growth rates were to continue at their present course (the so-called "constant fertility variant" or rate of natural increase) the world's population would reach at least ten billion by the year 2030, twenty billion by 2070, forty billion by 2110, and eighty billion by the year 2150.[1] Most social scientists believe the figure will be, at worst, between eleven and twelve billion. But some have not ruled out a population between fifteen and twenty billion.

While I have felt the oppressive weight of people—whether I envision them raging across the countryside, teeming over the concrete, slaughtering other species, burning down forests, or raping one another—I am still not quite conversant with the paradox of my own complicity. That, by association, as one more member of that species, I am as guilty, as out of control and blind as the next man. While my wife and I have had no child, we are two westerners, equal in ecologically destructive impact, I imagine, to at least four hundred of our brethren in the developing world. My response to that estimated ratio should be colossal guilt. Yet, in truth, I cannot trace, or visualize the known burden of myself upon nature. The quantum leap from my personal conduct and lifestyle to an imperiled world is vastly diffused and muted. Yet, there is no doubting the insoluble dilemma, that incessant proximity to more and more members of our own kind, who are at the crux of this biological configuration, of absolutely tragic dimensions. Such bipedal, carnivorous masses are unique in the annals of earthly experience, and surely outweigh all feeble, academic efforts to grapple with demographic theory. Even the theological struggle to explain, and resist, evil falls short of the psychological mayhem, the omnipresent paradox of so many *Homo sapiens*. "There is a concept which corrupts and upsets all the others," writes Jorge Luis Borges. "I refer not to Evil whose limited realm is that of ethics, I refer to the infinite."[2] So many people: six, twelve, fifteen billion people; ever dwindling privacy; the volatility of competing demands, desires, and information. The psyche is overrun by these many components of congestion, this malaise of contagion, these very doubts as to our own nature, and the meaning of so many separate human lives.

So far, in the span of my own life, we have more than doubled our number as a species. Over 90 percent of the growth of the human population has taken place in less than one tenth of 1 percent of our whole species' history. And because half the world's population is now under the age of twenty-four, a third younger than fifteen, it is clear that we have currently reached the base—not the top—of a demographic Mount Everest, or Chomolungma, as those Buddhists dwelling directly beneath the mountain call it.

Though this century has already witnessed an unprecedented human population explosion, we are presently poised to proliferate as never before. Three billion young people will enter their reproductive years in the next twenty years. To sustain even a *nonpetroleum*-based, well-fed economy at current levels of affluence, it has been pointed out that the U.S. population should exceed no more than one hundred million people. We are, as of late 1997, at a petroleum-based population of 270 million. I can think of no better image of this steadfast pyramid of human consumers, this total population dynamic, than that of a mountain like Chomolungma (29,032 feet), cresting above the surrounding Himalayan roof of the world. Where the analogy abruptly ends, however, is with the adjectives appropriate to such a sacred mountain as Chomolungma: wild, free, and magnificent, descriptions that no longer apply to most of the world. Ironically, already Chomolungma herself is showing signs of wear. The effects of overpopulation are starkly clear. Since 1951, thousands of climbers and trekkers to the mountain have left some forty thousand pounds of nondecomposing refuse strewn upon what is, in fact, one of the most fragile of ecosystems, an eight thousand meter peak.[3]

Some social scientists continue to ask, "At what point does the real population crisis set in? Or does it ever set in?" In parts of Egypt, that crisis has meant that school children obtain no more than three hours per day of instruction, so as to make way for incoming shifts of other students; in the Pacific Caroline Islands, the Yapese people were said to have been so overpopulated, and consequently destitute, that "families lived miserably on rafts in the mangrove swamps. . . and that sometimes four hungry men had to make a meal from a single coconut."[4] In 1722, 111 people were left on Easter Island. Polynesians had settled there as early as the third century A.D., and had attained a stable population size of seven thousand. But excessive deforestation meant that no more fishing boats could be constructed, and the eventually malnourished population split into two warring tribes that only succeeded, ultimately, in virtually wiping one another out.[5] Water scarcity in Pakistan, the absolute lack of new arable land in Kenya and Madagascar, are all crisis-level circumstances.

There is absolutely no doubting the links between human population growth—the daunting number of consumers—and environmental turmoil. It is known that, at a minimum, 75 percent of all global demand for fuelwood is the specific function of increasing numbers of consumers.[6] By the year 2030, at least eight billion people will reside in countries previously—but no longer—containing tropical rain forests from which their primary sustenance had once been extracted. Global reforestation is occurring at only a fraction of what would be necessary to ensure long-term fuelwood supplies as against the exponential growth of human numbers. Ninety-four percent of all population growth in the coming decades will likely occur in those developing countries with the most impoverished resource base. In Pakistan, even by the late 1970s there was fuelwood scarcity. Yet Pakistan's population is poised to more than triple in size in the coming two generations, while only 2 to 3 percent of the country's forest cover remains.[7] Where population is increasing most rapidly—from Myanmar to Cameroon—ecological deterioration tends to be the worst; and infant and child mortality, maternal mortality, and the extent of malnutrition and hunger, tend to be the highest.

The trends have long declared themselves. At present, for example, while the world population is growing by 1.8 percent per year, net grain output is growing at less than 1 percent per year. By the end of this century, the amount of arable land per person on the planet will be less than half of what it was in 1951. According to one model, because of the cumulative environmental impacts of overpopulation, global grain harvests will plummet by as much as 10 percent every forty months, on average, in the coming decades, and between fifty and four hundred million additional people will die from starvation.[8]

Nor has this net food deficit been mollified by the nearly eight billion tons of additional artificial fertilizer spewed into the atmosphere each year in the form of carbon dioxide emissions, at least two-thirds of which are the explicit result of overpopulation (i.e., more automobiles and electrification).[9] While future fossil fuel generation in the developed countries may be modified by gains in efficiency and the implementation of best available technologies, in the developing world per capita CO_2 emissions are projected to double in the coming generation. For governments in sub-Saharan Africa, where agricultural production has declined by more than 2 percent annually during the past twenty-four years, condemning at least thirty million people to starvation and chronic malnutrition, and 320 million others, or 65 percent of the total sub-Saharan population to "absolute poverty," such indicators are bewildering.

The sheer habit of finitude plagues any mind that attempts to reconcile seemingly irreconcilable conflict. We use the zero almost as casually as common change. But by 10^5—or one hundred thousand—we are no longer capable of visualizing the size. And this is precisely the point at which Aristotle, writing in Book VII of his *Politics,* suggested the emergence of a crisis in numbers. Human population, he said, is only in balance when it is "both self-sufficient and surveyable."[10] Beyond that surveyable, self-sufficient size, Aristotle advocated, by any standards, hideous alternatives—compulsory abortion, and the mercy killing of children born deformed, though he did not stipulate what kind of deformities. But what does "surveyable" mean in the twentieth century? A man surveys his property. But what about a place like Macao, the most densely human-populated corner of the planet, with 61,383 individuals per square mile over a region of ten square miles? In an essay he named "Despair Viewed under the Aspects of Finitude and Infinitude," (part of his larger work, *On Fear and Trembling*), Søren Kierkegaard psychoanalyzed an individual attempting to survey the unsurveyable. We can't see in the infrared, hear ultrahigh frequencies, nor single ourselves out from a cluster of 5.8 billion other people. The effort leads to loneliness, a kind of ecological existentialism, or insanity.

All of our physical capabilities, desires, and metaphors are conditioned by the need for stability, a precursor of so many of our formulations, general principles, hypotheses, and behavior. Hence, demographers have tended to establish rather arbitrarily a point of stabilization for the human population, much in the manner of Hegel, whose "dialectic" presupposed eventual synthesis and resolution in the human psyche. The World Bank and United Nations have each predicated their respective population projections according to this general impulse, appropriating a formulaic optimism as a means of asserting the inevitability of classic demographic transition. But the whole mental image of humanity's developmental triumphs, the very hope of family planning, is totally absorbed by blue sky. While there is some exceedingly good news (the increasing number of countries showing fertility replacement trends, for example), there is just as much reason for a sinking heart, if not outright panic.

GLOBAL SHOCK

THE BOMB IS now ticking. Every organism dimly perceives the growing shadow. In Oceanic Vanuatu the 1990 population of 151 thousand is expected to reach 205 thousand by the end of the 1990s. And, with its current high TFR of 5.53, the island population is expected to double by the year 2015, a mere generation away. Ten years later, in 2025 Vanuatu may well contain 348 thousand people. To feed and house such an increase in so small a region can only have the most devastating environmental consequences, reminiscent of Easter Island. Vanuatu is a surveyable problem. A dot in the ocean. And yet, even in this one workable microcosm, no solution to the population–environment collision has come to light.

Presently, eight to ten Paris-size cities a year are being added to the world's urban population. There is no way, as yet, to conduct real time population audits of these new megalopolises; no method by which the ecological or psychological impacts may be adequately measured. Too much is happening, too fast. Thought of differently, every eight months there is another Germany, every decade, another South America.[11] And while TFRs throughout the developing world (China excluded) have declined from 6.1 to 4.0 on average, and overall population growth from 2.1 to 1.7–1.8 percent per year, getting these numbers down any further is appearing next to impossible. In fact, because the base population is so much huger than ever before, runaway growth is outstripping the aforementioned declines. The numbers, then, are tragically deceptive. For the human race to check its growth even at 16.5 billion, it will have to reach a two-child (replacement) family by the year 2080. In the United States, at present, only 23 percent of the population actually conforms to a two-child norm.

A global demographic transition assumes that declining fertility will follow declining mortality, an assumption that is proving to be less and less tenable in most low-income countries like Indonesia and India. These countries are stricken with an average sixty-two-year life expectancy, and a mean infant mortality of ninety-four per one thousand, versus eight per one thousand in the industrialized countries.[12] More than half of the poor populations live in ecological zones that are biodiversity hotspots, those particularly vulnerable to further economically induced disruption. Eighty-five percent of all future megacities—ecological tinderboxes—are in the developing world. Each year, for example, Egypt, Ethiopia, and Nigeria add more people to the world than all of Europe combined. What we are seeing is the breakup of any predictability, just at the time when more and more government agencies and administrations are depending upon that presumed underlying orderliness to fulfill donor country targets, meet international treaty mandates, pay back loans, and get reelected. But ecological and economic fragmentation are rendering obsolete all classical demographic transition theory. Postindustrial fertility declines required a century in northwest Europe, but only thirty-five years throughout much of the Pacific Rim and Cuba. In Sri Lanka, China, and Costa Rica, diminished fertility did not coincide with noteworthy industrial development, whereas in Brazil and Mexico zealous industrialization has had little impact on continually escalating fertility rates.

By the year 2000, projections show that 1.2 billion women of reproductive age will have three children on average, and the number of those children under fifteen will have risen to 1.6 billion. By 2025 reproductive-age women will number 1.7 billion and their offspring also 1.7 billion. As technology enables women to conceive later in life, TFR data—sampled, typically, at one time—will tend to be less and less reliable. Moreover, male TFRs are yet to be accounted for. What this all means is that projections for future stabilization—be they population-oriented or ecological—are fraught with uncertainty.

Yet, according to the U.N., the U.S. Bureau of the Census, and the World Bank, demographic transition will effect a global human population stabilization in the middle of the coming century.[13] According to an executive summary of a U.N. document from its Population Division, the range of human stabilization is between six billion (clearly impossible) and nineteen billion for the year 2100.[14] These revised figures are based upon a replacement fertility rate of 2.06. But if fertility stabilization were just minutely higher, at 2.17, the world's population would hit nearly twenty-one billion in the year 2150! What is clearly terrifying to consider is that so miniscule an increase, multiplied by the human population over time, given all the current trends and variables, seems not only plausible, but dreadfully conservative. Demographers play a roulette game of chance. Yet, few people in government, or in science, dare to speak about a human population of twenty-one billion. Only the Vatican continues to uphold a belief that the world could carry on, even with forty billion people. Most scientists consider such convictions absurd. What is certain is the fact that human fertility is more combustible than ever before; its extent, advantage, brain power, carnivorous habits, footprint, hedonism, and malevolence, far in excess of the whole biological past combined.

What if, as outlined earlier, even the 2.17 figure is nothing more than demographic dreaming? What if a global average TFR of 3.0 persists, as it has for the past decade? After all, Africa is projected to remain at a TFR of six, its population expected to triple to 1.6 billion by 2025. And as of 1995, fifty-three countries still showed child mortality rates at or above one hundred per thousand. (In Europe, the average is thirteen.) Twenty countries in 1999 will still be officially considered malnourished, providing less than 90 percent of those respective populations' caloric requirements, engendering "stunting" and "wasting," as the conditions are known. And remarkably, sixty-eight countries containing 18 percent of the world's population are currently either maintaining or actually encouraging a rise in their fertility rates.[15] The major population centers—India, China, Indonesia, and the U.S., which until recently prided themselves on family planning—are all losing ground to wave after wave of new baby booms. Given the enormity of the world's present fertility base, the triggers seem to be transcending culture or technology. They are purely mathematical. In spite of all the talk of environmental mediation, international family planning, and the very best intentions, such mathematics indicate a war that has gotten totally out of our control.

PROJECTING INTO THE FUTURE?

POPULATION PROJECTIONS ARE based upon a host of assumptions. If the assumptions are off to any extent, so are the projections. The variables are exasperating. For example, population momentum ensures that all growth will continue for many decades before any assumed new norms are likely to set in. Human disaster tends to work in favor of more and more people. In many countries, economic success is also translating into higher fertility rates, as witnessed in Singapore and China. And, as for the much-touted principle of education, in Kerala it has had a major impact on fertility, but less so in California, Mexico, or Malaysia. And in poor Mali, the literacy rate has actually declined in the past two decades, not risen.

The biggest contradiction inherent to all stabilization projections is the very assumption that the human population will ever stabilize; or that the human condition is inevitably headed toward more wealth, more leisure, more security, when in fact all indications suggest the opposite. The standard of living, the so-called quality of life package, is rapidly diminishing for more and more people—billions of people in fact. Against such trends, how can anyone trust that fertility and mortality will eventually fall into some heavenly harmony? Economic and educational advantages are slipping for more people. On what grounds, then, can demography assume anything about demographic resolution?

Population experts have presumed that the conditions making for the most progressive region within a country will spread to all other regions in due time. In India and China these are doubtful deductions. For example, the replicability of the Tamil Nadu/Kerala TFRs, literacy rates, and IMRs may not be possible in any other Indian states, in which case, if India continues to grow, it will double, triple, and quadruple its size within a timeframe that is projected, instead, to stabilize. Zimbabwe has achieved a rather progressive contraceptive prevalence rate of over 30 percent and yet its TFR is still a high 4.4. The region of Chogoria in central Kenya is a good percentile point below the rest of the country in terms of TFR, but its success does not appear to be spreading elsewhere throughout that nation.

The entire North American growth rate of an annual 0.9 is projected to decrease to 0.3 by 2025 as a result of diminished net migration from Latin America. Yet statistics from California, the country's most populous state, show a doubling of numbers (comparable to Uttar Pradesh) and an enormous increase in migration (not unlike the situation in India's Bihar state). The notion that the world's total fertility rate is projected to decline from 3.3 to 2.9 in seven years, and then to 2.4 by 2025 is based upon nothing more than vague institutional optimism. "For countries with high fertility, the trend is assumed to be downward, and substantial fertility decline is projected."[16] Just like that!

Fifty countries currently show incomes under $610 per capita per year.[17] Another fifty-five or so are lower-middle income, from $610 to $2399. Still another thirty-three countries are, by any Western standards, poor. These include the Czech Republic and Brazil. All of these nations demonstrate the very economic adversity that has traditionally lent itself to higher and higher birthrates, not declines. While declining fertility assumptions by the World Bank and others are said to have no predictive relationship to socioeconomic factors, those are precisely the factors that have held sway during the initial fertility transitions in the two most populous countries in the world, and now appear to be doing so, contrary to most expectations, in Kenya. And if one assumption is incorrect, many probably are. For example, a higher TFR value will skew the anticipated decline in the proportion of individuals under the age of fifteen, meaning a larger percentage of childbearing females, and thus a larger built-in population momentum than expected. Optimism on this stage of life is a house of cards. Thus, the editors of the World Bank Working Papers caution a "universal qualifier that population will follow the indicated path if the assumptions prove to be correct."[18] And if the assumptions prove to be incorrect? Add a global recession and the mounting "trigger" of ecological collapse throughout the world, and all such population assumptions and projections go up in smoke.

To appreciate the sense of discrepancy that prevails within the demographic community, note that the World Bank Working Papers project that China will "remain the most populous country until 2120."[19] Yet dozens of independent demographers all predict that India will overtake China within two generations. Like some macabre game of chicken: two conflicting sets of data race toward a brink, crossing over the domains of urban and rural health care, ecology, religion, anthropology, politics, the world market economy, the shifting geopolitical landscape, the engineering, biotechnology, and military sectors, even ecotourism and telecommunications. The falling market for coconuts, the rising value of tennis shoes, the Pope's travel itinerary, new emergent contraceptive technologies, the age of certain political leaders, the extent of groundwater pollution, the death of mackerel, daily calorie supply, the scope of infant immunization, secondary school enrollment, the rate of inflation, political freedom, and civil rights, all enter into the equation of demographic projection.

In a recent study of women in twelve countries, it was shown that breast-feeding beyond the resumption of menstruation and sexual relations, following a birth had a "considerable contraceptive effect."[20] UNICEF says that breast-feeding could save 1.5 million lives a year, as well as sparing the 250 thousand children who are permanently blinded from vitamin A deficiency disease. Yet, few hospitals or doctors normally advocate breast-feeding as a form of contraception. And the same bias prevails with regard to the "rhythm method" which can be 97.5 percent effective, according to the World Health Organization. Even periodic abstinence has an 80 percent effectiveness rate, better than spermicides or sponges, about the same as a diaphragm, and just slightly less than the condom.

And yet, despite forty years of concentrated family planning worldwide, neither breast-feeding (which of course requires no genius, no literacy, no technology whatsoever) nor other natural methods have exerted the kind of population controls that many have hoped for. Experts argue it is because the educational component is lacking. Others attribute this missed opportunity to maternal morbidity, economic fallout, ecological stress, or lack of access to family planning services affecting at least three hundred million couples.[21] During the decade of the 1990s, another one hundred million couples will need family planning services just to maintain the status quo. According to a WHO/UNFPA/UNICEF statement, every year thirteen million children die before their fifth birthday and five hundred thousand women die from pregnancy complications, but "with current technology, the majority of these deaths could be prevented."[22]

There is no question that new technologies, and the greater application of existing ones, could alter the demographic outlook. UNICEF saves nearly two million children each year through the administering of measles vaccinations. Breast-feeding traditionally saves lives. But the demographic dangling modifier is more intractable than anyone ever imagined: Will such technologies and techniques increase or decrease the overall size of the human population, keeping in mind that it is precisely the advances in medical technology, the best-laid plans of humanitarianism, for example, that paved the way for India's and Africa's population booms?

Such data leaves the question wide open as to whether or not new technologies are likely to have any impact on curtailing fertility in the future.

Every factor influencing demographic projections confronts the same unknowable forces. Disaster breeds disaster. Medical technology devised and applied compassionately can inadvertently invoke even greater pain and suffering by keeping more people alive for longer periods and setting the groundwork for more and more children. Healthier children are understood to be the secret to fewer children. And yet, just the opposite can also be argued. There are no rules. Human nature, like every other force of nature, defies consistency.

And even where the highest TFRs might be expected eventually to come down (i.e., Rwanda from 6.2, Yemen from 7.2) other high TFRs are now going even higher—in Mozambique, Tanzania, and Niger, for example. And there are a host of other crucial quantitative observations that defy certitude or predetermination. For example, the World Bank estimates that by the year 2000 the developing world will suddenly start declining in growth— just like that. Why should it, coming right after the largest population growth rate in world history? And there are now the largest proportion of childbearing females ever! How can it be assumed that within one generation, twenty-two million fewer children will be born every year? The reason, of course, is that it simply "has to be" that way if fertility and mortality are going to even out, or harmonize, by the year 2150. This "harmony" is an arbitrary goal that says more about the human psyche and its perennial faith in the future, than it does about any hard science of numbers.

A good indication of the inherent vulnerability of such data is the total number of females in their childbearing years (fifteen to forty-four) as calculated in 1995 and again in 2150. In every significant country, there will be many more such women 155 years hence. Unless all other assumptions are fulfilled in the domains of health care, education, environmental remediation, and economic equality, these numbers indicate anything but stabilization.

In countries like Iran, Iraq, Pakistan, Egypt, India, Indonesia, Brazil, Mexico, Nigeria, the Philippines, Vietnam, and China, these inherent fertility faults in the smooth surface of mathematics—inherent volatilities of culture and economics, politics and religion, ecology and healthcare—provide no sure indication whatsoever of the planet's future. In China, 1998 will see 44 million girls added to the "teenage" sector, but in the year 2150, 53 million of them will be added. In India, overall there will be 260 million teenage girls in 1998, but in 2150, 370 million of them. In Malaysia, 1998 will see 3.5 million teenage girls, but the year 2150 will see over 8 million of them. In Pakistan, the gap is enormous: from a 1995 figure of 33 million teenage females to nearly 80 million females of childbearing age in 2150. Officials in many of these countries may insist all they like that there are no teen pregnancies, but the fact remains that millions of teenage girls are having babies and in nearly every country such teen pregnancies are on the rise, as they are dramatically in a place like Los Angeles.

Many of these young people, in over forty countries, in countless interviews and discussions with me, have expressed their common depression, sense of futility, and fatalism about the planet as they view it, adding fuel to their determination to enjoy life while they can. There are very few good arguments to dissuade them from having sex in a world where tigers and chimpanzees are going extinct. Even the prescriptions for "safe sex" lose cogency in a world so fraught with decay. Add to these intuitive syndromes one other astonishing fact: worldwide the average age of first menstruation is dropping! This trend corresponds with what must be seen as a global emphasis on earlier sex. Throughout Latin America, birthrates among teen mothers are extremely high—15 percent in El Salvador, for example. By the year 2000, there will be nearly 130 million teenagers in Latin America. Only 10 percent of them use any form of contraception, often erratically and hence, ineffectively. In Africa, 40 percent of all women have their first child before the age of eighteen. In at least one coastal district of Kenya, a country that has until recently placed a premium on female education, girls are getting married as early as the age of nine.

Only Brazil, among the fastest growing of large nations, will have a slightly lower fertile female count in the twenty-second century than it does now—by a few million. Yet, Brazil's population will have doubled from its

1990 figure of 150 million to over 300 million by then.[23] Again, according to the "harmony" (stabilization) scenario, China's and India's populations are expected to become stable by the year 2150, at 1.8 and 1.85 billion respectively, while Indonesia is expected to reach 375 million at that time. *The Working Papers* see Indonesia's population doubling by the year 2110, yet some government officials within Indonesia see it happening by the year 2040. Even in a defined, relatively small area—Shenyang, China, for example—projections are at odds. Shenyang's Environmental Protection Bureau has declared the city's annual population growth rate to be 1.5 percent. The U.N., however, estimates a growth rate of exactly double that.[24]

In sum, future contraceptive technologies and medical breakthroughs, increasing economic disparities, massive urbanization, emerging viruses susceptible to ecological disruption, a fast-growing population base among teenagers, and the unpredictability of fertility rebounds following disasters, all bode of population instability.

But, regardless of the imprecision and huge discrepancies of demographic projections, one unambiguous fact remains: the current size of the human population has wreaked unprecedented damage on the biosphere, and is going to accelerate that damage. Millions of plant and animal species will be driven to extinction. Hundreds of millions of innocent children, women, and men have been, and will be, slaughtered, in one form or another. A billion people are hungry. The ozone layer is thinning, with consequences that are lethal for every living organism. The air, water, and soil across the planet have been fouled. The forests in many countries are gone or nearly gone. And the mammary glands of every mother on Earth are now infiltrated with DDT and other harmful chemicals. These essential facts—truths that distinguish this century from any other in our history—are all the result of uncontrolled human fertility and thoughtless behavior. Even if we should somehow manage to merely double our population size by the next century, attaining, in other words, a number of twelve billion, the ecological damage will be catastrophic.

Oddly, despite this litany of woes, there is a new sense of ecological consciousness and stewardship throughout the world; a spirit of environmental community that is rapidly trying to mobilize in order to meet this disaster head-on. Whether a similar mobilization to meet the even more difficult crisis of as yet unborn children can be accomplished quickly, humanely, and firmly, will determine whether any kind of qualitative human future is even possible.

PHOTO BY M. TOBIAS

~Epilogue~
A Global Truce

The Power to Heal

T HERE ARE NO pat miracle cures for the crisis of human overpopulation, though countless temporary anodynes for those with the health, money, or leisure time to pursue them. Overpopulation and its ills, like the world war to which I have likened them, bring out the absolute worst in human nature, though this fact is initially disguised by its participants, our most elite corps, our very children, soon to become unwitting warriors. The system of human fertility is the machine that doesn't know it's broken. Confronting this paradox may well exceed the limits and tolerance of rationality, or of genes. Demographers, like philosophers, are well disposed toward a good debate. While Malthus has his share of followers, there are many, like those with the International Institute for Applied Systems Analaysis, who in 1997 declared that the world's population will never double again but, rather, should ease down to 10.4 billion by the end of the next century. But many others are less optimistic.

Yet, whether ten or twenty billion, the wars of overpopulation are more elusive, colossal, and unprecedented than all previous conflicts. Even ten billion is a number that is hard to fathom given that human behavior appears guided not by the urgings and imperatives of any collective goal or decision making process, but rather by individual appetites, in association with those few others in our lives to whom immediate gratification is tied—a spouse, children, one's parents, even one's rival. The "tragedy of the commons" (as the phrased was first voiced in a groundbreaking essay in 1968 by lifeboat ethicist Garret Hardin) is the tragedy of human individualism, sometimes positive, too often negative.

And yet, therein lies a profound hope. Having posited what I take to be fundamentally distinct about *Homo sapiens*—our individualism—I am thus led to this crucial observation, the one that must be mustered in defense of every tomorrow, namely, our capacity to express love. That is the power to heal, and it contradicts every gross approximation and generality of the masses.

Our innumerous acts of self-sacrifice, spiritualism, great art, and nonviolence transcend, and even outweigh, the more noticeable bursts of bedlam and barbarity throughout our history. While it is possible and tempting to condemn our species, there can be no greater emotion, no finer tears, than that recognition of our awesome potential. Herein lies the crux of our biological future, our *new nature.*

Sadly, ponderously, we are too many. This incredible dilemma imposes a near ethical impasse. But, true to our genetic disposition, we may still reconcile our numbers by focusing on those very traits that mark our individuality, our strength. The impact of overpopulation on all resident life forms is a global Holocaust. Our survival absolutely hinges upon those qualities of forgiveness, faith, art, and nonviolence that are generously distributed throughout our species, though perhaps less likely to be exhibited in large groups or bureaucracies.

As never before, the gift of our individual humanity must *inform* the collective. This challenge must engender personal missions of utmost conviction and urgency, focused upon extraordinary levels of decisiveness based upon empathy. There is no economic nirvana to which we can escape from the population explosion. We can only serve the world through honesty, directly and responsibly; by opening our eyes to the troubles all around us, and working toward change. A democracy provides no assurance of such change. Only individuals can do that.

I have argued throughout this book that two forms of action, in tandem, are essential if we are to end the war—namely, family planning at an enlightened, massive level and an equally dedicated global strategy for preserving and restoring biodiversity and vast regions of wilderness. Both endeavors will take money, lots of it, and the courageous selection of priorities and ecological hot spots from among so many imperatives. What new terms and conditions of survival will enable countless billions of rough moving, carnivorous primates, loosely known as human beings to forge a global truce that supports and sways not merely the poor and the rich alike, indigenous peoples, local lawmakers, taxpayers, even whole nations, but the entire global community of nations? Is the arithmetic even plausible, that a renaissance in individual ethics and efforts should somehow overturn a global genetic propensity, remaking the species? The critical mass, as it is so often referred to, is actually dependent upon the critical *person.* The continuation of our species hinges upon recognition that our individual morals are linked to an ecological bottom line.

Every personal encounter with anguish—either directly or secondhand—is actually a cogent building block for a new school of thinking that should radically change my person, and by logical inference, a world of persons. This is the ambition of every student who is still relatively unclouded and undiscouraged, to be able to hope clearly, to presume that human nature is malleable, that it can learn from, and be empowered by, its mistakes. As philosopher Robert Nozick has written, echoing the sentiments of Martin Heidegger, "The evolutionary basis of rationality does not doom us to continuing on any previously marked evolutionary track."[1] The cumulative force of rationality is a tantalizing haiku, an open book of enormous promise. But do we have the power, as a species, to appreciate cause and effect, to live together harmoniously, to be wise?

All genes evolved in the light of family and beauty, with a sense of the divine in nature, of altruistic bonds that can best be seen among mothers of every species. But it is more difficult to imagine that those same genetic impulses could have been prepared for the temptation to heal an entire country, or continent, or planet. As humans, our neurology cannot possibly be expected to extend the love of family, or the multispecial biophilia evident at a place like Amboseli, to the whole world. It is a nonrational, though necessary wish, born of a unique awareness—part information glut, part compassion—that has made many half-crazy with the zeal of an enormous ambition, the engendering of this new nature, the realizing of what it is, or can mean, to be truly human.

Belief systems are hard to alter. As "human exceptionalists" we have always considered ourselves somehow immune to brute nature. How could we have predicted that mass man, who has sought to transcend the harsh vagaries of "primitive biology," would have, in effect, created the most primitive nature of all, one more red in tooth and claw than anything nature ever devised?

Ironically, the hope for eventual balance is born in the very thickets and L.A.s of the population crisis. With enough aware people on the planet, there will be those who take up the selfless task of attempting to effect a difference. Certainly several thousand NGOS, and their millions of supporters, are trying. In fact, as of 1995, it was estimated that there were as many as five hundred thousand NGOs in the world. As the Chinese and their fifty million family planning volunteers have discovered, the sheer number of present cadres, of individuals taking the reins in modest, but decisive ways, offers the one and only blind antidote to the predicament of ourselves.

The world, by nature, is perfect. It needs no solutions. But if one accepts the premise—and it would be unimaginably stupid and evil not to—that biodiversity is necessary, that this planet has invested nearly four billion years in the propagation of wide-ranging life, then it must be conceded that human nature is somehow mysteriously in trouble, out of sync with the Earth's purpose and destiny. Yet, we have the power to heal ourselves, and we must do so if the biological world, of which we are a fragile part, is to survive.

By "World War III" I have meant to designate not only the concerted devastation our species is levying upon the whole planet, but the war we must wage to end this state of affairs.

THE ECOLOGICAL CONSCIENCE

THERE ARE ANY number of cultural examples, both contemporary and historical, to suggest qualities of lived (as opposed to merely thought) nonviolence and ecological sustainability.[2] Take, for example, the Jains, Todas, and Bishnoi of India, the Drukpa of Bhutan, the Lepcha of Sikkim, the Karen of the Thai–Myanmar border area, and the Tasaday of the Southern Philippines. Each bring to the table thousands of years of nonviolence and ecological sensitivity.[3]

Consider the Jains. The vast majority of the approximately seven million-strong Jain community are vegetarian, and engaged characteristically in those professions and businesses that only minimally harm the environment, and do not profit from any kind of animal product. While Jainism is arguably one of the oldest religions in the world, its "modern" renaissance was unleashed in the person of Mahavira (599–27 B.C.), an elder contemporary of Buddha. Mahavira spent most of his adult life naked, having renounced all possessions, including his clothing (as would Saint Francis nearly seventeen hundred years later). He walked throughout India discussing and formulating the rudiments of *ahimsa,* or nonviolence, in addition to other key Jain principles, such as tolerance and multiple-viewpoints, nonacquisition, abstinence, nonstealing, and truth. Mahavira reasoned that all living beings are endowed with a soul that must be respected and nurtured. Equally important to Jainism is the revelation that all souls, all biological beings, are interdependent (*parasparopagraho jivanam*). In fact, according to Jainism, it is humanity's duty to safeguard and shepherd that interdependency. Consequently most Jains, not merely those few monks who go naked or are clad in white robes, have adopted a philosophy of minimalist consumption.

In negotiating their way through the maze of destructive behavior that is endemic to most human life, the Jains have managed to a remarkable degree to impede the accumulation of ill thoughts, ill deeds, even inadvertent imposition. This, they say, is the only way to achieve peace. At every juncture of human behavior, the Jains have sought to enshrine gentleness, finding a viable path toward love that can be embraced by an entire community. This ecology of the soul (*jiva*) consists of care taken in all actions and thoughts: to forgive, to be universally friendly, compassionate, and affirmative; to exercise critical self-examination at all times, as well as restraint in all matters; to fast frequently, and meditate on nonviolence for forty-eight minutes at the beginning of every day (*samayika*); to follow a holy path that ultimately leads to total renunciation.

By definition, these behavioral codes are strictly ecological; and they extend to family planning. While they frown upon abortion, lay Jains are not at all averse to making practical choices based upon an empathetic concern for the pregnant woman. Jainism is one of the only religions in history that can claim to have granted totally equal status to men and women. The implications of this extend to the classroom, the bedroom, the workplace, and to the legislative domain. One result has been relatively small Jain families.

And in one other crucial manner, Jainism goes far beyond mere harmonious introspection: said Mahavira, "A wise man should not act sinfully toward earth, nor cause others to act so, nor allow others to act so. . . ."[4] It is this ecological and moral injunction that has endowed Jainism with its activist disposition and urgently contemporary character.

Vegetarianism has always been obvious to Jains. The increasingly modern revulsion to "hamburger colonialism" is one important key to environmental stability on the planet. Meat eating is obviously plausible under conditions observable, say, at the Serengeti, where the number of carnivores in relation to prey, is still in balance. But in a world of several billion humans, meat eating is disastrous. Human meat eating kills tens of billions of animals per year under unimaginably cruel circumstances; it also destroys untold millions of hectares of rain forest and pasture land needlessly, while deeply widening the gap between the rich and poor, between food-sufficient and food-deficient communities. The energy-intensive requirements to grow, spray, harvest, process, and transport a pound of meat multiplied by the total of meat-consuming humans, accounts for over 350 billion pounds of meat, each year, and a vast proportion of our fossil fuel and pesticide dependencies. But it is the ethical, not economic maxim which, hopefully, should ultimately sway the human heart, and this is where Jain idealism provides a unique blueprint for all twenty-first-century individuals.

Mahatma Gandhi was raised by a Jain tutor. Gandhi's revolution argued that, in essence, Jain economics and ethics were at the basis of any nonviolent, sustainable community. Gandhi was an optimist. He believed that even in an overcrowded world, compassion, joy, ecological integrity, and human dignity are possible.

A SUSTAINABLE FUTURE?

IT IS ESTIMATED that all of the population programs together have, historically, thus far prevented four hundred million people from being born (more than half in China). In the twenty-first century, if such family planning assistance continues and (hopefully) increases, four billion fewer people are expected.[5] Contraceptive prevalence has risen dramatically throughout the world—83 percent of married women in China, more than that on average in most rapidly industrializing countries, and 43 percent across much of the developing world. Child and infant mortality have dropped by a third in the developing countries, particularly among those couples availing themselves of contraception. The use of contraception has had an important impact on higher levels of adult female literacy.[6] If such data reflects even a semblance of what is actually possible, then it should be key to conceptualizing and enforcing all future political and economic priorities. Indeed, the U.N. slogan—"every child a wanted child"—needs to be facilitated in every country by the implementation of better contraceptive and health services.[7] That is not political rhetoric but an elegant summons to a true revolution in biological family values that is nonviolent to the core.

UNICEF stated in its 1992 *State of the World's Children* report, "the responsible planning of births is one of the most effective and least expensive ways of improving the quality of life on earth, both now and in the future, and one of the greatest mistakes of our times is the failure to realize this potential." The argument for drastically enhanced population funding should be clear enough. From a strictly national budgetary perspective, this is especially so. In the broadest sense, there is no greater economic, moral, and ecological recovery to be effected than through family planning. Yet, Americans spend more money on defense in twelve hours than is spent annually for family planning services. And those services are still held hostage by a Republican-dominated Congress that will not give money for family planning if, in any way, such funds are tied to medical termination of pregnancy—even if an agency gives money to a health clinic that provides literature in some Third World country on the possibilities for abortion. Our funding mindset has not really changed much from the turn of the century when people like Margaret Sanger were harassed by the police for passing out contraceptive literature.

There are distinct biases hampering the flow of sorely needed population assistance, just as the world has seen the least amount of food donations in forty years, according to a late 1997 report by the U.N. Food and Agriculture Organization. Of the 117 developing countries, nearly half of them will be dependent on foreign foodstuffs by the turn of the century.

There is clear evidence of "donor fatigue" in nearly every sector of human health and welfare. There may be underlying causes. Thomas Malthus argued against charity because, he said, it fostered population growth and hence, human misery. So-called lifeboat ethicists believe that by feeding starving children today, one is actually perpetuating a syndrome of starving children later on. The logical inference is that charity, compassion, aid, even medical assistance, increase population, which is certainly true if infant mortality rates are reduced. According to this same logic, by increasing the standard of living in an effort to engender smaller families, one may well be setting the preconditions for greater exploitation of the environment.

If that is the case, why do anything? In fact, why have smaller families at all if the end result will be the same, in terms of ecological impact? Does a smaller, wealthier family impact nature with the same severity as a larger, poorer one? It is a classic conceptual entrapment, an ethical no-win situation that can only be intelligently addressed on a case-by-case basis. Per capita CO_2 production in the U.S. is much higher than in Jordan, though the Jordanian TFR is nearly double that of the U.S. Poverty in Senegal has translated into an enormous amount of poaching; the Malaysian middle class is living off the spoils of tropical clear-cutting. In other words, there are no ecological guarantees that can be predicated merely upon family size or economic status. It is the combination of the two, under the particular, and widely varied, circumstances of human geography, that determines the extent of measurable environmental damage.

Aggressive prosperity cannot be held back, anywhere. And while there is no question that wealth has destroyed much of the world, it is hopeless to wage a war in defense of the Earth by combating such wealth. A more politically and ethically realistic solution will be to make that wealth work for nature and smaller families: to ecologically temper and redirect existing, and future profits in comprehensively well-planned, sustainable, and equitable fashions. Ecological sustainability will become the primary organizational impetus of the twenty-first century, but only if compelling economic systems support it.

At the 1994 Cairo Conference, delegates concluded that by the year 2015, to keep up with family planning needs, all contributions from developed and developing countries must equal nearly twenty-two billion dollars per year, in addition to six billion dollars for universal primary education. Of that, the United States would need to provide approximately

$1.85 billion per year. Yet, at present, our annual total contribution is under four hundred million dollars. In fact, the real dollar value of contributions to family planning by developed countries has been declining steadily. Currently, it is less than two dollars per capita per year. The platitudinous twenty-year Program of Action that resulted from the Cairo conference was neither binding nor precise, and seemed to reflect nothing but blurred language, formal compromises, and vague goals for the future, all handicapped by the Vatican's stance against birth control. Was it ever plausible to expect a few hundred politicians under an enormous media spotlight to design a blueprint that would transform the bedroom behavior of 2.5 billion sexually active individuals?

The real work is being done out in the trenches, by people like Nurse Alice in Nairobi; or in far less politicized conceptual environments and think tanks. Take the Greenpeace organization, for example, which has advocated a "Superfund for Workers" in the U.S. to help effect the inevitable transition to a clean energy economy. Others have promoted a Global Environmental Protection Agency; "compassion screens" for a new generation of investments; new types of energy and community development cooperatives, such as those engendered by A. T. Ariayartne throughout Sri Lanka, the Twin Oaks community in Virginia, or the Gaviotas commune between the Andes and Orinoco River in Colombia; and rural mobilization squads fueled by such successful low-scale lending organizations as the Grameen Rural Bank. From solar box cookers and tree planting schemes to the ultimate energy transformation on Earth—renewably produced hydrogen, coupled with fuel cells—the technology, the wisdom and passion to save the Earth is not in short supply. Ecotourism offers other effective means of targeting funds at biodiversity and indigenous culture revitalization, in addition to refamiliarizing many who have been desentizied, to the natural world.

Writes E. O. Wilson, "familiarity will save ecosystems, because bioeconomic and aesthetic values grow as each constituent species is examined in turn—and so will sentiment in favor of preservation . . . the better an ecosystem is known, the less likely it will be destroyed . . ."[8]

Such familiarity is in its adolesence. Nearly every Environmental Protection Agency the world over, including that of the U.S., has emerged in just the past twenty-five years. With this newfound agitation for a better world, countless international ecological treaties have been recently concluded, where no previous moderation, understanding, or protection under any laws existed.[9] And as free trade enriches the prospects for individual nations, so too the power of sanctions and popular boycott become important tools of ecologically minded trading partners. The U.S. Senate passed legislation in 1986 mandating the public's right to know what corporations are doing; and such "public right to know" laws are now being replicated throughout much of the Third World. But they entail, conversely, the responsibility of awareness on the part of the public, a fact public activist Ralph Nader has hit upon for many years. Our increasing concern about the environment, helped along by the renaissance in telecommunications, may be the most important single cause for optimism. A U.N. poll in the late 1980s suggests that the overwhelming majority of all people on the planet are concerned about the environment. Ecology may have more followers than any religion in history.

Awareness exacts a price. In a world of scarcity, political and ecological triage will inevitably figure. Even with a projected fifty-trillion-dollar annual economy, the increasing number of newborns on the planet will not make decisions any easier. Will one set out to assist Russia, Brazil, Indonesia, or Mali? The school system in Alabama or teenage mothers in India? And when conflicts arise, which are to become our national priorities in terms of intervention? Nuclear proliferation in Asia or illegal clear-cutting in Sumatra? Such questions have always weighed upon political leaders, in one form or another, but never before have ecological and population considerations played such dramatic roles in analysis and national determinations.

Individual men and women, boys and girls, are called upon to become policy makers, to think, to feel, to make those determinations, to take their lifestyles into greater consideration than ever before. By example they can inspire surprisingly huge assemblages of people. Ethical solutions, reasonableness, beauty, and inspiration, all have in their favor the force of silent majorities, the equivalent power of chain letters, the quiet seduction of an ideal.

From my perspective, it would be a very good thing indeed, if even a smattering of the Jain monks' daily vows infiltrated the consciousness of every nation. That would mean a life choreographed according to possibilities of nonviolence, the basis for any sustainable, compassionate, and equitable community on earth; universal one-child families, the only way to begin to slow down the human population explosion in those more than 150 countries and territories where there is a demographic problem; and an emphasis in our lives upon sharing, that human and humane capacity that best reflects the abundant generosity inherent to the creation.

Our species, by its very nature, has long been engaged in a war against the planet, a pattern that is ecologically insane. We know this to be true by now. Our acknowledgment itself is an act of meditation poised for selfless, even heroic change. Among more and more of the world's religious thinkers, there is a surge of ecologically aware activism. Buddhists in Thailand are fighting to save forests. Jews, Catholics, and Anglicans in the U.S. have sponsored a National Religious Partnership for the Environment. And in late 1997 the leader of some three hundred million Orthodox Christians, Bartholomew I, finally declared that "To commit a crime against the natural world is a sin. For humans to cause species to become extinct and to destroy the biological diversity of God's creation, for humans to degrade the integrity of the Earth by causing changes in its climate, stripping the Earth of its natural forests, or destroying its wetlands ... for humans to contaminate the Earth's waters, its land, its air, and its life with poisonous substances—these are sins."[10] It was the first time that word "sin" has ever been officially linked by the Church to human behavior toward the environment.

The same week Bartholomew made this pronouncement, demographers also made big news. They had gathered in New York at the request of the United Nations Population Division to examine the whys and wherefores of a silent revolution underway. In a not altogether unexpected trend, an inexplicable dynamic was shown to be at work, effecting smaller families in at least forty-five countries. According to the *World Population Prospects: The 1996 Revision,* world fertility rates were seen to be falling rapidly. One journalist, Ben J. Wattenberg, writing for the *New York Times* in a piece entitled "The Population Explosion Is Over," described the plight of fertility rates as "tumbling" and worried about a world underpopulated, topping out at about 8.5 billion in the year 2050; a world of "more lonely people, without siblings, uncles, aunts, cousins, children, or grandchildren."[11] The demographers who had assembled jointly predicted that by the year 2015, eighty-eight "countries and territories will have replacement levels at or below 2.1 children per woman."[12] Few of those countries cited were among the high-population nations. While the pattern seemed, indeed, to be spreading, the mathematical demon has not arrested, but actually reversed such causes for optimism in those dozens of high-fertility regions where abortion is illegal, or where tradition favors males, and where the inherent momentum has already predisposed those countries in question to gigantic and unsustainable populations (such as India, China, Pakistan, Indonesia, and Nigeria). As one long-time population expert, Bob Gillespie, responded (incredulous, like many others, that such a flawed perspective was given such attention) "He's got the numbers all wrong." The Population Institute responded by noting that 1997 saw more than eighty million newborns added to the planet; and that at least seventy-four countries will most likely double their population within thirty years. More than thirty-three countries in Africa still show TFRs exceeding six. Indeed, as we approach the end of the millennium, there are definitely two heated camps, working according to vastly different assumptions, and published data. This, too, will not make international family planning any easier, particularly as Congressional debate over America's contribution to the International Monetary Fund and its repayment of debt to the United Nations is increasingly tied to questions of federal funding of any private or government organizations overseas that provide abortion services. As president of the Population Institue, Werner Fornos, put it, "It would be arrogant on our part to think that the problem is over because the Caucasian race has balanced its population, and that we can now ignore the problems of the poorest of the poor."

As we have seen, there have been great strides in family planning, hundreds of millions of children prevented from being born since the time of Margaret Sanger. Fertility levels have plunged in many countries, no more so than in China. But the analysis of China's population explosion, and corresponding patterns of consumptive wildfires, and the difficulty so many other countries are having in pushing their fertility rates much lower, hardly makes for the euphoria that has prompted some demographers and journalists to cite the end of an era.

Nonetheless, we must remain optimistic if such new trends and attitudes are to gain fuel; to augur the kind of changes necessary to preserve the planet. Awareness itself, tempered by reason, must be nurtured and protected. It takes great courage to be an optimist, to be in love. There are important spiritual, behavioral, and self-fulfilling reasons for adopting a positive perspective.

Having delved into the labyrinth of population pain, it seems clear to me that, as a species, we need all the clarity-grounded optimism we can muster. Our children need to be informed and inspired, not daunted.

Although the planet is held captive by much that defines our personality and behavior, that aggression and its multiple tragedies need not be destiny.

But in reperceiving global fate beyond simple hope, certain sobering truths must be firmly absorbed and embraced. I quote: "The indispensable strategy for saving our fellow living creatures and ourselves in the long run, is, as the evidence compellingly shows, to reduce the scale of human activities. The task of accomplishing this goal will involve a cooperative worldwide effort unprecedented in history," write Paul Ehrlich and Edward Wilson, two of the leading ecologists of this century.[13] That invocation has similarly been endorsed by 1670 scientists in seventy-one countries, 102 of them Nobel laureates, who signed a population stabilization statement by the Union of Concerned Scientists, which declares, "Fundamental changes are urgent if we are to avoid the collision our present course will bring about . . . if vast human misery is to be avoided and our global home on this planet is not to be irretrievably mutilated."[14]

Throughout human history, hope and dread have always mingled. But never before have the risks been so permanent. Paradise is here, now, if only we will own up to it, accept it, and do our part to keep it true.

While timing is everything, we must all be prepared for a lifetime of service and diligence. The ethical and ecological responsibilities that being human entails will only increase as humanity finally comes of age.

~Endnotes~

1: The Balance of Nature

1. The work of Jostein Goksoyr, discussed in E. O. Wilson, *The Diversity of Life* (Cambridge, Mass.: Belknap Press of Harvard University, 1993), 144.

2. See Andrew M. Karmack, *The Tropics and Economic Development: A Provocative Inquiry into the Poverty of Nations* (Washington, D.C.: A World Bank Publication, 1976), 23.

3. Wilson, *Diversity of Life*, 210–11.

4. What finally upset the perfect balance achieved by the Pecos Indians were economic decisions taken by the Spanish in Mexico City, prompting one Francisco Vasquez de Coronado to lead his troops in search of the fabled Cibola, City of Gold. Whatever lessons of population stability and simplicity of lifestyle the North American indigenous peoples had to offer were, as yet, a few hundred years ahead of their time.

5. "Career-minded Singapore women have little time for marriage," "Agencies," *The Times of India*, September 20, 1997, 12.

6. See Wilson, *Diversity of Life*, 247–49.

7. See J. Smith's "Man's Impact upon Some New Guinea Mountain Ecosystems," in *Subsistence and Survival: Rural Ecology in the Pacific*, ed. T. Bayliss-Smith and R. Feachem (New York: Academic Press, 1977), 185–214; and Hagen, "Man and Nature: Reflections on Culture and Ecology," *Norwegian Archaeological Review* 172:5 (1), 1–22.

8. See Raymond Dart, "The Predatory Transition from Ape to Man," *International Anthropological and Linguistic Review* I (1953).

9. Wilson, *Diversity of Life*, 169.

10. See Ron Naveen, Colin Monteath, Tui De Roy, and Mark Jones, *Wild Ice: Antarctic Journeys* (Washington, D.C.: Smithsonian Institution Press, 1990), 37.

11. See author's film, *Antarctica: The Last Continent*, PBS, 1987; see also author's article "The Next Wasteland: Can the Spoiling of Antarctica Be Stopped?" *The Sciences* (March/April 1989), 18–25.

12. See Kim A. McDonald, "Penguins in Peril," in *The Chronicle of Higher Education*, January 5, 1994, A6, A7, A15.

13. See Catherine L. Albanese, *Nature Religion in America from the Algonkian Indians to the New Age* (Chicago: University of Chicago Press, 1990), 67.

14. Touche Ross Management Consultants, "Reducing Consumption of Ozone Depleting Substances in India; Phase 1: The Cost of Complying with the Montreal Protocol," Touche Ross Consultants, London, England, 1990, 55.

15. "Seeing Red over Green Issues," by Chen Ya and Xiong Lei, *China Daily* (Beijing), Feb. 12, 1993, 5

16. Lester R. Brown et al., *Vital Signs 1992* (New York: W. W. Norton, 1992), 60.

17. For Sargon quote, see Field-Marshall Viscount Montgomery of Alamein, *A History of Warfare* (Cleveland & New York: World Publishing, 1968), 33. For quotation from the massacre in Normandy, see S. L. A. Marshall, *Men Against Fire* (New York: William Morrow, 1947).

18. J. H. Fremlin, "How Many People Can the World Support?" in *Population, Evolution, and Birth Control*, ed. Garret Hardin (San Francisco: W. H. Freeman, 1969).

2: A Paradox of Souls: China

1. John Bongaarts, W. Parker Mauldin, and James F. Phillips, "The Demographic Impact of Family Planning Programs," *Studies in Family Planning* 21:6 (November/December 1990), 305.

2. See Jodi L. Jacobson, "Coerced Motherhood Increasing," in *Vital Signs*, by Lester Brown et al. (New York: W. W. Norton, 1992), 114–15.

3. There has, in addition, been some speculation about the year 2000, and its significance to the Chinese in terms of fertility. In his essay "Creating New Traditions in Modern Chinese Populations: Aiming for Birth in the Year of the Dragon," *Population and Development Review* 17:4 (December 1991), 663–86, Daniel M. Goodkin examines the fact that traditionally in many Chinese cultures there have been baby booms during dragon years. "The dragon will rise again in the year 2000, the gateway to the new millennium, and, for a phenomenon so dependent on an upwelling of emotion, the national symbolic significance of this should not be underestimated," he writes.

4. John S. Aird, *Slaughter of the Innocents: Coercive Birth Control in China* (Washington, D.C.: AEI Press, 1990), 20.

5. Paul Kennedy, *Preparing for the Twenty-First Century* (New York: Random House, 1993), 175.

6. In Beijing, as of 1989 there were an estimated 1. 3 million "floaters" (migrants) having as many children as they wanted. In Shanghai, the number of such migrants was suspected to be over 1. 8 million.

7. Virginia Abernethy, *Population Politics: The Choices that Shape our Future* (New York: Insight Books, 1993), 40, 290, quoting from *Cuba: The Demography of Revolution* (Washington, D.C.: Population Reference Bureau, 1981).

8. See Li Jingneng, "Reproduction Worship and Population Growth in China," Chinese *Journal of Population Science* 4:1 (1992), 27–32. Citing Ye Yangzhong, "A tentative study of the childbearing aspirations of contemporary farmers," *Population Studies* 4 (1988), 29, Li writes, "There is no question now that throughout rural China, the preferred family norm is two or more children."

See also Minja Kim Choe and Noriko O. Tsuya, "Why Do Chinese Women Practice Contraception? The Case of Rural Jilin Province," *Studies in Family Planning* 22:1 (Jan/Feb 1991), 39–51. Eighty-five percent of those rural married women with one child nevertheless continued to practice contraception, though most reported two as their ideal number.

9. See "China's Population and Development," *Country Report*, prepared by the Chinese Delegation to the Fourth Asian and Pacific Population Conference, Bali, Indonesia, August 1992.

10. Others like Professor Li Jingneng, director of the Institute of Population and Development Research at Nankai University in Tianjin, argue that the current birthrate is closer to fifty-four thousand per day, or thirty-eight per minute.

11. See Shanti R. Conly and Sharon L. Camp, "China's Family Planning Program: Challenging the Myths," *Country Study Series Number 1* (Washington, D.C.: Population Crisis Committee, 1992), 32.

12. See Song Jian, Tuan Chi-Hsien, and Yu Jingyuan, *Population Control in China* (New York: Praeger, 1985), 263–67.

13. Personal conversations with Professor Wu Cang Ping, Institute of Population Research, the People's University of China, Beijing.

14. Personal conversation with Qu Geping, former head of the Environmental Protection Agency for China.

15. See Ping Tu, "Birth Spacing Patterns and Correlates in Shaanxi, China," *Studies in Family Planning* 22:4 (1991), 255–63.

16. In fact, some regional statistics are known. Population planning in the decade of the 1970s had prevented approximately fifty-nine million births, and most of them were through induced abortions. In 1980, the rate of abortions in the country was estimated to be 574 per one thousand births. See H. Yuan Tien, with Zhang Tianlu, Ping Yu, Li Jingneng, and Liang Zhongtang, "China's Demographic Dilemmas," in *Population Bulletin* 47:1 (June 1992), 13.

17. See Conly and Camp, "China's Family Planning Program," 33.

18. By 1979, China's death rate had been stabilized at between 6 and 8 per thousand, its birthrate had dropped from 33.43 in 1970 to 17.82 per thousand, and its TFR had declined from 5.8 to 2.75.

19. See Aird, *Slaughter of the Innocents*, 21.

20. Ibid., 24.

21. See Tien et al., "China's Demographic Dilemmas," 7.

22. In both China and India, feminism is divided on this point: the fact that women bear the overwhelming burden of birth control. Family planners themselves are quick to point out that intervention and manipulation of the woman's biological cycle is a more effective means of birth control. Nearly all sterilizations in Asia are among women, though twenty years ago, the situation was reversed. Today, the unanimous (and obvious) consensus of family planners is that women need to be empowered to control their own bodies, to reinherit their own destiny,

to liberate that which men have coopted over time. But there is a price, which makes increasing rates of contraceptive use harder to achieve, particularly in poor countries or regions traditionally bound by cultural machismo.

23. See Tien et al., "China's Demographic Dilemmas," 9.

24. The government is presently studying social security systems throughout the world and asking government workers to pay 3 percent of their monthly paychecks into security funds. It is still constitutionally incumbent upon all children to eventually look after their parents. At present, it is alleged that some 25 percent of the aged in China enjoy the "five guarantees" of social security benefits. But the quality of these services vary. See Gao Zhanjun and Zhang Xueming, "Old-Age Insurance for 'Single Daughter Households' in Rural Changyi," in *China Population Today*, 9:2 (April, 1992).

25. Sheryl WuDunn, "China Village Prospers but Retains Old Ways," *New York Times*, Sunday, January 17, 1993, 8.

26. See James Thayer Addison, *Chinese Ancestor Worship* (Shanghai: Church Literature Committee of the Chung Hua Sheng Kung Hui, 1927), 15.

27. In Shaanxi province, nearly half of those parents who already had even two daughters, still wanted a third child, hoping it would be male. See Wei Jinsheng, "On the Operating Mechanism of Population Control," *Chinese Journal of Population Science* 4:1 (1992), 56; see also Li Jingneng, "Reproduction Worship and Population Growth in China," *Chinese Journal of Population Science* 4:1 (1992), 27–32.

28. This pathetic gender bias is noticeable in nearly every developing country, where the TFR continues to reside at about 4.6, excluding China. See "China: Accessibility of Contraceptives," *Asian Population Studies Series*, Number 103-B, Economic and Social Commission for Asia and the Pacific, Bangkok, United Nations 1991.

29. See W. J. F. Jenner and Delia Davins, ed., *Chinese Lives: An Oral History of Contemporary China*, quoted in Marlyn Dalsimer and Laurie Nisonoff, "Collision Course," in *Cultural Survival Quarterly* 16:4 (Winter 1992), 59

30. See Seung-kyung Kim, "Industrial Soldiers," *Cultural Survival Quarterly* 16:4 (Winter 1992), 54–56.

31. See Aird, *Slaughter of the Innocents*, 69, 92. The international organization, Asia Watch, has also reported on fertility-related atrocities in Tibet, including forced abortions, even the witholding of food ration cards from children.

32. See Zeng Yi et al., "An Analysis of the Causes and Implications of the Recent Increase in the Sex Ratio at Birth in China," *Working Paper* (Peking: Institute of Population Research, Peking University, 1992).

33. See Sten Johansson and Ola Nygren, "The Missing Girls of China: A New Demogaphic Account," *Population and Development Review* 17:1 (March 1991), 35–51.

34. See Aird, *Slaughter of the Innocents*, 44.

35. See Xie Zhenming, "An Evaluation of the Social Effectiveness of One-Child Policy in China," *Population Research* 7:1 (1990), 30–36.

36. See Aird, *Slaughter of the Innocents*, 83.

37. See Peng Xinzhe,"China's Population Control and the Reform in the 1980s," *Population Research* 7:3 (1990), 1–17, in which are discussed certain measures adopted on April 13, 1984 to relax the one-child policy, in particular the right for rural families to have a second child when judged necessary. "By 2005," says Peng, "every couple will be eligible to have two kids." See Maggie Farley, "China's One-Child Policy is Quietly Fading Away," *International Herald Tribune*, October 21, 1997, 1.

38. The evolution of slogans is fairly indicative of where Chinese family planinng has gone. In the early 1970s the saying was: "*wan-xi-shao*," literally, "later-longer-fewer." Then the refrain went, "one is not too few, two is good, three is too many." By 1979 the saying was, "one is best, at most two, never a third." See Elisabeth Croll, Delia Davin, and Penny Kane, ed., *China's One-Child Family Policy* (New York: St. Martin's Press, 1985).

39. The saying now is, "To charge nothing is not enough; the supplies must be sent straight into the home." See "China: Accessibility of Contraceptives," 6–7.

40. See Aird, *Slaughter of the Innocents*, 43.

41. See Conly and Camp, "China's Family Planning Program," 36.

42. It is of some interest to compare the difficulties, today, of lowering TFR, versus those gains accomplished twenty years ago in China. For example, in just one year, between 1973–74, China went from a TFR of 4.5 to 4.2. See "China's Population and Development," *Country Report*, prepared by the Chinese Delegation to the Fourth Asian and Pacific Population Conference, Bali, Indonesia, August 1992, 5. See also, Dr. Zhang De Wei, Project Leader, "Study of Stainless Steel Ring and Copper T IUD Efficacy, Use, Cost/Benefit, and Conversion in China," *UNFPA Project CPR/91/P43*, Project Report, May 21, 1992, Beijing.

43. According to consultants Stephen Shaw and Jonathan Woetzel of McKinsey & Co., as reported by Mark Clifford, "Consuming Passions," *Far Easten Economic Review*, February 11, 1993, 44.

44. See George Orick, "Combatting Poverty in Rural China: Change Comes to Anwang," *The Ford Foundation Report* 22:4 (Winter 1992), 3–7.

45. See Paul Ehrlich and Anne Ehrlich, *The Population Explosion* (New York: Touchstone Books, Simon and Schuster, 1990), 70.

46. "Tibet's Grasslands under Threat," *South China Morning Post*, September 26, 1992.

47. See Susan Woldenberg, "Tibet: Aerie or Abattoir?" in *The Animals' Voice Magazine* 6:1 (1993), 8–10.

48. *Tibetan Environment & Development News*, 6 (November 1992).

49. See Jeff Wise, "With Six You Get Bear Paw," *Esquire* (May 1993), 47 (in a section unfortunately titled by the magazine, "Man At His Best: The Enlightened Traveler").

50. See Ehrlich & Ehrlich, *The Population Explosion*, 129.

51. See Hu Angang and Wang Yi, "The Future Conflict between Population and Grain Output in China," *Chinese Journal of Population Science* 2:3 (1990), 202.

52. Hu and Wang have examined required grain output based upon a per capita grain requirement of eight hundred jin per year and have determined that China would have to achieve seven hundred jin per mu (1 mu = .067 hectares = .165 acres), which is equivalent to the highest petroleum-driven levels in Japan and France.

53. See Lester Brown et al., *Vital Signs 1992* (New York: W. W. Norton), 38.

54. See Dr. Qu Geping, *Environmental Management in China* (United Nations Environment Program, Beijing: China Environmental Science Press, 1991), 27.

55. See China's "Population and Development," *Country Report*, 17.

56. See Thomas Homer–Dixon, "Destruction and Death," *New York Times*, January 31, 1993, E17, adapted from an article in the February, 1993 issue of *Scientific American* and based on research at the Project on Environmental Change and Acute Conflict at MIT.

57. See Geping, *Environmental Management in China*, 5.

58. See *World Resources Report 1992–93* (The World Resources Institute, with the United Nations Environment Program and the United Nations Development Program, New York: Oxford University Press, 1993), 261–63.

59. See Sheryl WuDunn, "China's Consumers Start to Make a Splash," *International Herald Tribune*, February 16, 1993, 1, 12.

60. See Geping, *Environmental Management in China*, 134.

61. See "Some Very Bad News: An Interview with Amory Lovins," *Newsweek*, Asian Edition, February 15, 1993, 50.

62. Already the Chinese are following the Japanese model of cultivating fast-growing timber estates, or acquiring primary raw timber from other countries, such as New Zealand.

63. See Nicholas D. Kristof, "China's Headlong Sprint toward Wealth," *International Herald Tribune*, February 15, 1993, 1.

3: The Ecology of Pain: India

1. See Harald Muller, "Prospects for the Fourth Review of the Non-Proliferation Treaty," in SIPRI Yearbook 1990, *World Armaments and Disarmament*, Sipri–Stockholm International Peace Research Institute (New York: Oxford University Press, 1990), 557.

2. Seven years before that famine of 1970, India's Shastri government had frantically appealed to President Johnson for long-term food aid. But Johnson and the U.S. Congress had lost patience with India's problems, abolished food guarantees, pushing instead for self-help measures, and sporadic short-run food aid extensions, the precursors of later economically imposed austerity programs.

But this "short-tether" policy, as it was called, had failed to stabilize India's agricultural sector, pushing Indira Gandhi closer to Moscow, which in turn cemented nuclear assistance from the Soviets. Angered, Johnson then temporarily cut off all aid whatsoever to India in 1966. The politics of food aid, the outgrowth of failed population policies, thus encouraged nuclear proliferation.

3. See Seymour M. Hersh, "On the Nuclear Edge," *The New Yorker*, March 29, 1993, 56–73. See also Jennifer Griffin, "Pakistan, India Negotiate—but Tensions Increase," *Los Angeles Times*, January 16, 1994, M2.

4. Dr. George P. Cernada and Dr. A. K. Ubaidur Rob, "Pakistan's Fertility and Family Planning: Future Directions," *Journal of Family Welfare* 38:3 (September 1992), 47.

5. See V. A. Pai Panandiker and P. K. Umashankar, *Fertility Control-Induced Politics of India* (New Delhi, India: Centre for Policy Research and Family Welfare Program, 1991), 12.

6. See Donald P. Warwick, *Bitter Pills: Population Policies and Their Implementation in Eight Developing Countries* (Cambridge: Cambridge University Press, 1982), 28.

7. See Panandiker and Umashankar, *Fertility Control.*

8. India is often described according to ten biogeographic zones: Trans-Himalaya, Himalaya, Desert, Semi Arid, Western Ghats, Deccan, Gangetic Plain, North East India, Islands, and Coasts. Among the various biological subzones, "urban slum" is now considered India's latest environment. Taken together, India's landmass and coastal areas constitute not the richest, but the most diverse ecological tapestry in the world.

9. See Banwari, trans. by Asha Vohra, *Pancavati: Indian Approaches to Environment* (New Delhi, India: Shri Vinayaka Publications, 1992), 39.

10. Ibid., 94.

11. See the author's *Life Force: The World of Jainism* (Berkeley: Asian Humanities Press, 1991), 68; See also by K. C. Lalwani, *Sramana Bhagavan Mahavira: Life and Doctrine* (Calcutta: Minerva Associates Publications PVT., 1975), 176–83.

12. Christoph von Furer–Haimendorf, *Tribes of India: The Struggle for Survival* (Berkeley and Los Angeles: University of California Press, 1982), 305.

13. Ibid., 306. See also *The Originals* (Mumbai: CMM Productions, New Delhi: Doordarshan National Television Network, September, 1997).

14. See the author's essay, "The Ecology of Conscience," *Parabola Magazine* 22:3 (August 1997), 16.

15. See Catherine Dold, "Tropical Forests Found More Valuable for Medicine Than Other Uses," *New York Times*, Tuesday, April 28, 1992, B8.

16. In the Aukre region of Para state in Brazil, for example, environmental organizations are working with the Kayapo Indians to find alternative, sustainable sources of wealth in the forest, including new agricultural techniques and the harvesting of medicinals. But so far, the only market for these products has been a

single firm in England that sells Brazilian nut oil. Perhaps all the Kayapo will need are a few good marketing firms. But even then, according to Marguerite Holloway, once a "forest product such as latex becomes commercially important it is inevitably introduced into higher-yielding plantations. . . . Or the material is made synthetically. As a result, the price plummets, and small-scale extraction ceases to be profitable." In "Sustaining the Amazon," *Scientific American* (July 1993), 94.

17. See John Kurien and T. R. Thankappan Achari, "On Ruining the Commons and the Commoner: The Political Economy of Overfishing," Centre for Development Studies *Working Paper Number 232*, Tiruvananthapuram, Kerala, 1989, 37.

18. Examples of just some of the products overexploited for profit include mahua flowers, sal seed (an edible oil), tendu leaf, tusar silk cocoons, edible roots, and mushrooms. See H. S. Panwar, Ruchi Badola, Bitapi Sinha and Chandra-shekhar Silori, "The Wilderness Factor: Protected Areas and People: Compatible Strategies," *Sanctuary Magazine* 12:5 (1992), 77.

19. Population Crisis Committee, Washington, D.C., 1992.

20. According to *The Economic Times*, February 27, 1992, 40 percent of India is below the poverty line, a figure adopted officially by the Indian Government. But many others note that with an official per capita GNP of 5651 rupees, or between $160–80 dollars, depending on the currency exchange that day, 80 percent of all Indians are impoverished, even by developing country standards. See the "Text of Finance Minister's Speech," *Financial Express*, Bombay, Sunday, February 28, 1993, 6.

21. There are estimated to be some two hundred million middle- and upper-class Indians, leaving nearly eight hundred million poor or destitute.

22. See Rahul Pathak, "Did You Know," *India Today*, April 15, 1993, 54. The government is trying to upgrade the life of these half a billion or so individuals. The Rural Development Bill of 1991, or Panchayati Raj, was meant to ensure reg-ular elections to the local *panchayats*, or community governing boards. Each *pan-chayat* was to provide reservations for scheduled tribes in proportion to their population and one-third of all seats were to be reserved for women. As of the late 1990s, however, very few states had actually implemented the bill's provisions.

23. See Charlie Pye–Smith, *In Search of Wild India* (New Delhi, India: UBSPD, 1993), 24.

24. The young Alexander was reported by his biographer to have met sever-al naked yogic masters in the city of Taxila and been convinced that nonviolence and meditation were more powerful than conquest.

25. Pye–Smith, *In Search of Wild India*, 42.

26. See Museum of New Delhi painting number 47-110/1919.

27. For example, it was written in the *Isha Upanishad*, "This universe is the creation of the Supreme Power meant for the benefit of all his creation. Each indi-vidual life form must, therefore, learn to enjoy its benefits by forming a part of

the system in close relation with other species. Let not any one species encroach upon the other's rights." "Environment and Development: India's Approach," (New Delhi: Government of India, 1992), 7–8.

28. Yet to this day, after centuries of soil abuse, little more than 5 percent of eroded land in Kerala has ever been treated with conservation measures, and this paucity of restoration is characteristic of the whole country. See the *Kerala Report* (New Delhi: Government of India, 1985).

29. Pye–Smith, *In Search of Wild India*, 49.

30. Ibid., 53.

31. Ibid., 64.

32. By one estimate, there are 45,000 plants (7,000 of them endemic), and 75,000 animal species, including 2,000 species of birds, 850 species of mammals, and 450 species of reptiles in India. Of these, at least 1,500 plants are endangered, and 138 animals. B. K. Tikader, *Threatened Animals of India* (Calcutta: Zoological Survey of India, 1983). In addition, there are 250 cultivated species, 60 of which are endemic. See S. K. Saksena, *Environmental Planning Policies and Programmes in India* (New Delhi, India: Shipra Publications, 1993), 65. Other government figures show very different data: 340 mammals; 1,200 birds, 300 of which are over-winterers; 2,000 fishes; 140 amphibians; 420 reptiles; 5,000 species of algae; 1,600 lichens; 20,000 fungi; 2,700 bryophytes; 600 pteridophytes; 50,000 insects; 4,000 molluscs; and an unknown number of other invertebrates. Until recently, there were estimated to be as many as 50,000 varieties of rice in India, but that number is down to below 300 now. Twenty years ago, if not for the discovery of one existing wild rice strain in India, namely, Oryza nivara, the grassy stunt virus would have devastated rice fields from India to Indonesia. It took the testing of 6,273 different strains before the one resistant strain was discovered. Today, with biodepletion having gone on at such a high pace, few options exist for testing among multiple strains.

33. According to one report, rice yields have dropped by half, and wheat by as much as 78 percent in many large regions during just the past few years. See P. K. Joshi and Dayanatha Jha, "Environmental Externalities in Surface Irrigation Systems in India," in *Environmental Aspects of Agricultural Development* (International Food Policy Research Institute, Washington, D.C., 1990), 3–4.

34. See "Environment and Development: Traditions, Concerns, and Efforts in India," *National Report to UNCED* (New Delhi: Ministry of Environment and Forests, Government of India, June 1992), 20.

35. See Raj Chengappa, "Family Planning: The Great Hoax," *India Today*, October 31, 1988, 39.

36. See V. A. Pai Panandiker, "Dynamics of Population Growth: Implications for Environment and Quality of Life" (New Delhi: Centre for Policy Research, February 1992), 6.

37. See *The Life of the People of India* (ASI, Government of India, 1993). The document is forty-six thousand pages in length and represents the coordinated efforts of three thousand researchers studying 776 traits in each of the 4,635 larger communities of the country.

38. Mountain ecologists recommend a maximum of 11 percent sown area where forest is encroached upon by agriculture along steep slopes. See Michael Tobias, *Mountain People* (Norman: University of Oklahoma Press, 1986).

39. See K. B. Pathak and F. Ram who ask, "Under the given environment, are we expecting too much from 'BIMARU' [the heavily populated northern] states to achieve during a comparatively shorter period?" in "Pattern of Population Growth and Redistribution in India," *Demography India* 20:1 (1991), 7–14.

40. See H. Govind, "Recent Developments in Environmental Protection in India: Pollution Control," *Ambio* 18:8 (1989), 429.

41. See Soutik Biswas, "Troubled Waters," *India Today*, February 28, 1993, 133.

42. P. K. Surendran, "Delhi most polluted city in India," *Times of India*, February 6, 1993.

43. As a whole, Indian power plants produce some 30 million tons of coal ash per year.

44. See Mayank Chhaya and Nupur Basu, "Key Facts on the Issue in India— Child Labor: A Stubborn Social Problem," *India Abroad*, February 19, 1993, 19. See also, Olga Nieuwenhuys, *Childrens' Lifeworlds: Gender, Welfare, and Labour in the Developing World*, (London: Routledge, 1994).

45. Maneka Gandhi was the highest ranking woman in the Janata Dal, or People's Front Party, whose leader was Vishwanath Pratap Singh, Rajiv Gandhi's former finance minister who became prime minister, briefly, in 1989. Mrs. Gandhi was subsequently chosen to be minister of environment and forests.

46. See Bhattacharyya's essay, "Economic Development with Reference to Rural Economy and the Eco-Systems," in H. Ramachandran, ed. *Environmental Issues in Agricultural Development* (New Delhi: Concept Publishing Company, 1990), 49. "God forbid that India should ever take to industrialization after the manner of the West. . . . If an entire nation . . . took to similar economic exploitation, it would strip the world bare like locusts!" says Kamil Nath, the former minister of environment and forests who succeeded Mrs. Gandhi.

47. Increasingly dependent on its primary forests for sustenance, India nevertheless has no fuel wood policy; no national fodder policy. See Ravi Sankaran, "Dudhwa: A Forest Held to Ransom," *Sanctuary Magazine* 10:5 (September–October 1990), 81.

48. See Address by Kamal Nath, minister of environment and forests, India, to UNCED, June 1992, Government of India, New Delhi, 7.

49. Pye–Smith, *In Search of Wild India*, 13.

50. Nearly a dozen major chemical and timber companies throughout India have been exploring nonwood fiber alternatives to this forest crisis. The issues for

India, as for Indonesia, are twofold: first, will the impoverished classes have economic access to such alternative woods in time to save the existing forests; and second, will the political leadership ensure that forest plantations are developed on existing wastelands, rather than in primary forest areas?

51. See Asad R. Rahmani, "Save the Grasslands," *Sanctuary Magazine* 10:4 (July–August 1990), 24.

52. Ibid., 21.

53. It is estimated, for example, that each cow consumes on average 27 kilograms of fodder per day, which it scavenges from whatever is available. See S. S. Khanka, "Developments in Ghimtal Gadhera Catchment Area," in H. Ramachandran, ed., *Environmental Issues in Agricultural Development* (New Delhi: Concept Publishing, 1990), 150.

54. The native Indian blackbuck—a gloriously beautiful antelope—has been reduced from an estimated four million to something like forty thousand. See Pye–Smith, *In Search of Wild India*, 17.

55. Ibid., 155.

56. Outside of India, scientists allege that there are forty tigers left in China, three hundred fifty to four hundred in Siberia, four hundred in Sumatra, and fifteen hundred in Thailand and Malaysia.

57. See Ashwani Sharma, "Little protection for HP's protected species," *Times of India*, February 25, 1993.

58. As Madhav Gadgil of the Indian Institute of Science in Bangalore puts it, deforestation comes about because of "the use of state power to systematically undervalue biomass . . . and organize its supply to those in power at highly subsidized values." Pye–Smith, *In Search of Wild India*, 172. Traditional markets that are sustainable and value-added have been usurped by mass producers solely concerned with export of raw materials, which governments have increasingly subsidized, thus devaluing the natural resource and the labor force for purposes of quick profit. The syndrome is the same everywhere.

59. Ibid., 108.

60. Usha Rai, "A Quarter of Melghat Tiger Reserve to be Denotified," *Indian Express*, Feb. 25, 1993, 9.

61. See Ramesh Bedi and Rajesh Bedi, *Indian Wildlife* (New Delhi: Brijbasi Printers, 1984), 147–57.

62. Ibid., 24.

63. Ibid., 196.

64. Ibid., 270.

65. Similarly, when Sharon Camp of Population Crisis Committee in Washington (now called Population Action International) was asked whether she believed there was much hope for wildlife worldwide, her answer was an emphatic, "None." Asilomar Conference on Population and Environment, World Affairs Council of Northern California, Pacific Grove, California, April 30–May 2, 1993.

66. To protest such abuses, write to the Municipal Commissioner, Carmichael Road, Mumbai 400026.

67. See Saksena, *Environmental Planning Policies*, 41.

68. Rajiv Gandhi set up the National Wastelands Development Board, an eerie harbinger of restoration needs for the twenty-first century, with an aim towards implementing social forestry and wastelands development on protected plantations.

69. According to the Biogeographic Project, however, part of the National Wildlife Action Plan of the Wildlife Institute of India, one thousand square kilometers and a population of five hundred to one thousand is considered sufficient to ensure the genetic viability of a community. Many biologists would argue with such low figures.

70. See Ravi Chellam, "Wanted: Another Home for the Asiatic Lion," *Sanctuary Magazine* 12:5 (1992), 36–43.

71. See "Environment and Development: Traditions, Concerns, and Efforts in India," *National Report to UNCED* (New Delhi: Ministry of Environment and Forests, Government of India, June 1992), 13.

72. See H. Simon and Shri B. B. L. Sharma, *Training Modules for Incorporation of Family Welfare Messages* (New Delhi: National Institute of Health and Family elfare, 1990), 34.

73. Ibid., 88

74. Ibid., 39.

75. See Elisabeth Bumiller, *May You Be the Mother of a Hundred Sons: A Journey among the Women of India* (New Delhi: Penguin Books, India, 1991), 42.

76. See F. Max Muller, ed., *The Laws of Manu,* vol. 25 of *The Sacred Books of the East* (New Delhi: Motilal Banarsidass, 1967), section 9:2–3.

77. Today, some 4. 5 million marriages occur every year in India, and most brides are between fifteen and nineteen years old. See Dr. Mrs. M. R. Chandrakapure, inaugural address, director of health services, "New Interventions for a Small Family Norm," (Bombay: A Seminar Organised by Indian Merchants' Chamber, July 10, 1990). See also Raj Chengappa, "Family Planning: The Great Hoax," 44.

78. Bumiller, *May You Be the Mother,* 273.

79. See K. P. Bahadur, *Population Crisis in India* (New Delhi: National Publishing House, 1977), 31.

80. Private conversation at Dr. Bose's home, New Delhi, February 1993.

81. See "Equal Rights Must Start in the Cradle," *UNICEF News: Third World Women,* 76:3 (July 1973), 17. The Government's Department of Women and Child Development has summarized this bias by stating, "In a culture that idolizes sons and dreads the birth of a daughter, to be born female comes perilously close to being born less than human."

82. See Bumiller, *May You Be the Mother,* 39–40.

83. See Edward A. Gargan, "In 'Bollywood,' Women Are Wronged or Revered," *New York Times,* January 17, 1993, 11–12.

84. Bumiller, *May You Be the Mother,* discussed at length. See also F. Max Muller, ed., section 5.164.

85. Most noted among them: Parvati, Siva's consort, daughter of the Himalayas; Syama–Kali, dispenser of boons, dispeller of fear; Raksa–Kali, protectress; Smasana–Kali, creator and destroyer; Laksmi, guarantor of continued rule; Sakti–Maya-Devi, Durga, Uma, Sati, Padma, Candi, and countless others. See J. Campbell, Heinrich Zimmer, editor, *Philosophies of India,* Bollingen Series 26 (Princeton: Princeton University Press, 1969).

86. See Kavitha Shetty, "Cradles of Mercy," *India Today,* February 28, 1993.

87. Discussed in Bumiller, *May You Be the Mother,* 273.

88. See Rasheeda Bhagat, "Where Condoms Are Buried in the Ground," *Indian Express,* Madras, January 8, 1993.

89. Any contraceptive having to do with males has not done well in India since the mid-1970s. Family planning, in the back of the male's mind, is related to castration. One is thus talking about sexual potency. That has killed the male's participation in family planning. His ego is threatened, say Indian fertility counselers.

90. See Shanti R. Conly and Sharon L. Camp, "India's Family Planning Challenge: From Rhetoric to Action," *Country Study Series Number 2* (Washington, D.C.: Population Crisis Committee, 1992), 13

91. See Stanley Wolpert, *A New History Of India,* 2d ed., New York: Oxford University Press, 1982 267. By that time, India had slid economically to one one-hundreth the level of affluence and industrialization of England. See Paul Kennedy, *Preparing for the Twenty-First Century* (New York: Random House, 1993), 11. Many Indophiles have effectively reasoned that India's inability to keep pace with the Western Industrial revolution was strictly the result of subjugative British rule, the consequences of which have been an ever downward spiraling paralysis, a syndrome of poverty from which the country appears incapable of lifting itself. Others have argued that India's poverty was there long before the British arrived and if anything the East India Company mobilized the Indian labor force and created the infrastructure by which the country today is making, by some estimates, enormous strides. Put differently, England trained India and the proof can be gleaned from India's escalating GNP. Both perceptions are partly correct. The third, missing element, however, is the population boom which for most of India's recent history has skewed all comparisons.

92. See Simon and Sharma, *Training Modules,* 30.

93. See Dom Moraes, *A Matter of People* (New York: Praeger Publishers, 1974).

94. Today, the country's crude birthrate averages about thirty to thirty-three per thousand. But with its deathrate (of those over the age of five) of eleven per thousand, that makes for a net gain of over twenty per thousand per year—only moderately reduced since 1975. To achieve an NRR-1, or fertility replacement level, the precondition for eventual zero population growth, the country would need to achieve a birthrate of no more than twenty-one, and a death rate of seven, a net gain

of no more than fourteen per thousand. By comparison, the U.S. birthrate all time high was in 1947 at twenty-six and a half per thousand, but promptly shot back down to around fifteen per thousand. See "New Interventions for a Small Family Norm," A Seminar Organized by Indian Merchants' Chamber, Bombay, July 10, 1990. See also Paul R. Ehrlich, Anne H. Ehrlich, and John P. Holdren, *Ecoscience: Population, Resources, Environment* (San Francisco: W. H. Freeman, 1977), 100–101.

95. See S. Krishnakumar, "Kerala's Pioneering Experiment in Massive Vasectomy Camps," *Studies in Family Planning* 3:8 (August 1972), 177–92.

96. See V. H. Thakor and Vinod M. Patel, "The Gujarat State Massive Vasectomy Campaign," *Studies in Family Planning* 3:8 (August 1972), 186–92.

97. See "Shah Commission Third Report," 1978:153, quoted in V. A. Pai Panandiker and P. K. Umashankar, "Fertility Control-Induced Politics of India" (New Delhi: Centre for Policy Research and Family Welfare Program, 1991), 2.

98. Arrests were made under the Maintenance of Internal Security Act, the Defence of India Rules and the Indian Penal Code and Criminal Procedure Code. See Panandiker and Umashankar, "Fertility Control" (New Delhi: Centre for Policy Research and Family Welfare Program, 1991), 3–4.

99. See Ashish Bose, "India's Quest for Population Stabilisation: Progress, Pitfalls, and Policy Options," *Materials on Demogaphic Questions* (Herausgeber Wiesbaden: Bundesinstitut fur Bevolkerungsforschung, 1991), 23.

100. In Tamil Nadu, if a couple has two girls and then volunteers for one of the spouses to be sterilized, the government will give the two existing daughters each a bond that they will be able to cash when they are twenty.

101. See Chengappa, "Family Planning," 47.

102. Actually, the Tamil Nadu government had offered incentives for birth control as early as 1956.

103. Chengappa, "Family Planning," 40.

104. Conly and Camp, "India's Family Planning Challenge," 10.

105. Ibid., 38.

106. Those supplies include such items as sun-dried rags, bed sheet and blanket, a match-box and stove, a new razor blade, clean cotton, linen, scissors, cord ligatures, an enema can, a mucus sucker, two bowls, a torch, a weighing scale, antiseptics, mercurochrome, and methylated spirit. The government suggests that the *dai* advocate breast feeding five to six times a day or more, for fifteen to twenty minutes at a time. Because breast feeding inhibits ovulation, while providing the best nourishment for the newborn, it is considered the miracle form of contraception in India, as in most other countries.

107. For developing country comparisons and needs, see "Traditional Birth Attendants," *A Joint WHO/UNFPA/UNICEF Statement*, Geneva, 1992.

108. See T. V. Antony, "The Family Planning Programme Lessons from Tamil Nadu's Experience," *A Policy Paper* (Delhi: Centre For Policy Research, March 1992).

109. See A. Sreedhara Menon, *Political History of Modern Kerala* (Madras: S. Viswanathan Publishers, 1987).

110. B. A. Prakash, "Educated Unemployment in Kerala: Some Observations Based on a Field Study," *Working Paper Number 224* (Tiruvananthapuram, Kerala: Centre For Development Studies, 1988); See also B. A. Prakash, "Unemployment In Kerala: An Analysis of Economic Causes," *Working Paper Number 231* (Tiruvananthapuram, Kerala: Centre For Development Studies, 1989).

111. P. Sivanandan, D. Narayana, and K. Narayanan Nair, "Land Hunger and Deforestation: A Case Study of the Cardamom Hills in Kerala," *Working Paper Number 212* (Tiruvananthapuram, Kerala: Centre for Policy Studies, 1985), 15.

112. Rajaram Das Gupta, "Conditions of Cropping Intensity," *Working Paper Number 185*, (Tiruvananthapuram, Kerala: Centre for Development Studies, December 1983), 1. See also, K. P. Kannan and K. Pushpangadan, "Agricultural Stagnation and Economic Growth in Kerala: An Exploratory Analysis," *Working Paper Number 227* (Tiruvananthapuram, Kerala: Centre for Development Studies, 1988).

113. See K. Srinivasan, "India's Population Problems: Can We Afford to Shove Them under the Carpet?" *International Institute of Population Sciences Compiled Seminar Papers*, 1990, 19.

114. See Aditya Sinha, "Govt Fall Aborts Population Policy," *The Hindustan Times*, New Delhi, December 8, 1997, 9.

115. V. A. Pai Panandiker, "Dynamics of Population Growth: Implications for Environment and Quality of Life" (New Delhi: Centre for Policy Research, February, 1992). Presented at the International Conference on Population and Environment, University of Michigan, Ann Arbor, October 1990.

116. Bose, "India's Quest," 17, 20.

117. See "Quality of life and Problems of Governance in India" (New Delhi: Centre for Policy Research, 1990).

118. See *World Resources 1992–93*, A Report by the World Resources Institute in Collaboration with the United Nations Environment Program and the United Nations Development Program (New York: Oxford University Press, 1992), 237, 239.

119. Ibid, 240, 241.

4: Nature Held Hostage: Indonesia

1. Supplement to President's *Report to Parliament* on August 16, 1991.

2. See Leslie B. Curtin, Charles N. Johnson, Andrew B. Kantner, and Alex Papilaya, "Indonesia's National Family Planning Program: Ingredients of Success," *Occasional Paper Number 6*, Report Number 91-134-136, Population Technical Assistance Project (USAID–Jakarta and Office of Population Bureau for Research and Development, Washington, D.C.: Agency for International Development, December 11, 1992), 3.

3. See Widjojo Nitisastro, *Population Trends in Indonesia* (Ithica, N.Y.: Cornell University Press, 1970). See also "Recent Fertility Trends in Indonesia, 1971–87," *Working Papers Number 63*, East–West Population Institute, Honolulu: East–West Center, November, 1991.

4. *The Straits Times* (Singapore), February 2, 1993, 10.

5. "Biodiversity Action Plan for Indonesia," (Jakarta, Final Draft, BAPPENAS [National Development Planning Bureau], August 1991), 1:18.

6. Curtin et al., "Indoensia's National Family Planning Program," vii. See also Graeme J. Hugo, Terence H. Hull, Valerie J. Hull, Gavin W. Hones, *The Demographic Dimension in Indonesian Development* (New York: Oxford University Press, 1987).

7. Though according to research by the writer V. S. Naipaul, only a third of the Muslims in Indonesia actually live as Muslims. See V. S. Naipaul, *Among the Believers: An Islamic Journey* (New York: Vintage Books, 1982). Others have argued that, if anything, there is a strong Islamic revival taking place in Indonesia.

8. See Anju Malhotra, "Gender and Changing Generational Relations: Spouse Choice in Indonesia," *Demography* 28:4 (November 1991), 549–70. See also James A. Palmore and Masri Singarimbun, "Marriage Patterns and Cumulative Fertility in Indonesia," *Working Papers, Number 64* (East–West Population Institute, Honolulu: East-West Center, November 1991). See also Walter L. Williams, *Javanese Lives: Women and Men in Modern Indonesian Society* (New Brunswick, N.J.: Rutgers University Press, 1991).

9. According to J. Weeks, it is not Islamic religion, per se, but the inferior status of Muslim women, and their poverty, which causes their high fertility rates. Weeks points out that the patriarchal nature of Islamic society has limited the choices of women, which in turn dramatically impacts their freedom of contraceptive use. See J. Weeks, "The Demography of Islamic Nations," *Population Bulletin* 43:4 (December 1988). However, Donald P. Warwick writes, "One of the keys to the success of Indonesia's family planning program in rural Java was winning the neutrality and sometimes even the active assistance of local religious leaders. This was done mainly by consulting these leaders about the overall acceptability of family planning in their region and by showing them respect in other ways." See Donald P. Warwick, *Bitter Pills: Population Policies and their Implementation in Eight Developing Countries* (Cambridge: Cambridge University Press, 1982), 183.

10. And thus, the government has worked to enlist the Ministry of Religious Affairs and the leading Islamic organizations into population issues. Local Islamic leaders have accepted family planning, women's Qur'an reading groups have been formed, and over eight hundred Islamic medical facilities have been integrated into the government's own family planning efforts.

11. See Tahir Mahmood, *Family Planning: The Muslim Viewpoint* (New Delhi: Vikas Publishing, n.d.), 34.

12. B. F. Musallam, *Sex and Society in Islam: Birth Control Before the Nineteenth Century* (Cambridge: Cambridge University Press, 1983), 38.

13. See Paula M. Cooey, William R. Eakin, and Jay B. McDaniel, eds., *After Patriarchy: Feminist Transformations of the World Religions* (New York: Orbis Books, 1991), 238. See also Arvind Sharma, ed., with an introduction by Katherine Young, *Women in World Religions* (State University of New York Press. n. d.).

14. It should be pointed out, however, that one Companion, Hazrat Ali bin Abi Talib insisted that "unless the seven stages [*atwar*] were completed by the foetus its abortion would not be [construed as] burying [the fetus] alive." (Brackets my own) He recited verses 12, 13, and 14 of Sura Mu`minun of the Qur'an to emphasize his point and was himself confirmed by Hazrat Umar, another Companion, who said, "You [Hazrat Ali] stated the right thing. God bless you." See Tahir T. Mahmood, *Family Planning: The Muslim Viewpoint* (New Delhi: Vikas Publishing, n. d.), 31.

15. For the beginnings of the legal framework guiding the country's birth control efforts, see *Legal Aspects of Family Planning in Indonesia*, the Committee on Legal Aspects of the Indonesian Planned Parenthood Association, Law and Population Monograph Series Number 4, Law and Population Programme, The Fletcher School of Law and Diplomacy, 1971.

16. See Sheikh Abdul Rahman al-Khayyir, "The Attitude of Islam towards Abortion and Sterilization," *A Report of the Proceedings of the International Islam Conference* (Morocco, December 1971), published in *Islam and Family Planning* 2: 345–61, Beirut: International Planned Parenthood Federation, 1974, quoted on 243–44 of Paula M. Cooey, William R. Eakin, and Jay B. McDaniel, eds., *After Patriarchy: Feminist Transformations of the World Religions* (New York: Orbis Books, 1991).

17. See "Adding Choice to the Contraceptive Mix: Lessons from Indonesia," *Asia: Pacific Population & Policy Number 19*, Population Institute of the East–West Center, Honolulu, December, 1991.

18. See Siti Pariani, David M. Heer, and Maurice D. Van Arsdol, Jr., "Does Choice Make a Difference to Contracptive Use? Evidence from East Java," *Studies in Family Planning* 22:6 (Nov–Dec 1991), 384–90.

19. See *Indonesia Country Profile: Annual Survey of Political and Economic Background 92–93* (The Economist Intelligence Unit, New York: Business International, 1993). In a widely conflicting figure, however, the World Bank reports that adult literacy in Indonesia (encompassing both rural and urban), as of 1988, was 81 percent. See "Indonesia: Growth, Infrastructure, and Human Resources," *World Bank, Report Number 10470-IND*, Country Department III, East Asia & Pacific Regional Office, May 26, 1992.

20. The international nongovernmental family planning organization known as Pathfinder, led in Indonesia by Dr. Does Sampoerno, has also addressed the problem of Indonesia's rainy weather and inaccessible communities by launching a system of "floating clinics," boats that can reach remote islands and river bank

populations in West Kalimantan, South and Central Sulawesi, Riau Province, North and South Sumatra, Lampun, West, Central, and East Java, or, in other words, 69 percent of Indonesia.

21. See Robert Repetto, William Magrath, Michael Wells, Christine Beer, and Fabrizio Rossini, *Wasting Assets: Natural Resources in the National Income Accounts* (Washington, D.C.: World Resources Institute, 1989), 57–60.

22. See Budi Utomo, Sujana Jatiputra, and Arjatmo Tjokronegoro, *Abortion in Indonesa: A Review of the Literature* (Jakarta: Faculty of Public Health, University of Indonesia, May 1982).

23. See Curtin et al., "Indonesia's National Family Planning Program," ix, 28. See also World Bank, "Indonesia: Growth, Infrastructure, and Human Resources."

24. "Biodiversity Action Plan For Indonesia," 8.

25. Wilson, *The Diversity of Life*, 45.

26. *Indonesian Country Study on Biological Diversity* (Jakarta: Ministry of State for Population and Environment, KLH, 1992).

27. According to one researcher, the country contains at least five million, or between 10 percent and 17 percent of all known species. See Julian Caldecott, "Biodiversity Management in Indonesia," *Tropical Biodiversity* 1:1 (1992), 57–62.

28. As of 1988, the country contained 11,761,000 hectares of alleged wilderness (a four-thousand-square-kilometer section of totally undisturbed area), less than 1 percent of the total land area. See *World Resources 1992–93*, A Report by the World Resources Institute in collaboration with the United Nations Environment Program and the United Nations Development Program (New York: Oxford University Press, 1992), 263.

29. The analogy with Madagascar, however, does not hold in the long-term: Madagascar has a considerably smaller base of species diversity than Indonesia. See *World Resources 1992–93*, 304–5.

30. "Biodiversity Action Plan for Indonesia," 8.

31. A second, somewhat expanded ad ran as follows: "Indonesian Forests Forever; 2000 species of fauna PROTECTED. One-sixth of the world's bird species and one-eight of its mammal species will live here forever. The tropical forests of Indonesia, home to over 1500 species of birds and 500 species of mammals. Beautiful, unique & exotic. Of these inhabitants, some are dangerous, some helpless while some are even endangered. [sic] The Republic of Indonesia has taken steps to protect their natural habitat by designating 46 million acres as national parks, open to the public, and 75 million acres as protection forests, preserved in their natural virgin state and closed to commercial and recreational use. God gave them one of the world's most beautiful homes. We are their watchmen providing security 24 hours a day. Indonesia's forests are classified as parks, protection, production, and conversion areas, or agro-land. Parks: 46 million acres; protection: 75 million acres; production: 159 million acres; conversion: 75 million acres."

32. Quoted in Roderick Nash's *Wilderness and the American Mind*, 3d ed. (New Haven and London: Yale University Press, 1982), 271.

33. Ibid., 360.

34. Wahana Lingkungan Hidup Indonesia (WALHI), whose talented young executive director is Mr. M. S. Zulkarnaen. WALHI is the umbrella organization for some two hundred environmental NGOs and has successfully launched the first environmental lawsuits in the country.

35. At least twenty countries exceed 10 percent protection, while another twenty countries show 0. 0 percent protection. The United States shows an official figure of 10. 5 percent of its territory as biologically protected. Though it is more than likely that the discrepancies in Indonesia reflect discrepancies elsewhere. See *World Resources 1992–93*, 298–99.

36. See *National Strategy for the Management of Biodiversity*.

37. In addition, 14.5 percent from mining, 19.5 percent from manufacturing, and 16. 3 percent from trade and tourism.

38. See *Indonesia Country Profile*, 47–49.

39. "Biodiversity Action Plan for Indonesia," 17.

40. *Mistaking Plantations For Indonesia's Tropical Forest: Indonesia's Pulp and Paper Industry, Communities, and Environment* (Jakarta: WALHI and YLBHI, 1992), 13,15. The South–North Project for Sustainable Development in Asia includes WALHI (The Indonesian Forum for the Environment) and YLBHI (the Indonesian Legal Aid Foundation), the Project for Ecological Recovery (Thailand), Sahabat Alam Malaysia, the Philippines Rural Reconstruction Movement, PROSHIKA (Bangladesh), and Novib (Holland).

41. Ibid., 33.

42. Ibid., 41.

43. Thus, an editorial in *The Jakarta Post* of February 19, 1993, remarks that "timber trade should be developed further and not be curbed because without a market or the possibility of making fair profits there is no incentive at all to maintain forest resources, especially for the developing nations which are still struggling with massive poverty."

44. *Review Indonesia* 44 (February 13, 1993), 33.

45. See *World Resources 1992–93*, 48.

46. See James Gustave Speth, "Coming to Terms: Toward a North–South Bargain for the Environment," in *World Resources Institute Issues and Ideas* (Washington, D.C.: World Resources Institute, 1990), 4.

47. See Narendra Sharma and Raymond Rowe, "Managing the World's Forests," *Finance & Development* (Washington, D.C., June 1992), 31–33.

48. See Vincent Lingga, "Indonesia works hard to take care of its tropical forests . . . but is upset by constant international criticism," *The Jakarta Post*, February 18, 1993, 5.

49. Carl Whiting Bishop, with the collaboration of Charles Greeley Abbot and Ales Hrdlicka, *Man from the Farthest Past*, vol. 7 of the Smithsonian Series, (Washington, D.C.: Smithsonian Scientific Series, 1944), 357–58.

50. J. S. Parsons has called this politically effective system of inducements a "vertical and horizontal sense of commitment." See Parsons' "What Makes the Indonesian Family Planning Programme Tick," National Family Planning Coordinating Board, UNFPA, *Populi* 2:3 (1984), 10.

51. Private conversation with M. S. Zulkarnaen in Jakarta, February 18, 1993. See also WALHI and YLBHI documents, 54–58.

5: The Forgotten Ones: Africa

1. By that I do not mean to dismiss other primary agents of change, such as climatic perturbations, shifting curtains of rain that have, periodically, discombobulated probably every biome in Africa, not just the Sahara: oscillating predator-prey populations; the advance and retreat of glaciers; and natural feast and famine.

2. Patience W. Stephens, Eduard Bos, My T. Vu, and Rodolfo A. Bulatao, *Africa Region Population Projections, 1990–91 Edition (ARPP)*, Working Papers, Population and Human Resources Department (Washington, D.C.: The World Bank, February 1991), WPS 598, 26.

3. See E. K. Mburugu, *Factors Related to Stock Ownership and Population Movements; and Perception of Land Pressure and Other Environmental Changes among the Rendille in Marsabit District* (University of Nairobi, Integrated Project in Arid Land (IPAL), Technical Report Number F-2: Man in the Biosphere Program, n.d.), 2.

4. The Wildlife Conservation and Management Act of 1976 and the 1989 law enacting the Kenya Wildlife Service have thus far managed only minimally to ameliorate this marginalization crisis, a syndrome endemic to East Africa. See *Development Policy for Arid and Semi-Arid Lands (ASAL)* (Nairobi: Government of Kenya, September 1992), 28–29.

5. *World Population Prospects 1988* (New York: United Nations, 1989). Population density in Nairobi is currently estimated to be 1911 Persons per square kilometer, but this figure could be way off, considering discrepancies in data pertaining to the actual population size of Nairobi: from 1. 5 to 2. 5 million inhabitants, up from eight thousand in the year 1901 and 118,976 in 1948. See Stephens et al. *ARPP*, xvii.

6. See "Women at Risk," *Society*, 32 (Oct. 18), Nairobi, 1993, 30. See also Hugh O'Haire, "Think Again," *Populi*, (December 1993–January 1994), 8–10. Regarding the findings of a Berlin roundtable conference in late September 1993 ("Population Policies and Programmes: The Impact of HIV/AIDS"), writes O'Haire, ". . . the experts added that some sub-national regions and a small number of large cities could experience markedly reduced population growth for

short periods. But these downswings would be quickly canceled by immigration from surrounding areas." In fact, says O'Haire, "The view that AIDS will take care of the population problem is wrong."

7. Cited on page 41 of Thomas J. Goliber, "Africa's Expanding Population: Old Problems, New Policies," *Population Bulletin*, 44:3 (November 1989), Washington, D.C.: Population Reference Bureau, and derived from John Bongaarts and Frank Odile, "Biological and Behavioral Determinants of Exceptional Fertility Levels in Africa and West Africa and West Asia," African Population Conference, Dakar, 1988, Liege, Belgium: International Union for the Scientific Study of Population, 1988.

8. Ibid., 41–42.

9. Ibid., 42.

10. Mauritius's TFR dropped faster than any other country in history during the 1960s, from 5. 9 in 1962 (with a population of about seven hundred thousand) to 3. 4 in 1972, to 2.2 in 1983.

11. U.N. Secretariat, Population Policy Data Bank, Population Division, Department of International Economic and Social Affairs, 1989.

12. See *World Population Prospects: 1992 Revision* (New York: United Nations Department for Economic and Social Information and Policy Analysis), 150, 293.

13. *Kenya Demographic and Health Survey 1993: Preliminary Report* (National Council for Population and Development, Ministry of Home Affairs and National Heritage, Central Bureau of Statistics, Office of the Vice President and Ministry of Planning and National Development, prepared with technical assistance from Demographic and Health Surveys, Macro International Inc., Columbia, Maryland, under contract to USAID, September 1993), 13, 21.

14. See Association for Voluntary Surgical Contraception, *Kenya Assessment Program for Permanent and Long-Term Contraception Assessment Report* (National Council for Population and Development and the Ministry of Health, Division of Family Health, and US. A.I.D., 1992).

15. See note 13

16. Official family planning slogans in Kenya read, "*Nafasiza kazini haba, Zaa Watoto Wachache,*" or, "Jobs are scarce; have few children"; and "*Punguza Mzigo Wako Tumia Njia Ya Kupanga Uzazi,*" meaning, "Lessen your struggle, use a family planning method." Yet, many family planning officials themselves do not set the best example, coming from families of ten and twelve siblings.

17. See *Population, Resources, and the Environment: The Critical Challenges* (New York: UNFPA, 1991), 95. See also *Inventory of Population Projects in Developing Countries around the World 1991–92* (New York: UNFPA, 1992), 275–91; Wamucii Njogu, "Trends and Determinants of Contraceptive Use in Kenya," *Demography* 28:1 (February 1991), 83–99.

18. Stephens et al., *ARPP*, 77.

19. *World Population Prospects*, 519.

20. "United Nations Population Fund Proposed Projects and Programmes," recommendation by the executive director, assistance to the government of Kenya, support for a comprehensive population program, Fortieth session, May 1992, Governing Council of the United Nations Development Program, Geneva: UNFPA, 4.

21. Founded in 1923 by Dr. Clive Irine, a Scottish missionary and doctor; in 1956, management passed from the Church of Scotland to the Presbyterian Church of East Africa. In 1969, Mzee Jomo Kenyatta, the country's first president, led a famous Harambee, or community self-help jamboree, in which money was raised to expand the hospital to its current 290 beds.

22. See Howard I. Goldberg, Malcolm McNeil, and Alison Spitz, "Contraceptive Use and Fertility Decline in Chogoria, Kenya," *Studies in Family Planning* 20:1 (Jan–Feb 1989), 17–26.

23. See, John J. Dumm et al. "Helping Services Meet Demand: An Assessment of A.I.D. Assistance to Family Planning in Kenya" (Center for Communication Programs, Johns Hopkins University, 1992).

24. See *PCEA Chogoria Hospital Annual Report* (Chogoria, Kenya: 1992), 4.

25. See Professor Philip M. Mbithi, "Implication of Socio-Economic and Cultural Factors on Population and Development," *Report on the Second National Leaders' Population Conference* (NCPD, Republic of Kenya, September 1989), 43–44.

26. As a point of partial documentation, it should be noted that the Nairobi Vegetarian Society has fewer than forty members according to its president.

27. J. R Handby et al., "Population Changes in Lions and Other Predators," in *Serengeti: Dynamics of an Ecosystem*, ed. A. R. E. Sinclair and M. Norton–Griffiths (Chicago: University of Chicago Press, 1979), 249–62, cited by William Newmark, "The Selection and Design of Nature Reserves for the Conservation of Living Resources," *Managing Protected Areas in Africa: Report from a Workshop on Protected Area Management in Africa*, compiled by Walter J. Lusigi (Mweka, Tanzania: UNESCO, World Heritage Fund, 1992), 93.

28. Allen Bechky, *Adventuring in East Africa: The Sierra Club Travel Guide to the Great Safaris of Kenya, Tanzania, Rwanda, Eastern Zaire, and Uganda* (San Francisco: Sierra Club Books, 1990), 273.

29. Glory Chanda and Ackim Tembo, "The Status of Elephant on the Zambian Bank of the Middle Zambezi Valley," *Pachyderm Magazine* 16 (1993), 50.

30. See Fox, "Help for Tanzania," *HSUS* (Humane Society of the United States) *News* 38:4 (Fall 1993), 30–33.

31. See Michael Satchell, "Wildlife's Last Chance," *U.S. News & World Report*, November 15, 1993, 68–76.

32. *Kenya Wildlife Service: A Policy Framework and Development Program, 1991–96* (Nairobi–Kenya Wildlife Service, 1990), 4.

33. See Alison Wilson, "Sacred Forests and the Elders," in *The Law of the Mother: Protecting Indigenous Peoples in Protected Areas*, ed. Elizabeth Kemf (San Francisco: Sierra Club Books, 1993), 244–48.

34. See Robert A. Levine, "Maternal Behavior and Child Development in High-Fertility Populations," *Fertility Determinants Research Notes 2* (New York: The Population Council, September 1984), 4, cited in Goliber, "Africa's Expanding Population," 27.

35. The crisis is most pronounced in Taita Teva near Tsavo, in the Narok and Kajiado districts, and across the Laikipia District. See Joyce H. Poole, "Kenya's Initiatives in Elephant Fertility, Regulation, and Population Control Techniques," *Pachyderm Magazine* 16 (1993), 62. Publication of the World Conservation Union & WWF.

36. See *Kenya Wildlife Service: A Policy Framework*, 62.

37. See Poole, "Kenya's Initiatives," 64.

38. See *Sub-Saharan Africa—From Crisis to Sustainable Growth: A Long-Term Perspective* (Washington, D.C.: World Bank, 1989), 1.

39. See Stephens et at., *ARPP*, 99.

40. Most of Nigeria, however, is not seeing a CPR improvement. "The results of the 1990 Nigeria Demographic and Health Survey point to high fertility, low levels of contraceptive use, and high mortality and undernutrition among children." *DHS: Demographic and Health Surveys Newsletter* 5:1 (1992), 3.

41. See John Caldwell, I. O. Orubuloye, and Pat Caldwell, "Fertility Decline in Africa: A New Type of Transition?" *Population and Development Review* (1992), 214, 236. See also Susan H. Cochrane and S. M. Farid, "Fertility in Sub-Saharan Africa: Analysis and Explanation," *World Bank Discussion, Paper Number 43* (Washington, D.C.: The World Bank, 1989).

42. See Aj. Ahlback, *Industrial Plantation Forestry in Tanzania: Facts, Problems, Challenges* (Ministry of Natural Resources and Tourism, Dar Es Salaam, n.d.).

43. *Central Africa: Global Change Change and Development, Technical Report* (Landover, Maryland: Biodiversity Support Program, a Consortium of the WWF, The Nature Conservancy, World Resources Institute, U.S. Agency for International Development, 1993), V.

44. Peter Matthiessen and Mary Frank, *Shadows of Africa* (New York: Harry Abrams, 1992), 83.

45. See "Levels and Trends of Contraceptive Use as Assessed in 1988." *Population Studies* (New York: United Nations, 1989), 110, tables 2 and A. 11. 1.

46. See Annik Thayer–Rozat, *Plantes Medicinales du Mali* (Bordeaux: Ocoe Publishing, 1981).

47. See *Sub-Saharan Africa—From Crisis to Sustainable Growth*, 4.

48. The tenets of GATT and of free trade contradict this insular approach to the world, at least in boom economies. NAFTA, for example, is expected to drive fourteen million Hispanic immigrants into the U.S. in the coming decades, when America's population will double, well beyond U.S. Census pre-NAFTA projections. But in Africa, just the opposite is occurring: an artificial economy, kept minimally afloat by World Bank, IMF, African Development Bank loans, and by foreign aid, is also doubling its population every one to two

sexual generations, not from immigration, but from high TFRs and the continuing population momentum.

49. See *Plan d'Action sur la Strategie National pour la Planification Familiale*
(Bamako: Ministere de la Santa Publique et des Affaires Sociales a la Banque
Mondiale/Sante, Population et Hydraulique Rurale (PDSII), 1990). See also
"United Nations Population Fund Proposed Projects and Programmes," recom-
mendation by the executive director, assistance to the government of Mali,
Fortieth session, June 1993, Governing Council of the United Nations Develop-
ment Program, New York: UNFPA.

50. See Femi Ajayi et al., "Tools of the Trade: Do Farmers Have the Right
Ones?" *African Farmer* 5 (November 1990), 5

51. *KDHS*, 29.

52. Two other noteworthy Kenyan women have made a profound difference
for the country, as well. Wangari Matthai started out in the Girl Scouts, and eventually initiated a Green Belt movement that has effected the replanting of hundreds of thousands of seedlings. In December 1997, she ran for president of
Kenya. Similarly, forty-three-year-old Sophia Kiarie founded a nursery which to-
date has distributed over six hundred thousand seedlings throughout the country. And she has campaigned to conserve forests by the use of efficient stoves
designed by engineers with the Bellerive Foundation in Geneva. Today, a few
thousand Kenyans use the stoves, while an estimated million households apply
the so-called "C2C Cooking to conserve" principles of conservation. See "Kenya:
Creating Islands of Green," *Environmental Impact: An Occasional Magazine of the
Bellerive Foundation*, 1993, 7.

53. See Patricia C. Wright, "Ecological Disaster in Madagascar and the
Prospects for Recovery," *Ecological Prospects: Scientific, Religious, and Aesthetic
Perspectives*, ed. Christpher Key Chapple (Albany: State University of New York
Press, 1994), 11–24.

54. Nampaa Sanogho, *Les Elephants du Gourma* (Bamako: Water and
Forestry Department [DNEF], 1980). See also Robert Olivier, *The Gourtna
Elephants of Mali: A Challenge for the Integrated Management of Sahelan
Rangeland* (Nairobi: UNEP, 1983).

55. John Boorman, *West African Butterflies and Moths: A West African Nature
Handbook* (London: Longman House, 1978). See also W. Serle, G. J. Morel, and W.
Hartig, *A Field Guide to the Birds of West Africa* (London: Collins Publishers, 1986).

56. See Peter Warshall, *Mali: Biological Diversity Assessment* (Office of Arid
Lands Studies, University of Arizona, Natural Resources Management Support
Project A.I.D., Bureau of Africa, Office of Technical Resources, Natural Resources
Branch, Project no. 698-0467, Prime Contractor: E/Dl, Washington, D.C., March
1989), 87.

6: The Price of Development

1. See Eina S. Bakker, *An Island Called California* (Berkeley and Los Angeles: University of California Press, 1971), xi.

2. William R. LaFleur, *Liquid Life: Abortion and Buddhism in Japan* (Princeton, N.J.: University Press, 1992), 96–98.

3. Ibid., 135.

4. International North Pacific Fisheries Commission, *Final Report of 1990 Observations of the Japanese High Seas Squid Driftnet Fishery of the North Pacific Ocean* (Seattle: Alaska Fisheries Science Center, Seattle, 1991), 193–95, table 24; quoted in *World Resources 1992–93*, a report by the World Resources Institute in collaboration with the United Nations Environment Program and the United Nations Development Program (New York: Oxford University Press, 1992), 181.

5. The U.S. Census Bureau predicts a population of 309 million in the year 2040.

6. See Alex Shoumatoff, *The World Is Burning: Murder in the Rain Forest* (Boston: Little, Brown, 1990), 76.

7. See Paul Ehrlich and E. O. Wilson, "Biodiversity Studies: Science and Policy," *Science* 253 (August 16, 1991), 760.

8. *World Resources 1992–93*, 119.

9. Ibid., 78.

10. Wilson, *The Diversity of Life*, 230, 242.

11. Ibid., 254–58.

12. See Robin Poulton and Michael Harris, *Putting People First: Voluntary Agencies and Third World Development* (London: Macmillan, 1992); quoted in Robert Lacville, "Wisdom: Ancient and Modern," *Guardian Weekly*, February 21, 1993, 14.

13. Five countries in Africa, two in North/Central America, ten in Asia, two in Europe (Luxembourg and Malta), and one in Oceania. Syria has no protected land, nor does the United Arab Emirates, Iraq, Cambodia, Somalia, or Jamaica. *World Resources 1992–93*, 298–99.

14. Neither wealth, nor the size of human population by itself is a necessarily predictable indication of the likely measure of impact on surrounding habitat. For example, Namibia has all of 22 people per 1000 hectares, but zero percentage of its land could be described as wilderness. Canada and Australia are the two regions with remaining sizable wilderness and low populations and population densities. Twenty-nine percent of little Iceland is wilderness, its density a mere twenty-five people per one thousand hectares. Nepal—despite its vast, wild Himalayas—has a high density, 1,399 people per one thousand hectares, and zero wilderness.

15. Conversation with Paul Papanek, chief, Toxics Epidemiology Program, County of Los Angeles Department of Health Services, January 1993.

16. Joseph Brodsky, "Blood, Lies, and the Trigger of History," *New York Times*, August 4, 1993.

17. David Rothenberg, *Is It Painful to Think? Conversations with Arne Naess* (Minneapolis and London: University of Minnesota Press, 1993), 108.

18. Paul R. Ehrlich and Anne H. Ehrlich, *The Population Explosion* (New York: Touchstone Books, Simon & Schuster, 1990), 134.

19. Peter A. Morrison, "Testimony before the House Subcommittee on Census and Population," RAND Corporation, May 26, 1992, 5.

20. Paul Kennedy, *Preparing for the Twenty-First Century* (New York: Random House, 1993), 221.

21. "The poor disadvantaged tend to suffer disproportionately from environmental degradation but it is extremely difficult to generalize about the impact of poverty on environment. Thus, although extreme poverty may preclude investment in environmental improvement that has a long payoff, it is also true that the richest countries pose the main threat to the ozone layer and the global climate. . . . It is increasingly being recognized that most environmental problems are less the result of individual large-scale development projects that have gone wrong, than the combined consequences of millions of relatively small-scale activities, unsustainable agricultural practices, small-scale polluting activities, and individual decisions to exploit tropical forest resources." Jeremy Watford and David Wheeler, "Integrating Environmental Issues into Economic Policy Making," *Environment Bulletin: A Newsletter of the World Bank* 4:2 (Spring 1992), 6.

22. See Sergio Munoz and Juanita Darling, interview with "Jaime Serra Puche," *Los Angeles Times*, August 1, 1993, M3.

23. Kennedy, 102.

24. For an overview of the Seveso disaster, see Michael Tobias, *Voice of the Planet* (New York: Bantam Books, 1990), and film series by same title, Turner Broadcasting Service (TBS), 1990.

25. Global Assessment of Soil Degradation, World Map on Status of Human Induced Soil Degradation, sheet 2, Europe, Africa, and Western Asia, United Nations Environment Program International Soil Reference and Information Center, Nairobi, 1990.

26. *World Resources 1992–93*, 177.

27. See "The Price of Pollution," *Options*, International Institute for Applied Systems Analysis, Laxenburg, Austria, September 1990, 5.

28. Brian Gardner, "European Agriculture's Environmental Problems," paper presented at the First Annual Conference of the Hudson Institute, Indianapolis, Indiana, April 1990, 7.

29. *World Resources 1992–93*, 66.

30. See Kathleen Hunt, "Death and Life in a Company Town," *Los Angeles Times Magazine*, July 11, 1993, 14.

31. See Carey Goldberg, "Flaring Siberian Gas: Torches Light Way to EcoDisaster," *Los Angeles Times*, July 25, 1993, Al, A10.

32. See Richard A. Nuccio, Angelina M. Omelas, and Ivan Restrepo, "Mexico's Environment and the United States," *In the U.S. Interest: Resources, Growth, and Security in the Developing World*, ed. Janet Welsh Brown (Boulder, Colo.: A World Resources Institute Book, Westview Press, 1990), 19–58.

33. Julia Preston, "A Mother's Success: Some Babies Lived," *International Herald Tribune*, February 16, 1993, 1, 7.

34. *World Resources 1992–93*, 27.

35. Chauncey Starr, Milton F. Searl, and Sy Alpert, "Energy Sources: A Realistic Outlook," *Science* 256 (May 15, 1992), 961–86.

36. See "Element One," (PBS, 1996), a one-hour documentary focused on the hydrogen/fuel cell economy, distributed by the Video Project, Ben Lomond, California.

37. Norman St. John–Stevas, *The Agonizing Choice: Birth Control, Religion, and the Law* (London: Eyre & Spottiswoode, 1971), 20–21.

38. Ibid., 222.

39. See Joseph A. McFalls, Jr., "Population: A Lively Introduction," *Population Bulletin* 46:2 (October 1991).

40. Claudia Morain, "A Freedom Fighter Packs for Washington," *Los Angeles Times*, March 8, 1993.

41. See Peter A. Morrison, "California's Demographic Outlook: Implications for Growth Management," Santa Monica, Calif.: RAND Corporation, 1991, P-7738.

42. See "Population Projections by Race/Ethnicity for California and Its Counties 1990–2040," *Report 93 P-1: Official Population Projections* (Sacramento: Demographic Research Unit, April, 1993).

43. See "Travel and Related Factors in California: 1991," *Cal Trans Annual Summary* (Los Angeles: Cal Trans, 1992).

44. See *Regional Growth Management Plan* (Los Angeles: Southern California Association of Governments, February 1989).

45. Relative per capita emissions are actually the highest in the United Arab Emirates, Qatar, Brunei, Bahrain, even Cote d'Ivoire and Luxembourg. See *World Resources 1992–93*, 209–10.

46. Mary D. Nichols and Stanley Young, *The Amazing L.A. Environment: A Handbook for Change* (Los Angeles: The Natural Resources Defense Council/ Living Planet Press, 1991), 72.

47. Two hundred agricultural chemicals used in California that might be harmful to human reproductive health have been identified under the state's Birth Defects Prevention Act of 1986. See Deborah B. Jensen, Margaret Tom, and John Harte, *In Our Own Hands: A Strategy for Conserving Biological Diversity in California* (Berkeley: California Policy Seminar Research Report, 1990), 110–11.

48. Ehrlich and Ehrlich, *Population Explosion*, 88. Other reports have shown agricultural inefficiency or crop losses of between 5 and 30 percent. See John Bongaarts, "Can the Growing Human Population Feed Itself?" *Scientific American* 270:3 (March 1994), 40.

49. "Land's End," by Meredith Grenier, *The Santa Monica Outlook*, March 17, 1993, Bl.

50. *Sliding Toward Extinction: The State of California's Natural Heritage, 1987*, written at the request of the California Senate Committee on Natural Resources

and Wildlife, commissioned by the California Nature Conservancy (prepared by Jones & Stokes Associates, Sacramento: November 1987), 19–25.

51. Ibid, 26, 28. At least 15,211,000 acres of those are given over today to cities and irrigated agricultural lands.

52. Ehrlich and Ehrlich, *Population Explosion*, 29.

53. Jensen et al., *In Our Own Hands*, 59, 66.

54. *Annual Report on the Status of California State Listed, Threatened, and Endangered Animals and Plants* (State of California, Sacramento: The Resources Agency, Department of Fish and Game, 1991), 12–13.

55. See Paul Dean, "To Catch a Thief," *Los Angeles Times*, January 10, 1993, E2.

56. *U.S. Environmental Quality: 23d Annual Report*, 12–15.

57. See Maura Dolan, "Endangered Species Act Battles for Its Own Survival," *Los Angeles Times*, Dec. 21, 1992.

58. Cary Fowler and Pat Mooney, *Shattering: Food, Politics, and the Loss of Genetic Diversity* (Tucson: University of Arizona Press, 1990), 19.

59. *World Resources 1992–93*, 24.

60. Peter W. Kelly, *Thinking Green! Essays on Environmentalism, Feminism, and Nonviolence* (Berkeley, Calif.: Parallax Press, 1994), 96.

7: Demographic Madness

1. Joseph A. McFalls Jr., "Population: A Lively Introduction," *Population Bulletin*, 46:2 (October 1991), 34.

2. Quoted in Kirk J. Schneider, *The Paradoxical Self: Toward an Understanding of Our Contradictory Nature* (New York and London: Insight Books, 1990), 17.

3. See Barry James, "At the Peak of the Litter," *International Herald Tribune*, February 26, 1993, 1.

4. E. E. Hunt, "The Depopulation of Yap," *Human Biology* 26 (1954), 20–51 quoted in Virginia D. Abernethy, *Population Politics: The Choices that Shape Our Future* (New York: Insight Books, 1993), 62.

5. See John Keegan, *A History of Warfare* (New York: Alfred Knopf, 1993), 26

6. Norman Myers, *Population, Resources, and the Environment: The Critical Challenges* (New York: UNFPA, 1991), 49.

7. Ibid., 74.

8. See G. C. Daily and P. R. Ehrlich, *An Exploratory Model of the Impact of Rapid Climate Change on the World Food Situation* (Stanford, Calif.: Morrison Institute for Population and Resource Studies, Stanford University, 1990).

9. See P. Harrison, "Too Much Life on Earth?" *New Scientist* 126 (1990), 28–29.

10. See Martin P. and Naomi H. Golding, "Population Policy: Some Value Issues," in *Arethusa* 8:2 (Fall, 1975, special issue on "Population Policy in Plato & Aristotle,"), 355.

11. Special report, *Christian Science Monitor*, July 8, 1992, 9–16.

12. *World Resources 1992–93*, a report by the World Resources Institute in collaboration with the United Nations Environment Program and the United Nations Development Program (New York: Oxford University Press, 1992), 30. See H. Jeffrey Leonard, *Environment and the Poor: Development Strategies for a Common Agenda* (New Brunswick, N.J.: Transaction Books, 1989), 5–7, 19.

13. *Demographic Indicators of Countries: Estimators and Projections as Assessed in 1980* (New York: United Nations, 1982), 3–28; "Population Profile of the United States 1983–84," *Current Population Reports*, Special Studies, Series P23, no. 145 (Washington, D.C.: U.S. Government Printing Office, 1985), 4–6; *World Development Report 1984* (New York: Oxford University Press, 1984).

14. *Long-Range World Population Projections: Two Centuries of Population Growth, 1950–2150* (New York: United Nations, n.d.).

15. Peter J. Donaldson and Amy Ong Tsui, "The International Family Planning Movement," *Population Bulletin* 45:3 (November 1990), 6.

16. See My T. Vu, Eduard Bos, and Ann Levin, *Europe and Central Asia Region, Middle East and North Africa Region: Population Projections, 1992–93 Edition*, Policy Research Working Papers, Population, Health, and Nutrition, Population and Human Resources Department, PS 1016 (Washington, D.C.: World Bank, November 1992), xii.

17. Mozambique is the poorest, at eighty dollars per capita, followed by Tanzania, Somalia, Nepal, Laos People's Democratic Republic, Guinea–Bissau, Malawi, Bangladesh, Chad, Ethiopia, and Bhutan—all poorer than India.

18. Vu et al., *Europe and Central Asia*, vii.

19. Ibid., xxiii.

20. Deborah Guz and John Hobcraft, "Breast-Feeding and Fertility: A Comparative Analysis," *Population Studies* 45:1 (March 1991), 91–108.

21. Lester R. Brown et al., *Vital Signs 1992* (New York: W. W. Norton, 1992), 76.

22. Geneva: WHO, 1992, 1.

23. See My T. Vu, Eduard Bos, and Ann Levin, *Latin America and the Caribbean Region (and Northern America) Population Projections 1992–93 Edition*, Policy Research Working Papers: Population, Health, and Nutrition, Population and Human Resources Department (Washington, D.C.: World Bank, November 1992), WPS 1033.

24. See Cynthia B. Lloyd, "The Contribution of the World Fertility Surveys to an Understanding of the Relationship between Women's Work and Fertility," *Studies in Family Planning 1991* 22:3, 144–61. See also "Shenyang Environmental Assessment: Phase 1, Summary of Existing Information and Recommendations for Action" (Denver, Colo.: China Environmental Fund, 1994), 2.

Epilogue: A Global Truce

1. Robert Nozick, *The Nature of Rationality* (Princeton: Princeton University Press, 1993), 177.

2. See Colin Spencer, *The Heretic's Feast: A History of Vegetarianism* (London: Fourth Estate, 1993). See also Christopher Key Chapple, *Nonviolence to Animal, Earth, and Self in Asian Traditions* (Albany: State University of New York Press, 1993), 113–14. See also Ashley Montagu, ed., *Learning Non-Aggression: The Experience of Non-Literate Societies* (Oxford: Oxford University Press, 1978); and Michael Tobias, *Ahimsa: Nonviolence* (Denver, Colo.: KRMA/PBS, 1987), a one-hour documentary about Jainism.

3. See Michael Tobias, *Life Force: The World of Jainism,* 2d ed. (Fremont, Calif.: Asian Humanities Press, 1998). See also the author's essay, "The Ecology of Conscience," *Parabola Magazine* 22:3 (August 1997), 14–19. See also, Michael Tobias, *A Vision of Nature: Traces of the Original World* (Kent, Ohio: Kent State University Press, 1995).

4. Hermann Jacobi, trans., *The Akaranga Sutra, Jaina Sutras* (New Delhi, India: Motilal Banarsidass, n.d.) book 1, lecture 1, lesson 3, 4–5.

5. John Bongaarts, W. Parker Mauldin, and James F. Phillips, "The Demographic Impact of Family Planning Programs," *Studies in Family Planning* 21:6 (Nov–Dec 1990), 305.

6. *World Resources 1992–93,* a report by the World Resources Institute in collaboration with the United Nations Environment Program and the United Nations Development Program (New York: Oxford University Press, 1992), 87.

7. *United Nations, World Fertility Survey: Major Findings and Implications* (Vaarburg, Netherlands: WFS, International Statistical Institute, 1984), quoted by Norman Myers in *Population, Resources, and the Environment: The Critical Challenges* (New York: United Nations Population Fund, 1991), 111.

8. Wilson, *The Diversity of Life,* 320.

9. See Hilary French, *After the Earth Summit: The Future of Environmental Governance,* Worldwatch Paper Number 107 (Washington, D.C.: Worldwatch Institute, March 1992), 28.

10. See Larry B. Stammer, "Harming the Environment is Sinful, Prelate Says," *Los Angeles Times,* November 9, 1997, A3.

11. See Ben Wattenberg, "The Population Explosion is Over," *The New York Times Magazine,* November 23, 1997, 60–63.

12. Barbara Crossette, "How to Fix a Crowded World: Add People," *New York Times,* November 2, 1997, 1, A4.

13. Paul Ehrlich and E. O. Wilson, "Biodiversity Studies: Science and Policy," *Science* 253 (August 16, 1991), 761.

14. "World Scientists' Warning to Humanity," Union of Concerned Scientists, Cambridge, Mass.: April 1993.

~Index~